**Oracle Press™**

# Oracle Database 12c Release 2 New Features

Bob Bryla

Robert G. Freeman

New York   Chicago   San Francisco
Athens   London   Madrid   Mexico City
Milan   New Delhi   Singapore   Sydney   Toronto

24.00

**Cataloging-in-Publication Data is on file with the Library of Congress**

McGraw-Hill Education books are available at special quantity discounts to use as premiums and sales promotions, or for use in corporate training programs. To contact a representative, please visit the Contact Us pages at www.mhprofessional.com.

**Oracle Database 12c Release 2 New Features**

1 2 3 4 5 6 7 8 9   LCR   21 20 19 18 17

ISBN    978-1-259-83719-7
MHID       1-259-83719-X

| | | |
|---|---|---|
| **Sponsoring Editor**<br>Wendy Rinaldi | **Technical Editors**<br>Peter Sharman<br>Michelle Malcher | **Production Supervisor**<br>Pamela Pelton |
| **Editorial Supervisor**<br>Janet Walden | **Copy Editor**<br>Bill McManus | **Composition**<br>Cenveo® Publisher Services |
| **Project Editor**<br>Patty Mon | **Proofreader**<br>Paul Tyler | **Illustration**<br>Cenveo Publisher Services |
| **Acquisitions Coordinator**<br>Claire Yee | **Indexer**<br>Karin Arrigoni | **Art Director, Cover**<br>Jeff Weeks |

*To the gang at home, particularly my kids, who will always be the kids that I watched the movie* The Master of Disguise *with too many times to count.*

—Bob Bryla

*This book is dedicated to all those who saved the life of my wife, Carrie, as she spent the Christmas of 2016 in a coma, and spent the winter of 2017 recovering from that coma. The doctors, nurses, therapists, social worker, and everyone else who took a situation where mortality was most likely and made life the end result.*

*This book is dedicated to all of those who helped me, during that time, to take care of a 3-year-old and a newborn while I was trying to juggle more than I knew how. This book is dedicated to all those who offered prayers and comfort during that time, and who continue to root for Carrie and my family. So many names, too numerous to mention.*

*This book is dedicated to my sister Ginger, who dropped everything to come and stay with my kids—to give me time to focus on Carrie and recover from strep throat that hit at the same time. It's dedicated also to Jen, a good friend, who stepped in and helped watch the kids at times. She allowed me moments of quiet and time to get ready for the terror of being a 51-year-old new dad who has to take care of a 3-year-old crazy-pants child and a tiny newborn.*

*The book is dedicated to the wonderful folks at Businessolver, who provided me the flexibility I needed to take care of Carrie— the many hours away at doctors, therapists, and all of the things that go with recovery. Thanks to all my co-workers, too numerous to list, and the expressions of concern that I received.*

*Finally, it's dedicated to Wendy Rinaldi—who recognized that I was in deep need of help, and for taking this project off my hands when I could not bring myself to do it. This book has always been my baby, my love—and giving it away was painful.*

—Robert G. Freeman

# About the Authors

**Bob Bryla** is an Oracle 9*i*, 10*g*, 11*g*, and 12*c* Certified Professional with more than 20 years of experience in database design, database application development, training, and Oracle database administration. He is the primary Oracle DBA and database scientist at Epic in Verona, Wisconsin. Bob has served as a technical editor for a number of Oracle Press books, including several certification study guides for Oracle Database 10*g*, 11*g*, and 12*c*. You can also find him on Lynda.com teaching Oracle Database fundamentals in bite-sized videos. Bob has also been known to watch science fiction movies, tinker with Android devices, and refinish antique furniture in his spare time.

**Robert G. Freeman** is the author of a number of books that cover a wide range of Oracle Database topics. From backup and recovery to new features to Oracle GoldenGate and more, Robert has written on the subject. Robert has been working with Oracle Database for longer than he cares to admit. Robert currently lives in Des Moines, Iowa, and is the proud husband of Carrie, proud father of seven children, and enjoys numerous things including swimming in his backyard pool, traveling, and flying airplanes.

# About the Contributor

**Eric Yen**, OCP, CISSP, is a Senior Principal with Oracle's National Security Group. He has been working with Oracle databases since version 7.3.2. Directly recruited to Oracle out of college, Eric developed his passion to learn, understand, and implement database technology early in his career.

### About the Technical Editors

**Pete Sharman** is a freelance technical architect specializing in Oracle Database and High Availability architecture. He worked with Oracle for 22 years in a variety of roles, from education to consulting to development, most recently for 5 years as a Principal Product Manager with the Enterprise Manager product suite group. Pete is a member of the OakTable Network, and has presented at conferences around the world, including Oracle OpenWorld (both in Australia and the United States), RMOUG Training Days, the Hotsos Symposium, Miracle Open World, and the AUSOUG and NZOUG conferences. Pete has previously authored a book on how to pass the Oracle8*i* Database Administration exam for the Oracle Certified Professional program, co-authored a book on Enterprise Manager, and co-authored a book on Oracle Database Cloud technology. He is based in Canberra, Australia.

**Michelle Malcher** is a data and security professional with several years of experience in database development, design, and administration. She has expertise in security, performance tuning, data modeling, and database architecture of very large database environments. As an Oracle ACE Director, she enjoys sharing knowledge about best practices involving database environments. Her experience is focused on designing, implementing, and maintaining stable, reliable, and secure database environments to support business and important business processes. Michelle has held several positions on the IOUG Board of Directors. She has authored articles for the IOUG *Select Journal* and a book, *Oracle Database Administration for the Microsoft SQL Server DBA* (Oracle Press/ McGraw-Hill Education, 2010), and is a co-author of *Oracle Database 12c: Install, Configure & Maintain Like a Professional* and *Securing Oracle Database 12c* (Oracle Press/McGraw-Hill Education).

# Contents

**vii**

# Acknowledgments

Many technical books need the expertise of more than one person, and this one is no exception. The people I collaborated with regarding this book at Oracle Open World, in Oracle Support, and in the Oracle Partner Network are too numerous to mention, but all played an important role in this book.

Thanks also go out to all the people at McGraw-Hill Education (and those who work with MHE) who pulled me in at the last minute to finish off the book in a somewhat timely manner, including Wendy Rinaldi, Claire Yee, and Patty Mon. Thanks also to Michelle Malcher, who gave me good advice in each chapter, which did add the final polish to those chapters. Extreme thanks to Robert G. Freeman, my co-author, without whose help this book would not have been published in a timely manner. I will have to remind him again about the time I wrote one chapter for his Oracle Database 10g RMAN book many, many years ago.

Many of my professional colleagues at Epic were a source of both inspiration and guidance: James Slager, Scott Hinman, Maggie Yan, Joe Obbish, and Lonny Niederstadt. In this case, the whole is truly greater than the sum of its parts.

I would be remiss to not mention the mostly nontechnical support of my friends and family in Wisconsin—and hot yoga. I found much inspiration for writing this book while experiencing extreme perspiration three times a week (and no less than three times a week!).

If you have any questions or comments about any part of this book, please do not hesitate to contact me at rjbdba@gmail.com.

—*Bob Bryla*

So much has changed since my last book. I suppose that this is not the place for a personal historical chronology, but there are a few things I must mention as a part of the acknowledgments. However, to understand who I am acknowledging, I think a little bit of what happened to me, on my way to the printing press, is called for.

I've had a few tragic events happen around me while I've been engaged in this thing called writing. If you will allow me just a moment, I'd like to share a few experiences with you—as a part of my overall acknowledgments.

Back in 1995, I had been a DBA in Oklahoma City, Oklahoma, for maybe three years. I was just starting to become interested in presenting on Oracle topics and I was putting together the first abstracts I would submit to some Oracle conference (I can't recall which one it was now). April 19, 1995 was a sunny day and it was no different than any other day. I drove to work, realized that I'd forgotten my laptop, and asked my wife, at the time, to bring it to me. She loaded it in our van, along with our three preschool-aged kids, and dropped it off and kissed me goodbye. Then, literally just 2 to 3 minutes later—just as I sat down at my desk—the loudest sound you can imagine erupted. Glass flew everywhere, false ceilings collapsed, and fluorescent lighting fixtures fell to the ground. In the eerie silence that followed, punctuated with the faraway sounds of a few car alarms and fire alarms, we looked out what was left of our office window to see the shattered remains of the Alfred P. Murrah Federal Building.

In the story of the Oklahoma City bombing, there are many miracles, and that I am alive is probably one. However, that my wife and kids are alive is a genuine miracle. Normally, she would have turned left at the intersection in front of the Murrah building, but instead—and to this day she does not know why—she turned right. Had she turned left, the death toll would have certainly increased by four that day. I am grateful she turned right. That day, and the days afterwards, we watched people do amazing things, go through amazing things, and we watched people suffer great happiness and sadness.

Some years later, in 2011, I was living in Jacksonville, Florida. I was in the middle of writing a book at the time that the events of 9/11 occurred. I can't say that I was directly impacted by the events of 9/11 as much as I was by the Oklahoma City bombing. Indirectly, the attack brought back memories of Oklahoma City and it also reinforced the appreciation I felt for all those who took part in the monumental efforts to save lives. In the midst of the horrors of the absolute disdain for life, we saw the amazing efforts of those who cherish and protect life.

Flash forward to 12/14/2016. During this time, I was in the midst of trying to write *Oracle Database 12c Release 2 New Features*. Frankly, writing a new features book is frustrating in many respects. You only have beta software to start with, you don't know when the product will ship, and yet, you still have a schedule to keep. At the same time, my wife Carrie was pregnant with our newest arrival, who would be named Abigail (Abbie for short!). I won't go into a lot of detail, but we had some challenges with the pregnancy and I was already way behind on the book. The saving grace was that Oracle had not yet released Oracle Database 12c Release 2.

Abbie was born on 12/14/2016—and I'd done the new dad thing before. I figured that I'd get caught up on the book and that everything would be OK. I am not sure my editors shared my sense of confidence in my ability to deliver—but they stuck with me.

Then, several days later, I was feeding Abbie at 5:30 A.M. on Monday morning when my wife said she needed to call 911. The ambulance came, they packed her up, and off she went, leaving me with two kids and not a clue what to do. After some phone calls and scrambling about, I got the kids taken care of and made my way to the hospital. To make a long story short, they could not figure out what was wrong with my wife, and at around 7 that evening she was wheeled into emergency surgery.

She then spent the next two weeks in a coma. After that, it was (and still is) a long road to recovery. She is doing much better now, and as I stated in the dedication, I owe a debt of gratitude to many people.

So, first, I need to acknowledge Wendy Rinaldi and Bob Bryla. When I told Wendy what was going on, she immediately took steps to remove the burden of finishing this book from my plate. I'll be honest, I was hesitant—this book has always been my baby. She was right though; I simply did not have the time to get it done.

Thanks to Bob for stepping in and picking up a very rough piece of work. My understanding is that he went pretty much heads down on this project. Thanks for getting it done, Bob!

Thanks to the whole Oracle Press staff who participated in this project: Claire Yee, Patty Mon, and Janet Walden.

Thanks to my old friend Pete Sharman for technical editing yet another book for me.

I am also thankful to the folks at Oracle who continuously produce a great product in Oracle Database.

—*Robert G. Freeman*

I would like to thank all those who are willing to share their knowledge and continue to make the Oracle Community a better place. Also, I want to thank some of the brightest people I ever worked with and all those who could not be mentioned by name (you know who you are).

—*Eric Yen*

# Introduction

Welcome to *Oracle Database 12c Release 2 New Features*! We're excited about this book, and very excited about how much Oracle Database 12*c* Release 2 expands the extremely cool features introduced in Oracle Database 12*c* Release 1. If you have picked up this book, then we have little doubt that you are also excited about the enhancements included in Oracle Database 12*c* Release 2.

There's something else worthy of mention here in the introduction. While we wrote the initial chapters of this book using pre-release versions of Oracle Database 12*c* Release 2, the final version of this book was tested on the real deal. The results you see in the code throughout this book are from the production database release. We've always done the books in this series that way, because we understand that it's important. In the past, we've seen many things change between pre-release versions and the production release, and we've read other books that were clearly written with pre-release code that didn't work in the production release. You won't find any of that here. As a result of this approach, our book took a bit longer to get to press, but we think it's worth the extra time, and we hope you do too.

If you find that you like this book, please go to your favorite online place to buy books and leave a kind comment. Five-star reviews are always welcome! If you have feedback for us, please send an e-mail to rjbdba@gmail.com with your thoughts and comments or ping Bob on Twitter: @rjbdba. We always look to improve our books, and if you find an error, we want to correct it. Enjoy this book—it's short and sweet but jam-packed with great examples of the best new features in Oracle Database 12*c* Release 2—rock on!

# CHAPTER
1

Getting Started with
Oracle Database 12c
Release 2

Welcome to *Oracle Database 12c Release 2 New Features*, covering Oracle's latest release. I've done my best to provide as much coverage of the many new features in Oracle Database 12*c* Release 2 as fits in a book of this size. Oracle Database 12*c* Release 1 was a big release with a number of new and changed features. Oracle Database 12*c* Release 2 adds many more features and enhances all of the new ones introduced in Release 1!

This first chapter describes everything you need to know to get started with Oracle Database 12*c* Release 2. This includes the following topics:

- Downloading Oracle Database 12*c* Release 2

- Preparing the OS to install Oracle Database 12*c* Release 2

- Installing Oracle Database 12*c* Release 2 (software-only install)

- Preparing to install Oracle Database 12*c* Release 2 Grid Infrastructure

- Staging Oracle Database 12*c* Release 2 Grid Infrastructure (preinstall)

Even on a single-instance, nonclustered database, we want to use Grid Infrastructure (GI) to leverage Automatic Storage Management (ASM). As the preceding list indicates, we're doing a software-only install of Oracle Database, so it doesn't matter whether we set up GI before or after that. The GI setup is "preinstalled" and as such the staging of GI is much easier than in past releases. In any case, you will need to create a GI instance, with storage, before creating your first database, and you'll find the details on that process in Chapter 2. Let's start looking at Oracle Database 12*c* Release 2!

# Downloading Oracle Database 12*c* Release 2 Components

The initial release of Oracle Database 12*c* Release 2 is available on both OTN (www.oracle.com/technetwork/database/enterprise-edition/downloads/index.html) and via Oracle's eDelivery service (https://edelivery.oracle.com). Oracle Database 12*c* Release 2 is considered a "base release" even though it builds on the features introduced in Oracle Database 12*c* Release 1. Some Oracle documentation calls Oracle Database 12*c* Release 2 a "patch set," but since you can do a clean install with no existing databases on your server, I'm calling it a "base release." When patch sets come out every quarter, they will only be available via Oracle Support (https://support.oracle.com).

**NOTE**
*If you want to experiment with the new features of
Oracle Database 12c Release 2 in a preinstalled
environment, you can get prebuilt virtual machines
(VMs) for use with Oracle Virtual Box or Oracle VM
here: www.oracle.com/technetwork/community/
developer-vm/index.html. These VMs are not
intended for use in a production environment.*

If you get the files via the Oracle eDelivery service, here are the packages and
descriptions:

- **V839960-01**  Database
- **V840012-01**  Grid Infrastructure
- **V840019-01**  Global Service Manager
- **V839967-01**  64-bit Linux client
- **V839968-01**  32-bit Linux client
- **V266898-01**  Fusion Middleware

Via OTN, here are the filenames:

- **linuxx64_12201_database.zip**  Database
- **linuxx64_12201_grid_home.zip**  Grid Infrastructure
- **linuxx64_12201_gsm.zip**  Global Service Manager
- **linuxx64_12201_client.zip**  64-bit Linux client
- **linuxx86_12201_client.zip**  32-bit Linux client
- **linuxx64_12201_examples.zip**  Sample schemas and code
- **linuxx64_12201_gateways.zip**  Oracle Gateways

For your initial installation of Oracle Database 12*c* Release 2 and Grid
Infrastructure, you will need only the database and grid packages.

# Preparing the Operating System for Oracle Database 12*c* Release 2

In the examples that follow, I'll be using **V839960-01-database.zip** and **V840012-01-grid.zip** to perform the installations. I'll also be using Oracle Linux 7.3, although most of these guidelines will apply to all hardware and software platforms. Table 1-1 lists the relevant file systems, directories, and raw disk devices in addition to the OS default locations used for all of the examples in this chapter and throughout the book.

At the OS level, there are a number of steps that you need to complete before you start your Oracle Database software installation(s). If the server on which you are going to install Oracle Database 12*c* Release 2 is already running some other release of Oracle Database, then you might have already performed many of these steps. Regardless, it's a best practice to review all of the requirements associated with a new release of Oracle Database and ensure that your current hardware and software meet those requirements.

The following list highlights the most important tasks that you should complete before you install Oracle Database 12*c* Release 2. This list isn't exhaustive (but covers the most important things to check), and it's certainly not hardware specific, so you need to consult the installation guide for your specific hardware and OS combination for a more detailed list of things to do. Many of the tasks will seem very familiar to those who have been working with Oracle Database for a long time.

- Review the Oracle Database Installation Guides (hereafter generically referred to as the install guides) and Readme files. In many cases, Oracle makes the Readme files accessible online so that you don't even need to extract the database software to read them.

- Make sure your OS platform has all required updates installed.

| Device or File System | Contents |
|---|---|
| **/media/zipfiles** | Installation source files |
| **/install** | Staging area for database installer files |
| **/u01/app/oracle** | Oracle "base" for all products and configuration information: $ORACLE_BASE |
| **/dev/sdc1-/dev/sdf1** | ASM disks for DATA disk group |
| **/dev/sdh1-/dev/sdi1** | ASM disks for RECO disk group |

**TABLE 1-1.** *Key Installation File Systems and Devices on the Linux OS*

- Make sure your platform meets the minimum hardware and software requirements. In particular, if you're moving from a much earlier release of Oracle, make sure that the OS version is one supported by Oracle Database 12*c* Release 2. You can find which OS versions are supported (down to individual package versions) either from the My Oracle Support portal (using the Certification Search function on the Certifications tab) or by reviewing the install guide for your particular OS platform.

- Create the required OS groups and users. Note that a new administrative role, SYSRAC, is available to provide more granularity with respect to management of Oracle Real Application Clusters (RAC)–related components. You may wish to create a new OS group to support this new role.

- Check and configure the required kernel parameters for your OS platform. This information is platform specific and is contained in the install guide for your OS platform.

- Check whether any patches to Oracle Database 12*c* Release 2 are required prior to the install.

- Finish the preinstall steps.

Let's look at each of these tasks in some additional detail next.

## Review the Installation Guide and Readme Files

It's always a good practice to review the install guide a few times before you install Oracle Database, especially if you're dealing with a new release. The install guide provides you with a concise list of steps that you should perform as you prepare to install Oracle Database 12*c* Release 2.

> **NOTE**
> *For Oracle Database 12c Release 2, the installation guides are at http://docs.oracle.com/database/122/ nav/install-and-upgrade.htm.*

Additionally, you will find a Readme text file available online that you can review before you download the install media. It's a good idea to read the online version of the Readme file because it contains the most current list of the various files in the install package and what the purpose of each is. That way, you don't end up downloading files you don't need. Readme files are also available in each file of the install media with specific instructions on how to install the files that are on that image. You will also often find other Readme files in other locations within the media that address specific products that you might be installing.

Finally, My Oracle Support usually provides additional documentation online that supplies the most current information with respect to any issues you might encounter when installing Oracle Database 12*c* Release 2. You will find a link to this My Oracle Support documentation in the Readme files both online and on the install media. It's a really good idea to read this supplementary documentation before you start installing and upgrading databases to Oracle Database 12*c* Release 2.

## Make Sure Your OS Platform Has All Required Updates Installed

Review the install guide for your specific OS platform to ensure that you are running on a version of that OS that supports Oracle Database 12*c* Release 2. Additionally, check that guide, the associated Readme files, and the My Oracle Support portal to make sure that you have installed all the OS patches and fixes that are required before installing Oracle Database 12*c* Release 2. On Oracle Linux, this is as easy as running **yum update** from a user logged in as **root**.

## Make Sure Your Platform Meets the Minimum Requirements

Before you begin your install, make sure the platform on which you will be installing Oracle Database 12*c* Release 2 meets the minimum hardware and software requirements. Of course, minimum requirements are just that—*minimum* requirements—and don't ensure peak performance of your databases. Total requirements of the platform with respect to disk space, memory, and CPU usage are impacted by other factors such as plans to add databases in the future, the nature of the processing that occurs in the databases, and so on.

Oracle Database 12*c* Release 2 is fully supported on Oracle Linux (OL) 6.x and 7.x as well as on the equivalent Red Hat Enterprise Linux (RHEL) releases. Otherwise, the general minimum server requirements vary by platform. To give you an example, the following sections outline some of the stated requirements for a Linux x86-64 (64 bit) install on Oracle Linux.

### Oracle Database 12*c* Release 2 Software Storage Requirements

A Linux x86-64 install has the following software storage requirements for the two Oracle Database 12*c* Release 2 editions and Grid Infrastructure:

- Oracle Database Enterprise *or* Standard Edition: 7.5 GB
- Oracle Grid Infrastructure: 8.6 GB

The space requirements for GI seem a bit steep, but keep in mind that at the heart of GI is another very specialized Oracle Database plus the software required to manage high availability (HA) configurations such as RAC and ASM. The benefits of ASM alone justify the disk space required for the software itself! Also keep in mind that the disk space requirements for the database itself, backups, redo log files, and so forth depend on your application, but to create an empty database with all of the options, it will occupy about 2 GB. Each additional database will be about the same size unless you are using Oracle's Multitenant Architecture (container databases)—which you should also be using, but those enhancements are a topic for another chapter!

The **/tmp** directory requires a minimum of 1 GB of space. If you do not have enough space in **/tmp**, then either increase the amount of space in that file system or set the TMP or TMPDIR environment variable in the Oracle environment.

## Oracle Database 12*c* Release 2 Memory Requirements

The Oracle Database 12*c* Release 2 memory requirements for a Linux x86-64 install are as follows:

- Oracle Database: minimum of 1 GB (recommend 2 GB of RAM or more).

- Swap space:

    - If you have between 1 GB and 2 GB of memory on your system, then you should allocate 1.5 times the amount of RAM for swap space.

    - If you have more than 2 GB of memory on your system, then you should allocate an amount of swap space equal to the amount of memory available on the system, up to 16 GB.

- Oracle Grid Infrastructure (GI): at least 8 GB.

**NOTE**
*To reiterate, these are* minimum, *bare-bones requirements for database memory. Typically, you will want a great deal more memory on your system. The amount of memory that you will need is very dependent on the nature and number of the databases that you intend to run on the system.*

## Operating System Requirements

As of this writing, Oracle Database 12c Release 2 supports the following Linux distributions:

- Oracle Linux 7.x and Red Hat Linux 7.x distributions for x86-64

- Oracle Linux 6.4 and Red Hat Linux 6.4 distributions for x86-64

- SUSE Linux Enterprise Server 12 SP1

You can use a command such as **uname -a**, **cat /etc/oracle-release**, **cat /etc/ redhat-release**, or **lsb_release -id** to determine the distribution and version of Linux that is installed. Here is an example of checking both the Oracle and Red Hat versions of the OS (the version number should be the same with minor differences in the details):

```
[root@ol7base ~]# cat /etc/oracle-release
Oracle Linux Server release 7.3
[root@ol7base ~]# cat /etc/redhat-release
Red Hat Enterprise Linux Server release 7.3 (Maipo)
```

You will also want to determine whether the required kernel errata is installed by using the **uname -r** command, as shown here:

```
[root@ol7base ~]# uname -r
3.8.13-118.16.4.el7uek.x86_64
```

The installation guide indicates that I need to be on the Linux kernel 2.6.x (version 6.4) or later, or kernel 3.8.x (version 7.3) or later, therefore I have the correct server release installed. The current install guide (or updated Readme file) will contain the latest minimum release level required. The Linux distributions from Oracle and Red Hat differ mainly in the availability of the Unbreakable Enterprise Kernel (UEK), which as you might expect has many additional HA features. Unless you are in a 100 percent Red Hat shop or have other licensing issues, Oracle Linux is by far the best choice given that the vast majority of Oracle Database's development and testing is performed on that platform.

For Linux distributions, a number of packages must be installed. Check the current install guide for a list of these required packages. Use the **rpm** command to query the system to determine if the correct packages are installed. For example, I might want to check that the correct release for **binutils** (binutils-2.17.50.0.6 or later as of this writing) is installed. I can use the following command to check this information:

```
[root@ol7base ~]# rpm -q binutils
binutils-2.25.1-22.base.el7.x86_64
```

But there is a much easier way to go about this! If you are using Oracle Linux and are signed up with the Unbreakable Linux Network (https://linux.oracle.com), you can take advantage of the Oracle preinstallation RPM. Simply subscribe to the relevant preinstallation channel and then use **yum** to install the correct preinstall RPM, as shown here (note that the name of the package might well change over time, so make sure you check the documentation for the correct name):

```
[root@ol7base ~]# yum install oracle-rdbms-server-12cR2-preinstall
Resolving Dependencies
--> Running transaction check
---> Package oracle-database-server-12cR2-preinstall.x86_64 0:1.0-2.el7 will be
installed
--> Finished Dependency Resolution
. . .
Installing:
 oracle-database-server-12cR2-preinstall      x86_64       1.0-2.el7
ol7_latest        18 k
. . .
Total download size: 18 k
Installed size: 52 k
Is this ok [y/d/N]:
Installed:
  oracle-database-server-12cR2-preinstall.x86_64 0:1.0-2.el7
Complete!
[root@ol7base 12.2.0]$
```

When you run this package, it creates the OS groups and users that are required, sets various kernel parameters, and performs other required preinstall actions. The installation guides provide a great deal more information on how to use this feature.

## Create the Required OS Groups and Users

If this is the first install on the system you are using, then you need to create the Oracle environment. The process to do this has not changed in Oracle Database 12*c* Release 2. You still create (default names given in parentheses) the Oracle inventory group (**oinstall**), the OSDBA group (**dba**), the Oracle software owner (the **oracle** OS account), and the OSOPER group (**oper**). A new OS group called the RAC Administrative Group is available in Oracle Database 12*c* Release 2 and you may want to consider adding a new group to support the functionality of the RAC administrator. Otherwise, for a smaller infrastructure with a single DBA, the only roles you'll probably need are the **oinstall** and **dba** groups. To further divide responsibilities, you can create the **grid** user to own the GI software directory.

**NOTE**
*If you use the Oracle preinstall package, these users and groups are created for you automatically.*

## Configure the Kernel Parameters

On a new system, you need to set the OS kernel parameters if you have not used the Oracle RDBMS preinstall RPM referenced earlier in the chapter. Refer to the Oracle Database 12c Release 2 install guide for your specific OS for recommended minimum values. The Oracle install guide for your OS also provides you with the recommended minimums and methods to determine the current settings and reset those settings if required.

**NOTE**
*I often find that the minimum values for the parameters recommended by Oracle quickly become insufficient for larger database installations. If you are not familiar with the operating system you are working with, you should discuss the recommended settings with an experienced OS administrator and determine if higher values are advisable.*

I often find that one of the places that I run into problems is with the resource limits defined for the account that owns the Oracle database software and runs the background processes upon database startup (typically this is the **oracle** user). Make sure that the limits for the **oracle** account are set to at least the minimum values listed in the install guide.

## Check for Patches

Something else to consider when installing Oracle Database 12c Release 2 is that there may be a patch set that you should apply. In fact, I'm a strong believer in keeping all production databases up to date with each quarterly Oracle Database proactive bundle patch (BP), Patch Set Update (PSU), or at a minimum, the Oracle Security Patch Update (SPU) after performing the appropriate regression testing in a QA environment. By the time you read this, there will likely be at least one quarterly BP, PSU, or SPU available for Oracle Database 12c Release 2, so consider applying the most recent version to the base database software install.

All BPs, PSUs, and SPUs can only be found on the My Oracle Support website. If applicable, you would install the BP, PSU, or SPU after you have installed the base Oracle Database software. Figure 1-1 shows the hierarchical content of Oracle quarterly patch sets.

A quarterly SPU is included in each PSU, and a BP includes everything in the PSU. Bundle patches will have additional fixes that are generally not critical but include things like optimizer fixes or enhancements. As a result, BPs may require a higher level of regression testing before deploying them in your production environment.

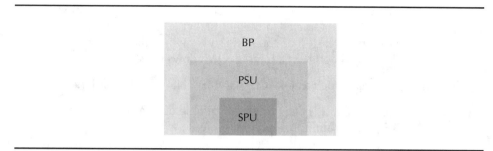

**FIGURE 1-1.**   *Quarterly database patch content*

**NOTE**
*Future patch sets will not have stand-alone SPU patch sets—you will be required to install a PSU or BP to get the security fixes. The SPU+PSU gives you the minimum set of patches to ensure a secure database environment with the most important database fixes that affect the vast majority of database users.*

## Finish the Preinstall Steps

You are almost ready to install the software for Oracle Database 12*c* Release 2 (database and GI). Before you can begin the install, you need to complete the following steps:

- Determine the location of the ORACLE_BASE directory. If you already have a previous release of Oracle Database installed on the system, then you should use the same ORACLE_BASE directory that is already defined. This is not required but highly recommended. For the examples throughout this book, this will be **/u01/app/oracle**:

```
[oracle@ol7base ~]$ ls -l /u01/app/oracle
total 8
drwxr-xr-x.  2 oracle oinstall    6 Aug 31  2016 12.1.0
drwxr-xr-x. 69 oracle oinstall 4096 Mar  3 17:32 12.2.0
drwxr-xr-x.  2 oracle oinstall    6 Mar  3 21:32 checkpoints
drwxrwxr-x. 21 oracle oinstall 4096 Mar  3 21:27 diag
drwxr-xr-x.  3 oracle oinstall   19 Mar  3 21:25 product
[oracle@ol7base ~]$
```

- Ensure that you can start an X terminal session (if installing on Linux) so that you can run the Oracle Universal Installer (OUI). Alternatively, if you are using a Linux desktop on the same server where the software will be installed, you will not need a remote X Windows server.

- Unset parameters such as ORACLE_HOME, TNS_ADMIN, and the like.

- Make sure that the PATH environment variable does not include an existing **$ORACLE_HOME/bin** from a previous release.

**NOTE**
*In earlier Oracle Database releases, it was common to set ORACLE_HOME to the location of the new ORACLE_HOME before starting a new software install. It is now recommended that you set the ORACLE_BASE parameter instead. When ORACLE_BASE is set, the OUI creates an ORACLE_HOME path that is compliant with Oracle's Optimal Flexible Architecture (OFA). It is recommended that you accept the ORACLE_HOME path that the OUI recommends.*

# Installing Oracle Database 12*c* Release 2

Now that you have made sure your system is ready to install Oracle Database 12*c* Release 2, you can begin the installation process. For purposes of demonstration, in this section I am showing the steps for installing Oracle Database 12*c* Release 2 Enterprise Edition on Oracle Linux x86-64. In this section you will

- Prepare the installation environment

- Install Oracle Database 12*c* Release 2 using the OUI

- Stage the Oracle Database 12*c* Release 2 Grid Infrastructure software

**NOTE**
*Oracle Database 12c Release 2 cannot be installed over an existing ORACLE_HOME location, so you will be installing into a new ORACLE_HOME.*

The ZIP files are at **/media/zipfiles** and you are extracting them into the **/install** directory identified at the beginning of the chapter:

```
[oracle@ol7base 12.2.0.1]$ pwd
/install/db/12.2.0.1
[oracle@ol7base 12.2.0.1]$ ls -l /media/zipfiles/*.zip
-rwxrwx---. 1 root vboxsf 3453696911 Mar  1 17:19
    /media/zipfiles/V839960-01-database.zip
-rwxrwx---. 1 root vboxsf 2994687209 Mar  1 17:30
    /media/zipfiles/V840012-01-grid.zip
[oracle@ol7base 12.2.0.1]$ unzip /media/zipfiles/*database*.zip
. . .
[oracle@ol7base database]$ pwd
/install/db/12.2.0.1/database
[oracle@ol7base database]$ ls
install  response  rpm  runInstaller  sshsetup  stage  welcome.html
[oracle@ol7base database]$
```

The actual database installer files are now ready to run from **/install/db/12.2.0.1/database**.

## Prepare the Installation Environment

Before you can start the install, you first need to set up the environment so that you can run an X Windows session, and then you need to log in as the **oracle** user. There are many ways to run an X Windows session. In the examples that follow, I am logged directly into the server. You could use other methods, like VNC or SSH tunneling with X Server software on your laptop. As with many things, there are a number of ways to get the job done.

Before performing the install, set the ORACLE_BASE directory to **/u01/app/oracle**:

```
export ORACLE_BASE=/u01/app/oracle
```

Now you are ready to start the Oracle Universal Installer and begin the database install.

## Install Oracle Database 12*c* Release 2 Using the OUI

To begin the install process, **cd** to the directory in which you extracted the install media. From that directory, you will find the **runInstaller** program, which is used to start the database software install. Then, start the **runInstaller** program as shown in this example from a Linux OS prompt:

```
[oracle@ol7base database]$ ./runInstaller
```

This launches the Oracle Universal Installer.

**NOTE**
*Depending on your operating system software, you may need to perform additional steps before you can start the **runInstaller** program. Additionally, the way you actually start the **runInstaller** program may vary by platform. This is all documented in the install guide for your platform.*

During the install, the OUI presents you with several screens for entering your install information. The look and feel of the OUI has not changed a great deal since Oracle Database 11g Release 2 or Oracle Database 12c Release 1, so if you have installed either of those releases, this process should feel familiar to you.

Figure 1-2 shows the first screen that you will see when you start the OUI, prompting you to enter your email address and your My Oracle Support password to get automated security updates. You can also choose to skip this step and move on if you prefer. Either way, click the Next button.

**NOTE**
*If you do choose not to include an email address, the OUI will ask you if you are sure you wish to remain uninformed of critical security issues. You can simply click Yes and proceed with the install.*

Figure 1-2 also provides a good template for the general way the rest of the OUI screens look. There are buttons at the bottom right of the screen that allow you to proceed to the next step, return to the previous step, cancel the install, or proceed with the install when you have answered the required questions. The left pane is a navigation pane that shows the list of installation steps so that you can easily see which step you are currently on, which steps you have completed, and which steps remain to be completed. A Help button is found at the bottom left, which you can click to access help with the specific screen you are on.

The next OUI step is the Select Installation Option screen, shown in Figure 1-3. From this screen you can decide what kind of install you wish to perform.

The Select Installation Option screen gives you three options:

■ **Create and configure a database** Installs the Oracle Database 12c Release 2 software and also creates a small Oracle database and configures the networking associated with that database. This is probably a good choice if you don't have a PSU or BP to apply after the database software install. By creating a database, you can test the success of the database software install.

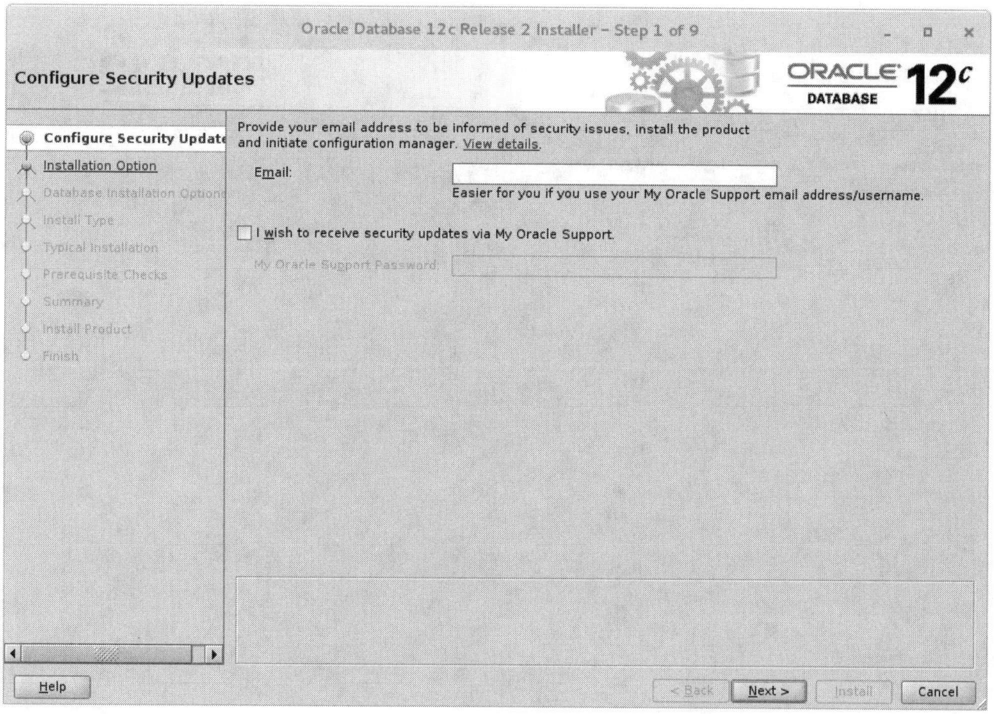

**FIGURE 1-2.**   *OUI Configure Security Updates (and marketing) screen*

- **Install database software only**   Installs the Oracle Database 12c Release 2 software only. You would need to manually create a database afterward using the Oracle Database Creation Assistant. This is the option I typically choose if I have a PSU or BP that I want to apply. In that case, I first apply the base Oracle Database software install, then I install the BP and any other patches that might be required. After I've installed the patches, I then create a test database to test the database software install.

- **Upgrade an existing database**   Starts the Oracle Database Upgrade Assistant, which will give you an option to upgrade an existing database to Oracle Database 12c Release 2.

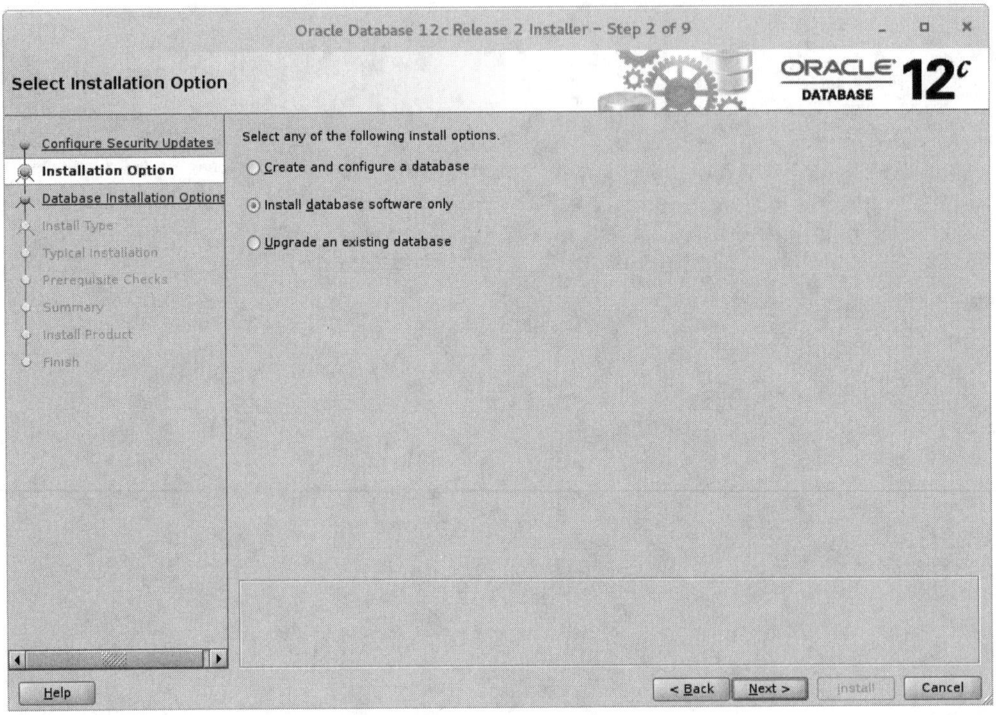

**FIGURE 1-3.** *OUI Select Installation Option screen*

As you can see, which option you should choose depends largely on whether you have PSUs or BPs that you want to apply after the initial database install. After you click Next, you will see the Select Database Installation Option screen, shown in Figure 1-4.

The Select Database Installation Option screen enables you to select the type of install you want. You have three options to choose from:

- **Single instance database installation**   Indicates that you want the installer to install a single instance of the Oracle Database software.

- **Oracle Real Application Clusters database installation**   Indicates that you want the installer to install a RAC-compatible version of the Oracle

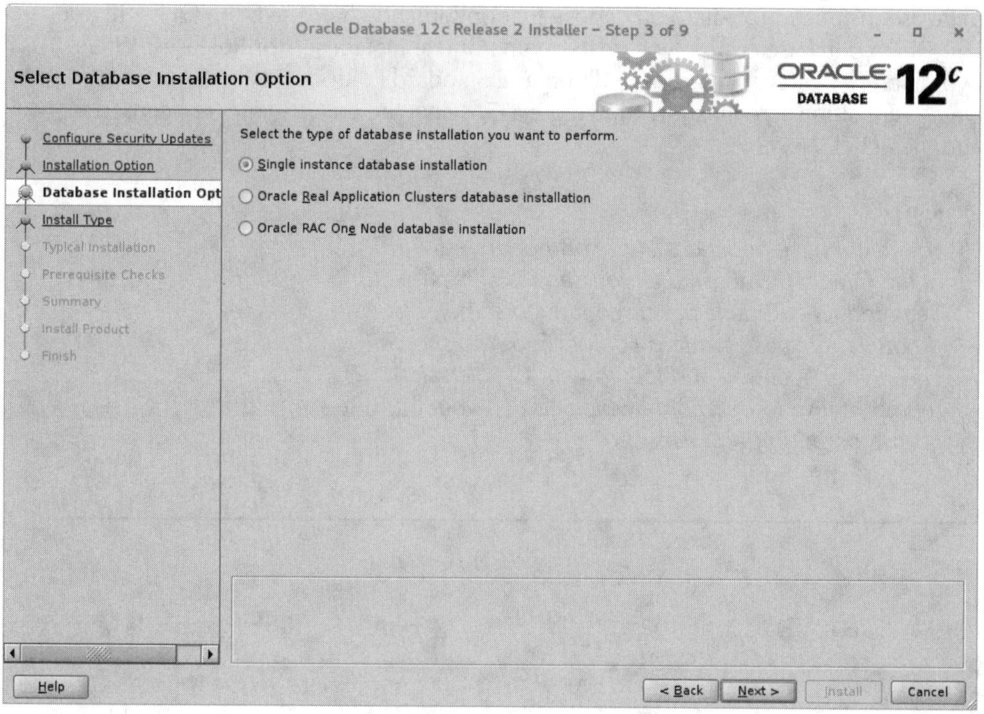

**FIGURE 1-4.**   *OUI Select Database Installation Option screen*

Database software. Oracle RAC is a high-availability option that provides the ability to access an Oracle database from more than one database server.

- **Oracle RAC One Node database installation**   Indicates that you want the installer to install a version of the Oracle Database software that will support Oracle RAC One Node. Oracle RAC One Node provides high availability for single-instance Oracle databases by providing the ability to fail over to a passive database node and also positioning your infrastructure to use Oracle RAC when the time comes.

For the purposes of the most common scenario, choose "Single instance database installation." After you choose that option and click Next, the OUI will ask you which database edition you wish to run. Oracle Database 12c Release 2 offers two different editions: Enterprise Edition and Standard Edition. On the Select Database Edition screen, shown in Figure 1-5, select the edition you are licensed for and then click Next.

**NOTE**
*You might have noticed that the number of editions of the Oracle Database that you can install has been reduced. Oracle has discontinued some of its products, such as Standard Edition Two. You should check your licensing and talk to your Oracle sales representative to determine which edition your license permits you to use.*

Oracle Database 12c Release 2 Installer – Step 4 of 10

**Select Database Edition**

ORACLE **12**c
DATABASE

- Configure Security Updates
- Installation Option
- Database Installation Options
- **Database Edition**
- Installation Location
- Operating System Groups
- Prerequisite Checks
- Summary
- Install Product
- Finish

Which database edition do you want to install?

⊙ Enterprise Edition (7.5GB)

Oracle Database 12c Enterprise Edition is a self-managing database that has the scalability, performance, high availability, and security features required to run the most demanding, mission-critical applications.

○ Standard Edition 2 (7.5GB)

Oracle Database 12c Standard Edition 2 is a full-featured data management solution ideally suited to the needs of medium-sized businesses. It includes Oracle Real Application Clusters for enterprise-class availability and comes complete with its own Oracle Clusterware and storage management capabilities.

Help    < Back    Next >    Install    Cancel

**FIGURE 1-5.** *OUI Select Database Edition screen*

Next, the OUI presents the Specify Installation Location screen, as shown in Figure 1-6. It is from this screen that you choose the location for ORACLE_BASE, which is the base location from which the Oracle Database software will be installed. ORACLE_BASE is part of the Oracle Optimal Flexible Architecture (OFA) feature, which supports the ability to store many different versions of the Oracle Database software on a given database server. The OUI provides a default value for the ORACLE_BASE parameter and it is the same directory we created for that purpose earlier in this chapter, so the default value is perfect!

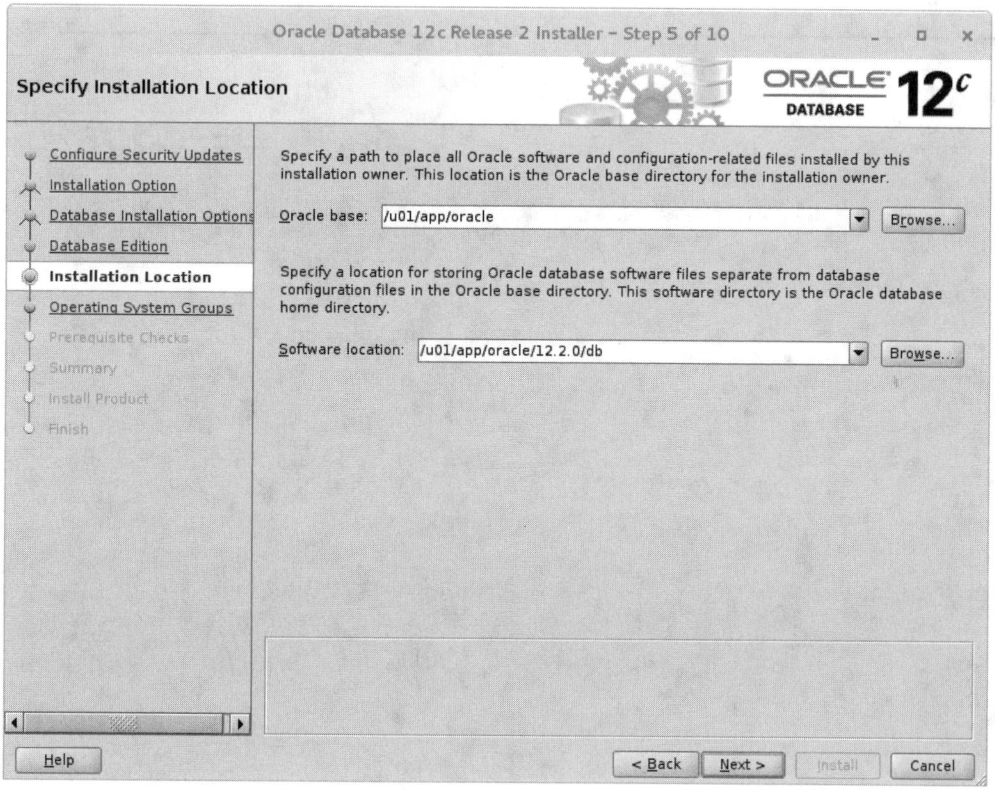

**FIGURE 1-6.**    *OUI Specify Installation Location screen*

After setting the ORACLE_BASE parameter, set the ORACLE_HOME parameter. The ORACLE_HOME parameter should always start with the ORACLE_BASE parameter. The installer will provide a recommended location to install the Oracle Database software. Make sure that this location is associated with the OS file system that you want the Oracle Database software to be installed on. The OFA standard does define a particular format for the directory naming location that the installer will follow—so use caution when considering changing the default setting for ORACLE_HOME.

Once you have set the ORACLE_BASE and ORACLE_HOME locations, click Next. The OUI presents the Create Inventory screen, shown in Figure 1-7, which

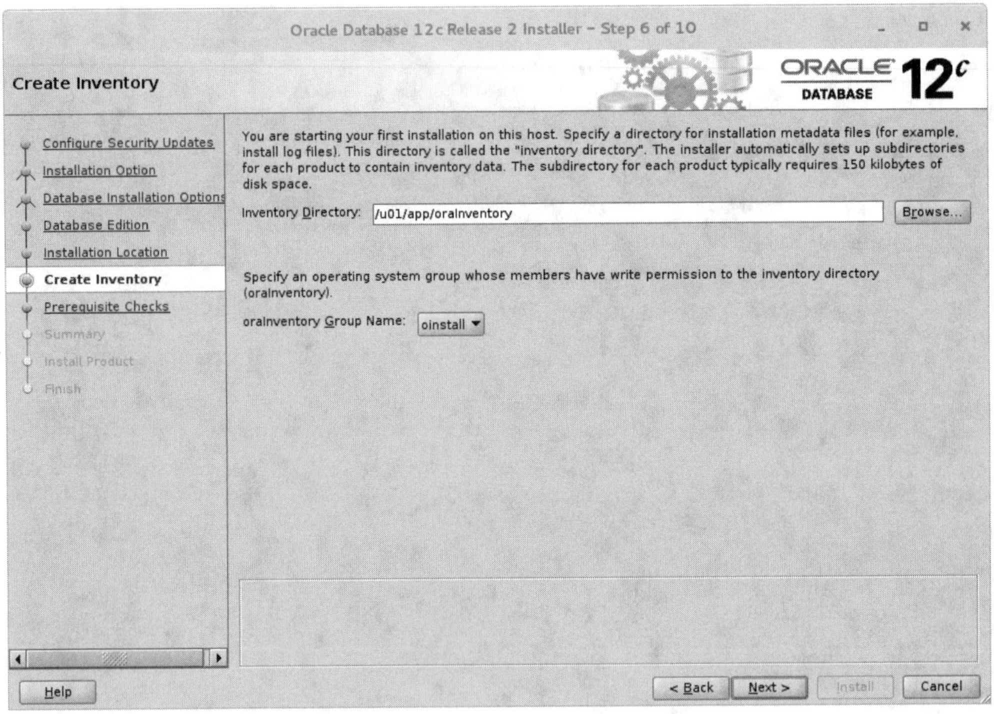

**FIGURE 1-7.** *OUI Create Inventory Directory*

defines where Oracle stores the Oracle inventory. Note that this screen typically is only relevant for a system that does not already have Oracle Database software installed. The inventory contains a list of Oracle software, versions, and locations for all Oracle products installed on this server. Typically, you should not need to change anything in this screen, in which case you can just click Next to proceed to the Privileged Operating System Groups screen, shown in Figure 1-8.

It is in this screen that you can choose the various operating system groups that are associated with the various database privileges, such as SYSDBA, OSOPER, OSBACKUPDBA, and so on. Select the OS groups that you want to assign to the specific privileged groups and click Next. At this point, the OUI will begin to perform the prerequisite checks. If there are any OS or database settings that don't comply with Oracle's minimum requirements, you'll see this on a findings screen.

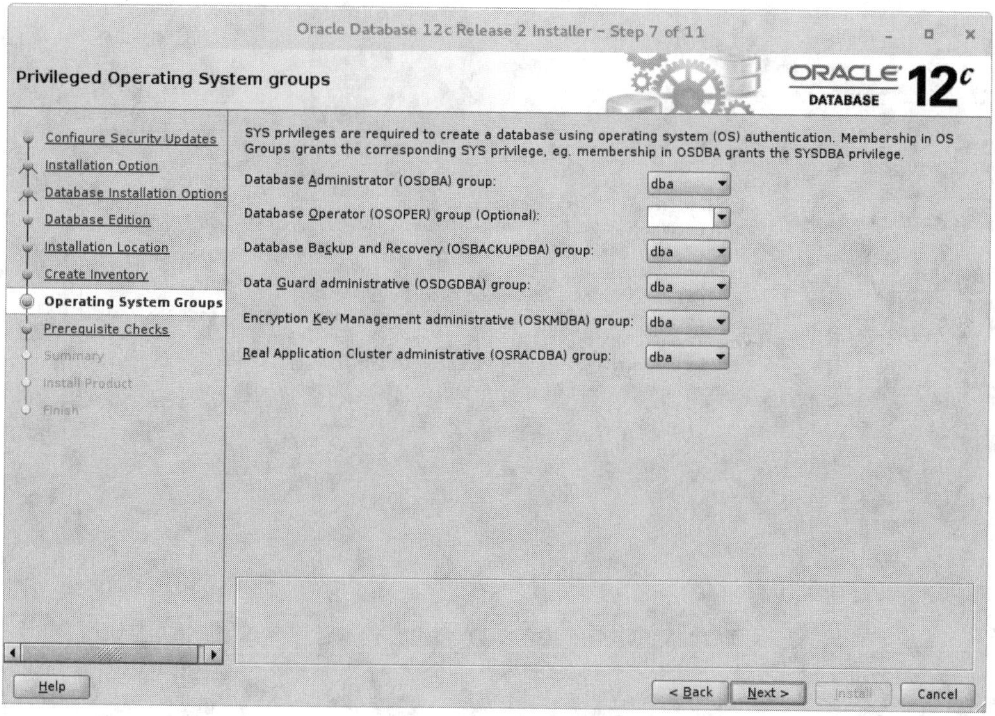

**FIGURE 1-8.** *OUI Privileged Operating System Groups screen*

Some findings can actually be corrected by the OUI. In those cases, you can click the Fix and Check Again button to correct the problem. Sometimes, you will find that the problem reported is one that can be ignored, but otherwise fix the requirements and retry the prerequisite check.

The Summary screen, shown in Figure 1-9, provides a review of the operations that the OUI is going to be completing. If you wish to change something, you can click Back and return to previous screens. If, after reviewing all of the configuration settings, you are ready to begin the database install, then click the Install button.

The Install Product screen shown in Figure 1-10 appears and indicates the install progress. Toward the end of the product install, the OUI will present you with the Execute Configuration Scripts dialog box, as shown in Figure 1-11. This dialog box will indicate that you should run one or more scripts from the **root** OS account. You should run each script as **root**, in the order listed in the OUI screen.

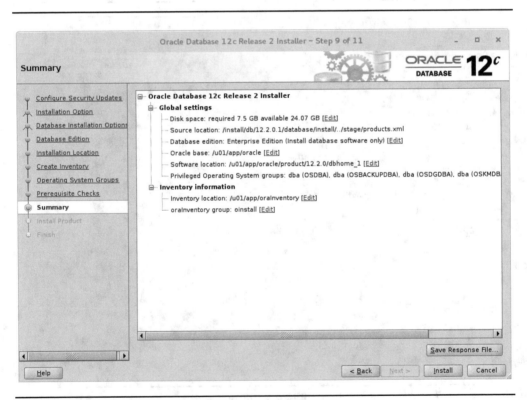

**FIGURE 1-9.** *OUI database install Summary screen*

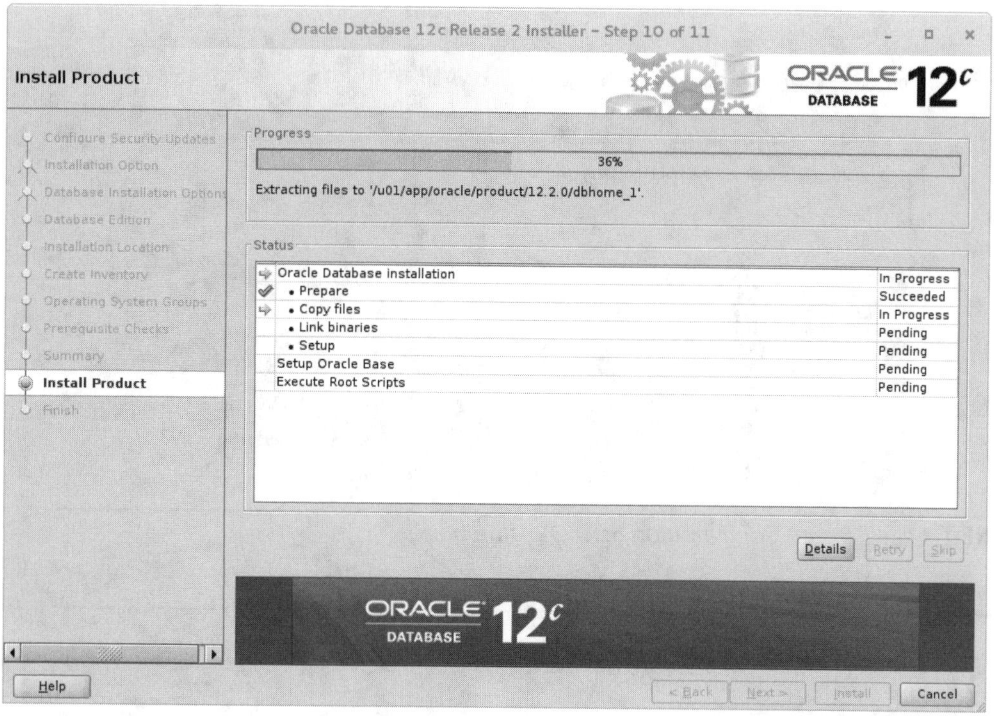

**FIGURE 1-10.**   *OUI Install Product progress screen*

When you run the root.sh script from the $ORACLE_HOME that you just created, it will ask if you want to install the Trace File Analyzer (TFA), a tool that Oracle uses for problem diagnosis. I recommend that you install the TFA when prompted. If you do not install the TFA, the **root.sh** terminal session will provide you with a link to the location of the TFA should you wish to install it later. Note that if you already have the TFA installed, then you won't see this message.

After you run the configuration scripts, click the OK button in the Execute Configuration Scripts dialog box. At this point, Oracle will indicate that the install has completed successfully, as shown in the example in Figure 1-12. Click Close to complete the install. When you click Close, Oracle will give you an option to move the log file, which is currently in a temporary location, to a permanent location. If you wish to do so, select a new location to which to move the log file and then click the Move and Exit button. Otherwise, complete the install process by clicking the Exit button.

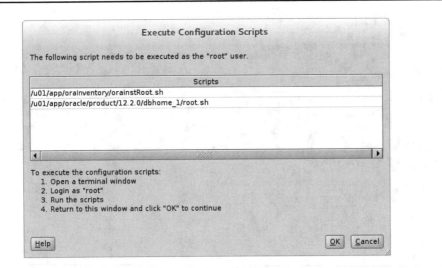

**FIGURE 1-11.** *Execute Configuration Scripts dialog box*

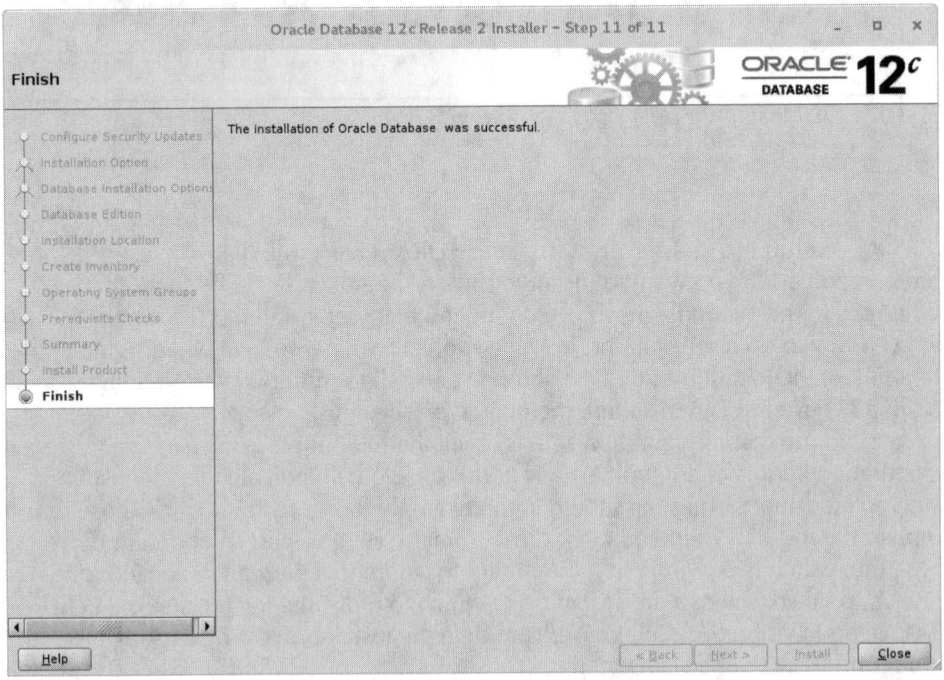

**FIGURE 1-12.** *OUI Database install completion screen*

# Installing Oracle Database 12*c* Release 2 Grid Infrastructure

The Grid Infrastructure setup is optional but recommended even for a single-instance database given the features of ASM alone. You will find out in the sections that follow how to stage the GI installation since it is handled a bit differently from a database software installation—essentially, the GI software is prestaged, so there is no need to run a "software only" installation.

## Prepare to Install Oracle Database 12*c* Release 2 Grid Infrastructure

As with the database part of the installation, you need to create a directory under $ORACLE_BASE for the GI home. It's essentially another Oracle home to support the components of Grid Infrastructure—in particular, ASM. The preinstall tasks are easy in that you must ensure that the **oracle** user owns the GI home, as in this example that we'll be using throughout this book:

```
[oracle@ol7base oracle]$ cd /u01/app/oracle/12.2.0
[oracle@ol7base 12.2.0]$ mkdir grid
[oracle@ol7base 12.2.0]$ ls -l
total 0
drwxr-xr-x. 2 oracle oinstall 6 Mar  2  2016 db
drwxr-xr-x. 2 oracle oinstall 6 Mar  3 17:20 grid
[oracle@ol7base 12.2.0]$
```

## Stage Oracle Database 12*c* Release 2 Grid Infrastructure

The GI software is already preinstalled as part of the ZIP file package. Therefore, before creating your ASM instance (which we'll do in Chapter 2), all you have to do is unzip the GI package into the directory you just created in the previous section:

```
[oracle@ol7base 12.2.0]$ cd grid
[oracle@ol7base grid]$ ls -l /media/zipfiles/*.zip
-rwxrwx---. 1 root vboxsf 3453696911 Mar  1 17:19
    /media/zipfiles/V839960-01-database.zip
-rwxrwx---. 1 root vboxsf 2994687209 Mar  1 17:30
    /media/zipfiles/V840012-01-grid.zip
[oracle@ol7base grid]$ unzip /media/zipfiles/V840012-01-grid.zip
. . .
  lib/libclntshcore.so    -> libclntshcore.so.12.1
  lib/libjavavm12.a       -> ../javavm/jdk/jdk8/lib/libjavavm12.a
```

```
    lib/libodm12.so        -> libodmd12.so
    lib/libagtsh.so        -> libagtsh.so.1.0
    lib/libclntsh.so       -> libclntsh.so.12.1
    lib/libocci.so         -> libocci.so.12.1
[oracle@ol7base grid]$
```

# Deinstalling Oracle Database 12*c* Release 2

To deinstall Oracle Database 12c Release 2 (or earlier releases), you need to download and install the Oracle Database deinstallation tool ("deinstaller"). The deinstaller package is contained in the various install images in the Oracle Database Install file collection. To deinstall a release of Oracle Database, make sure that you download the deinstaller that is associated with the specific release that you want to remove. For example, if you want to deinstall an Oracle Database 12c Release 1 ORACLE_HOME, then you would use the deinstaller for Oracle Database 12c Release 1, and not the deinstaller for any other release.

Be careful when you use the deinstaller because it will remove configuration files contained in the ORACLE_HOME that you are going to delete. For example, assume you have two Oracle Database 12c Release 1 ORACLE_HOMEs. All of your databases might be running from the single ORACLE_HOME, but the listener that serves those databases might be configured and running out of the ORACLE_HOME you are planning on removing.

When I remove an ORACLE_HOME in Linux, I always use the **lsof** utility to determine if that ORACLE_HOME has any files open. I also use utilities like **ps** to determine if any processes are running that are using software in those ORACLE_HOME directories.

# Summary

This chapter has guided you through the installation of Oracle Database 12c Release 2. You learned how to use the OUI to properly install the Oracle Database software as well as how to set up Grid Infrastructure installation. If everything goes wrong, the Oracle deinstallation utility can remove the Oracle Database software. In the next chapter we will discuss creating a new Oracle 12c Release 2 database and upgrading an existing database to Oracle Database 12c Release 2. We will also discuss downgrading from Oracle Database 12c Release 2 if that is required.

# CHAPTER
## 2

# Installing or Upgrading to Oracle Database 12c Release 2

This chapter covers both installing Oracle Database 12c Release 2 and Grid Infrastructure from scratch and upgrading your existing Oracle databases to Oracle Database 12c Release 2. In this chapter we cover the following topics:

- Installing Oracle Database 12c Release 2 Grid Infrastructure (ASM)

- Creating a new Oracle Database 12c Release 2 database

- Upgrading a non-multitenant Oracle database (including pre–Oracle Database 12c databases)

- Upgrading a multitenant architecture Oracle database

- Deprecated and desupported features in Oracle Database 12c Release 2

We'll start off this chapter by installing Oracle Database 12c Release 2 Grid Infrastructure (GI) of which ASM is the most important component, especially in a single-server environment. This deployment is required in a Real Application Clusters (RAC) environment, but even in a single-instance, single-server environment, using Automatic Storage Management (ASM) makes storage management… well, more automatic, with less DBA and OS storage administrator involvement, while at the same time ensuring the best performance from your storage subsystem.

Once ASM storage is in place, you can install one or more new databases. If you install multiple new databases, they all can share the ASM disk groups created during the Grid Infrastructure install. Ideally, all of your database upgrades would involve creating new databases on the new version and then migrating the data only using tools like Oracle Data Pump. In reality, however, few DBAs have the luxury of that option unless they are migrating the database to a new server with additional storage.

Regarding database upgrades, a bit of a disclaimer is in order. The upgrade process can be very complex because it involves a number of different permutations based on the hardware your database is running on, the Oracle Database release you are moving from, the database features you are using, security you have implemented, your tolerance for outage, and many other considerations. Because of these complexities, it's not possible for this chapter to be anything close to a comprehensive guide to upgrading to Oracle Database 12c Release 2. Instead, this chapter provides you with some best practices with respect to upgrading your databases and gives you some idea of things you should and should not do; consider this chapter to be more of an introductory swimming lesson than a guide to crossing the English Channel. It is a place to get your feet wet, a summary of the basic methods and tasks involved in upgrading to Oracle Database 12c Release 2.

That being said, before you attempt to upgrade your production databases, please make sure you thoroughly read the *Oracle Database Upgrade Guide* and the Readme files associated with the database distribution and become comfortable with the entire upgrade process. Also, I recommend doing a few test upgrades in a test environment until you're comfortable with the process.

Another important thing to note is the list of desupported features at the end of this chapter. In particular, if you are using Advanced Replication, you should know that it's been desupported as of this release. That might well impact your database upgrade plans just a wee bit. Other changes like desupported parameters can cause upgrade problems, so make sure you carefully review the last part of this chapter.

With those caveats in mind, let's take a look at how you can upgrade to Oracle Database 12*c* Release 2, starting with the installation of Grid Infrastructure!

# Installing Oracle Database 12*c* Release 2 Grid Infrastructure

Having a robust storage environment is a foundation for any type of database, whether it be a data warehouse or an online store. Oracle ASM, part of Oracle Database 12*c* Grid Infrastructure (GI), provides this foundation by managing and optimizing your database storage so you don't have to. In the following sections, we'll pick up where we left off in Chapter 1 with the Grid Infrastructure preinstall to create the ASM instance using the Oracle Universal Installer (OUI), add the default disk group for application storage, then use the Oracle ASM Configuration Assistant (ASMCA) to create a fast recovery area to hold database backups, copies of control files, archived redo log files, and more!

Before proceeding with the ASM setup, look at Table 2-1 for the list of raw devices we'll use for storage. Four of the raw devices are for the DATA disk group and two are for the RECO disk group. Since we're installing GI on Oracle Linux, we can take advantage of the ASMLib driver, managed via the **oracleasm** command, and those device names are exposed in the directory **/dev/oracleasm/disks** and also identified in Table 2-1.

| Raw Device Name | Size | oracleasm Disk Name in /dev/oracleasm/disks | Disk Group |
|---|---|---|---|
| /dev/sdb | 32 GB | ASM01 | DATA |
| /dev/sdc | 32 GB | ASM02 | DATA |
| /dev/sdd | 32 GB | ASM03 | DATA |
| /dev/sde | 32 GB | ASM04 | DATA |
| /dev/sdh | 100 GB | ASM07 | RECO |
| /dev/sdi | 100 GB | ASM08 | RECO |

**TABLE 2-1.**   *ASM Raw Device and ASMLib Storage Locations*

With the Grid Infrastructure software already staged in **/u01/app/oracle/12.2.0/grid** from Chapter 1, here are the steps we'll use to get ASM up and running and ready for a database installation:

- Configure the Oracle Database 12*c* Grid Infrastructure software with the DATA disk group

- Add the RECO disk group using the remaining raw disks

## Configure Grid Infrastructure and Start ASM

The **/u01/app/oracle/12.2.0/grid** directory contains the script **gridSetup.sh**, which performs the same function as the very familiar **runInstaller** script you see when you install the database software. Start the setup from that directory as follows:

```
[oracle@ol7base grid]$ pwd
/u01/app/oracle/12.2.0/grid
[oracle@ol7base grid]$ ./gridSetup.sh
Launching Oracle Grid Infrastructure Setup Wizard...
```

The first step of the OUI wizard, Select Configuration Option, is shown in Figure 2-1. Choose the second option, Configure Oracle Grid Infrastructure for a Standalone Server, instead of the first option for configuring a new cluster.

Click Next to move to the Create ASM Disk Group step, shown in Figure 2-2, where you create the initial disk group (defaults to DATA). You'll also see the available disks for new disk groups. I'll use the first four 32 GB disks for the DATA disk group and use the remaining two for the RECO disk group that is added in the next section.

**NOTE**
*If you do not see the disks in the expected location, click Change Discovery Path to inform the OUI of the location of your storage.*

For the Redundancy setting, be sure to specify External if your disks are already striped or mirrored on a storage area network (SAN). Otherwise, if they are local physical disks, specify either Normal or High to let ASM handle the disk redundancy— Normal means that two sets of disks are paired and High means three sets of disks are paired. Since I'm relying on the SAN for mirroring, the total disk space for the DATA disk group will be approximately 125 GB. You'll select Flex if you're setting up an ASM disk group for an ASM Flex cluster.

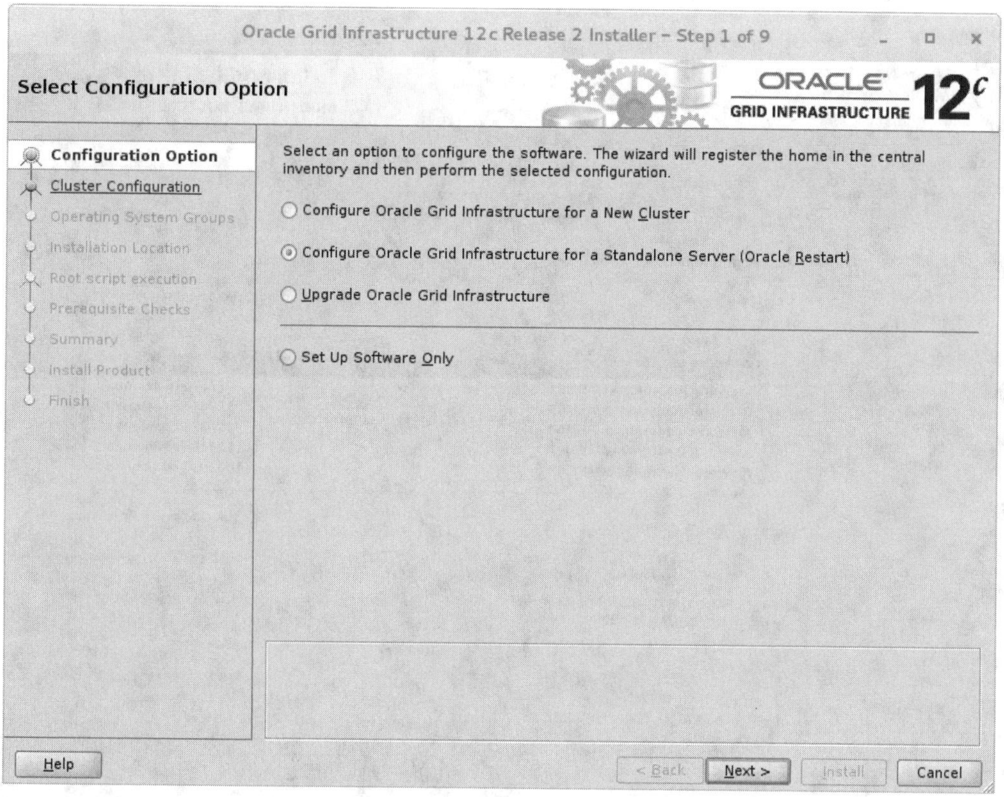

**FIGURE 2-1.**   *Selecting a Grid Infrastructure configuration option*

Click Next to move to the Specify ASM Password step, shown in Figure 2-3. Specify a SYSASM password for the ASM instance. The SYSASM privilege is analogous to the SYSDBA privilege on a database instance.

Click next to move to the Management Options step, which lets you specify an Enterprise Manager Cloud Control instance to manage and monitor this ASM instance. Provide the hostname and credentials for the Cloud Control instance.

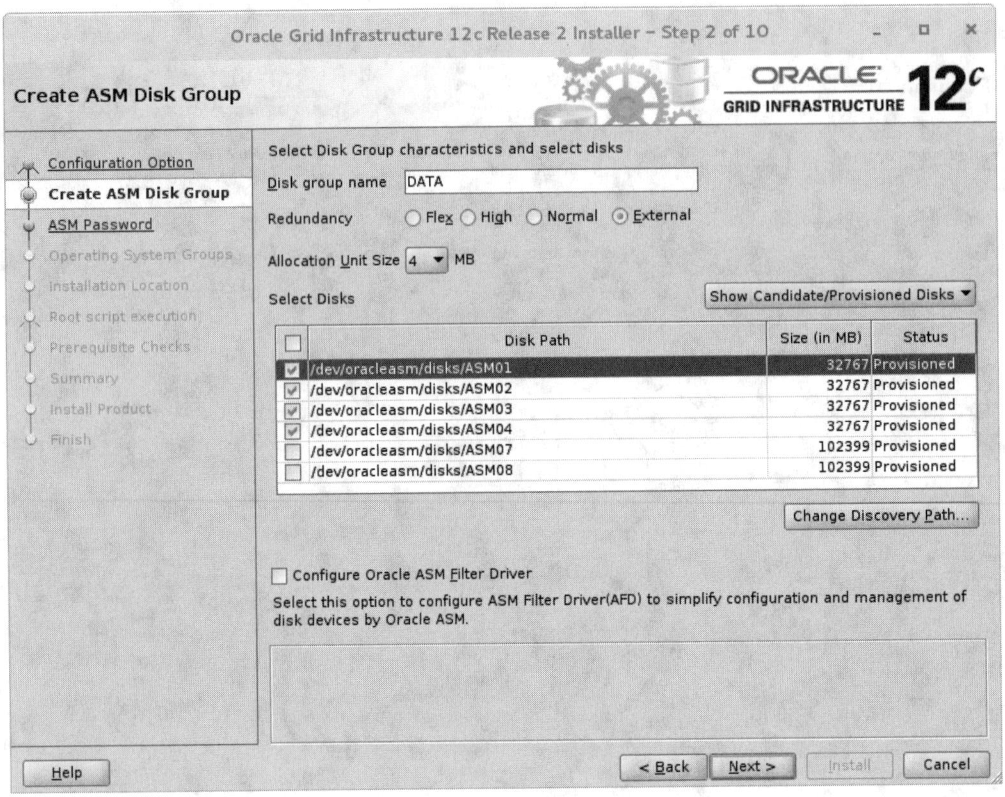

**FIGURE 2-2.** *Selecting grid disks and redundancy for the DATA disk group*

Click Next to move to the Privileged Operating System Groups step, shown in Figure 2-4, where you specify the OS groups you want to use to authorize users for the OSASM, OSDBA, and OSOPER roles within the ASM instance. If your environment is small or you don't need fine-grained levels of responsibility, you can use the OS **dba** group for any or all of these.

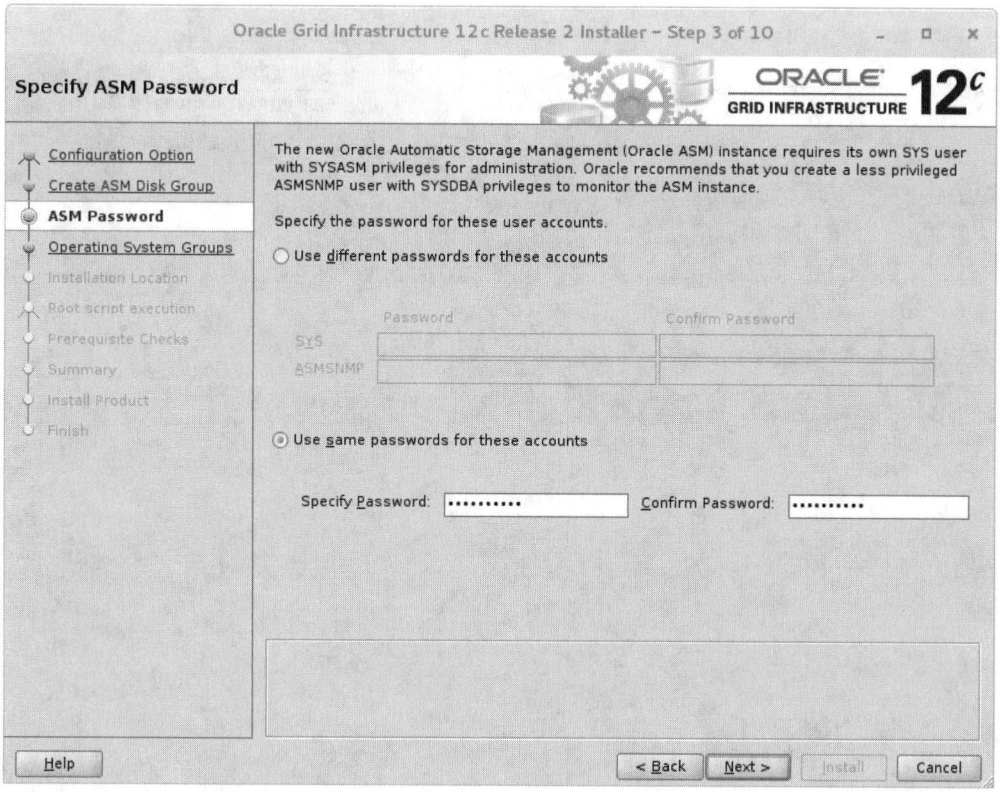

**FIGURE 2-3.** *Specifying a password for the SYS account in the ASM instance*

Click Next to move to the Specify Installation Location step, shown in Figure 2-5, where you can specify the location for ORACLE_BASE, which in this case is **/u01/app/oracle/12.2.0** and is the same ORACLE_BASE for the database instance. As the installer points out, the GI home directory is the same as the software location (**/u01/app/oracle/12.2.0/grid**).

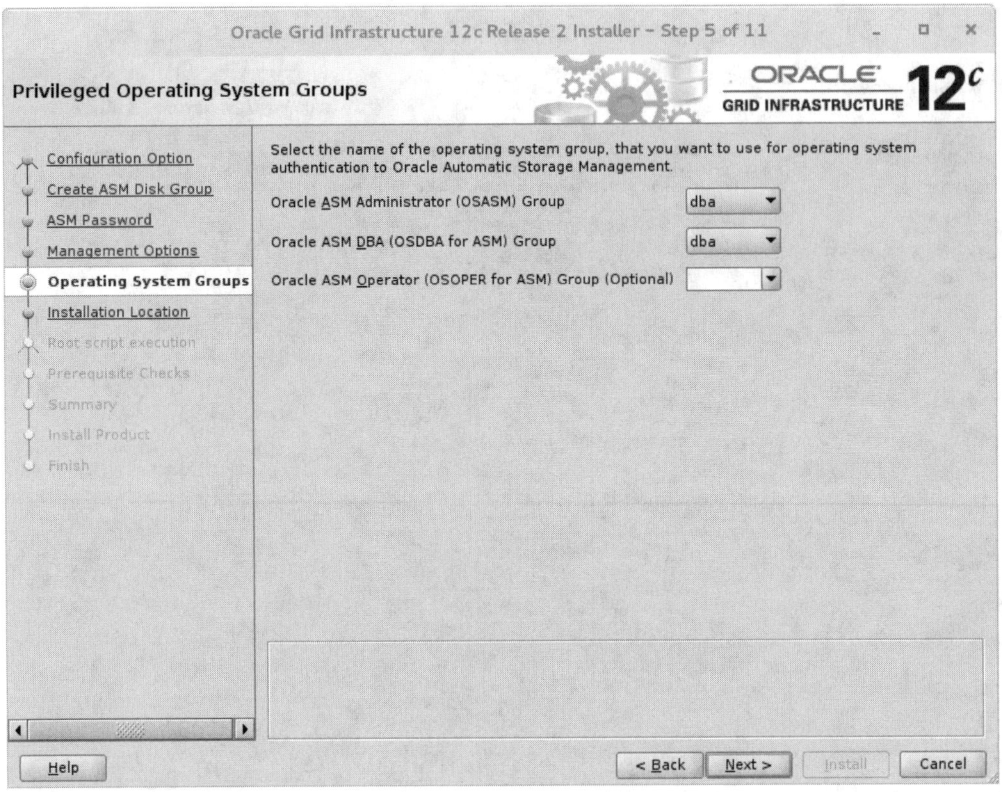

**FIGURE 2-4.** *Selecting OS groups for ASM administration*

Click Next to move to Create Inventory step, shown in Figure 2-6, where you specify the location of the Oracle Inventory directory. This directory is typically located in ORACLE_BASE.

Click Next to move to the Perform Prerequisite Checks step, in which you can configure the OUI to automatically run the required scripts as the **root** user and alert you to any deficiencies in your system configuration. In this scenario, I'm skipping

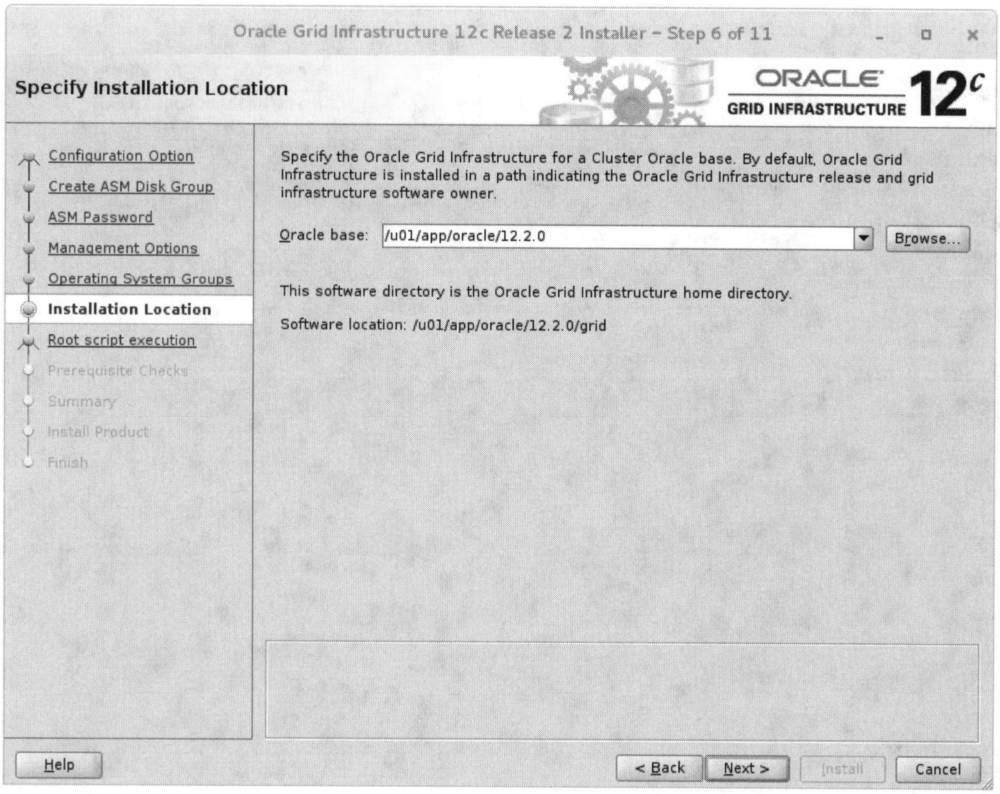

**FIGURE 2-5.** *Specifying the GI installation location*

this window and I'll run those scripts manually. Figure 2-7 shows an example result of running the prerequisite checks, alerting that the system doesn't have enough physical memory to run GI. If you get a warning such as this, fix the issue(s) before you start the GI stack.

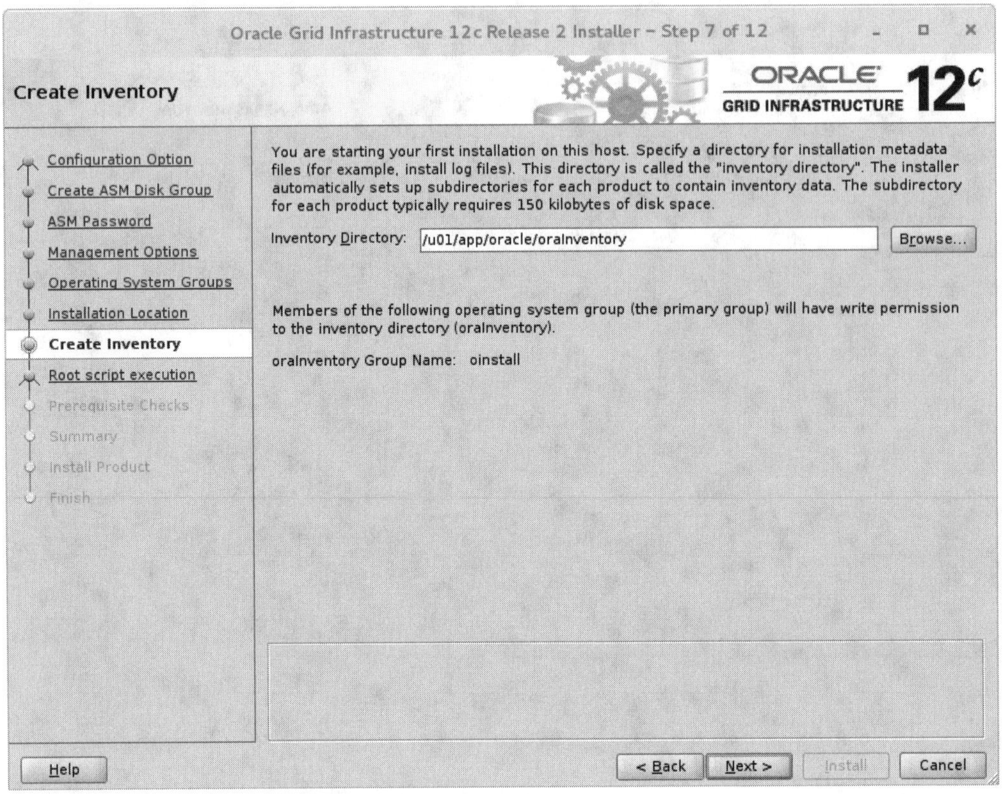

**FIGURE 2-6.** *Choosing the Oracle inventory location*

Before starting the installation process, the OUI shows you a summary of the configuration. Click the Install button to proceed. Figure 2-8 shows the progress of the installation.

After completing the first stage of the installation, the OUI specifies the two scripts that you need to run as **root** to complete the GI setup, as shown in Figure 2-9. After you run the scripts, click OK to finish the install via the OUI.

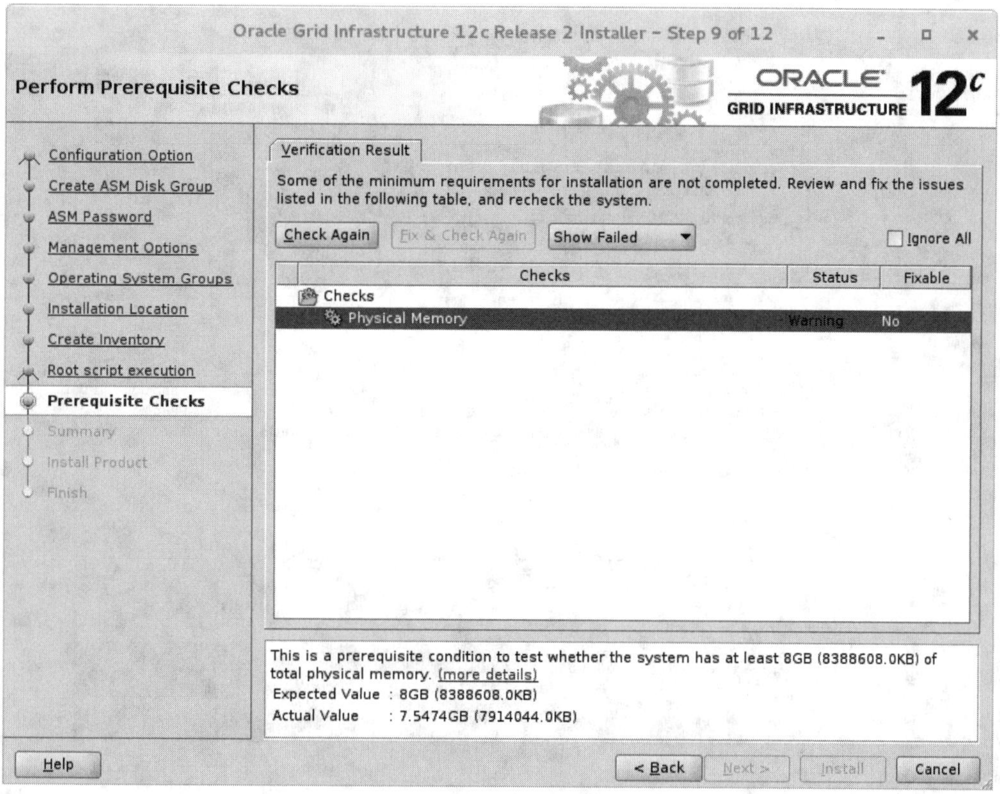

**FIGURE 2-7.** *Result of running prerequisite checks*

An ASM instance is now running. The file **/etc/oratab** shows the new entry for the ASM instance:

```
# Multiple entries with the same $ORACLE_SID are not allowed.
#
#
+ASM:/u01/app/oracle/12.2.0/grid:N
```

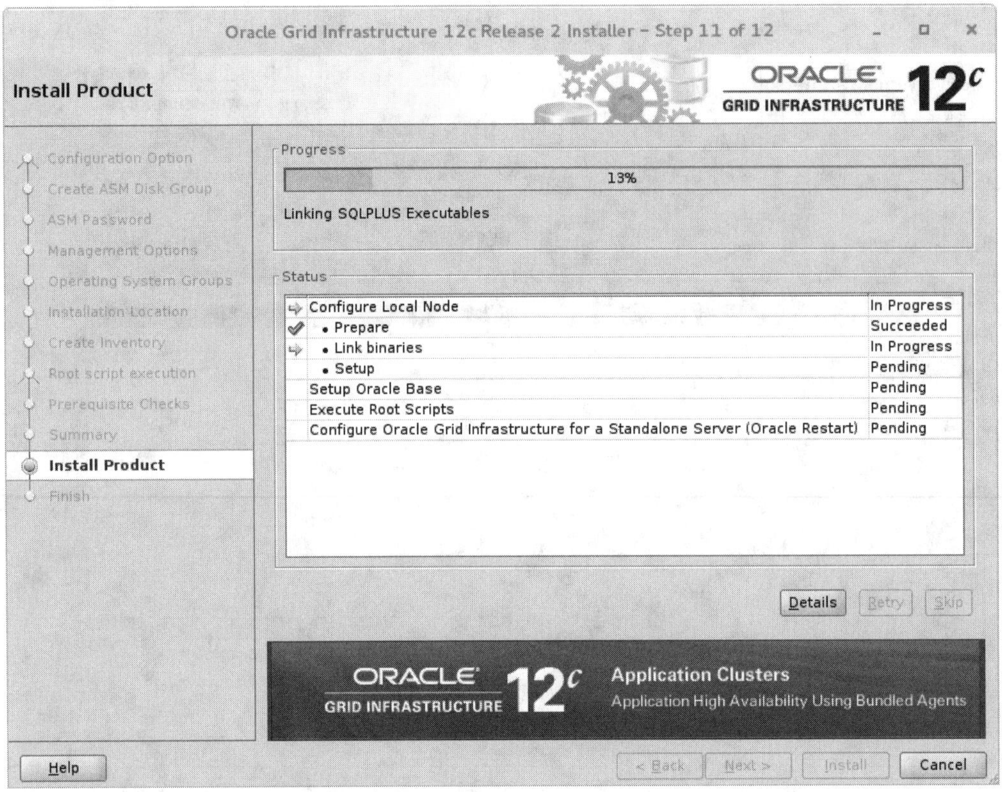

**FIGURE 2-8.** *Installation progress*

Connecting to the ASM instance itself, you can view the size of the DATA disk group:

```
[oracle@ol7base ~]$ sqlplus / as sysasm
SQL*Plus: Release 12.2.0.1.0 Production on Tue Mar 7 16:20:29 2017
Copyright (c) 1982, 2016, Oracle.  All rights reserved.
Connected to:
Oracle Database 12c Enterprise Edition Release 12.2.0.1.0 - 64bit Production
SQL> select name, free_mb, total_mb from v$asm_diskgroup;
NAME                               FREE_MB    TOTAL_MB
------------------------------- ---------- ----------
DATA                                130920      131056
SQL>
```

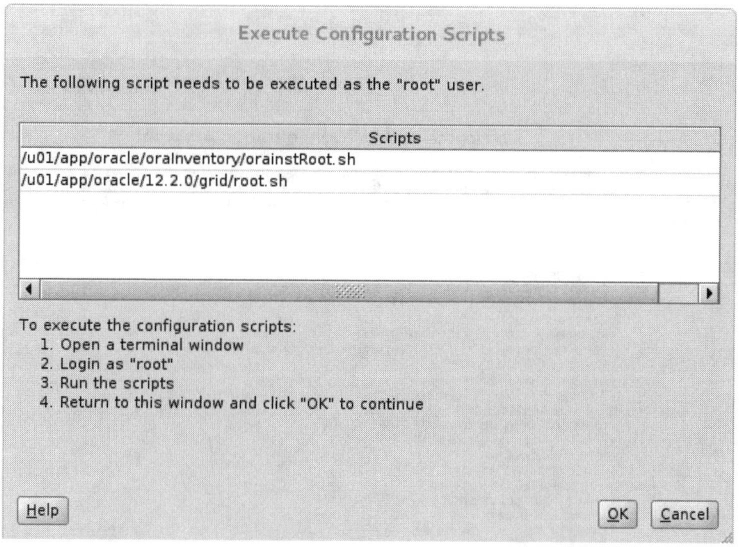

**FIGURE 2-9.** *Scripts to run as root*

Next, we'll create the RECO disk group for recovery-related files—then proceed with creating a database using the new ASM storage!

## Add the RECO Disk Group Using asmca

Now that you have an ASM instance running with storage for the primary disk group DATA, you need to set up the RECO disk group using the remaining disks before creating a new database. You want to make sure you have disk space for every database's control files, redo log file copies, and backup files. To add disks to an existing ASM instance, use the **asmca** utility as follows after setting up the environment for accessing the ASM instance:

```
[oracle@ol7base ~]$ . oraenv
ORACLE_SID = [orcl] ? +ASM
The Oracle base remains unchanged with value /u01/app/oracle/12.2.0
[oracle@ol7base ~]$ asmca
```

The first window you see when you launch **asmca** is a menu of options that includes the current ASM configuration. Figure 2-10 shows the menu for the existing disk group DATA.

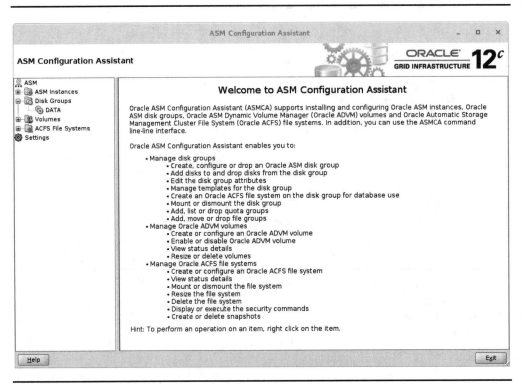

**FIGURE 2-10.** *ASM Configuration Assistant Welcome screen*

To add the new disk group RECO, right-click Disk Groups in the left pane and select Create. Add the remaining available disks, ASM07 and ASM08. Select both of those, enter RECO as the disk group name, and, as with the DATA disk group, specify External redundancy. Click OK to create the new disk group. Figure 2-11 shows the status of all disk groups after RECO has been created.

Here's what the disk group configuration looks like from the command line:

```
SQL> select name, free_mb, total_mb from v$asm_diskgroup;
NAME                                     FREE_MB    TOTAL_MB
------------------------------------ ---------- ----------
DATA                                     130920      131056
RECO                                     204692      204792
SQL>
```

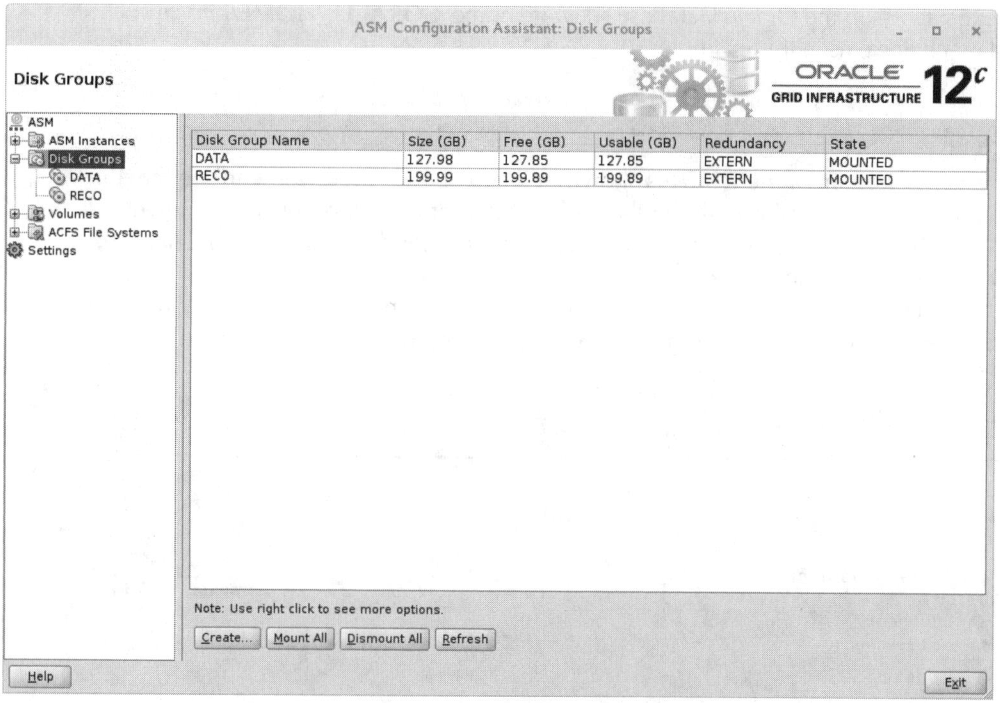

**FIGURE 2-11.**    *ASM Configuration Assistant disk group status*

# Creating a New Oracle Database 12*c* Release 2 Database

This is the moment you've really been waiting for. Your server is ready, you have the database software ready, and you've just created an ASM instance to manage your storage. It's time to create a database. And not just any database—a multitenant database. You *could* create a standalone database in Oracle Database 12*c* Release 1, and you can still create a standalone database in Oracle Database 12*c* Release 2. But there are no disadvantages—only advantages—to creating a multitenant database even if your container database (CDB) has only one pluggable database (PDB). In future releases of Oracle Database, you won't be able to create standalone databases, so you might as well start taking advantage of the multitenant architecture right now.

In the following scenario you'll use the Database Configuration Assistant (DBCA) to create a new database called REL2017 with a single pluggable database called DEV01.

To start the process, open a command window on your Linux desktop, navigate to the executables in the Oracle Database software home (**$ORACLE_HOME/bin**), and launch **dbca**, as in this example:

```
[oracle@ol7base bin]$ cd /u01/app/oracle/12.2.0/db/bin
[oracle@ol7base bin]$ ./dbca
```

The first step of the DBCA is shown in Figure 2-12, where you can see that I'm creating a new database. If I had already created other databases on this server, I would have the option to modify settings for another database, drop a database, or manage pluggable databases.

Clicking Next moves you to the Select Database Creation Mode step, shown in Figure 2-13. I am specifying my container (CDB) name as REL2017, since I want to

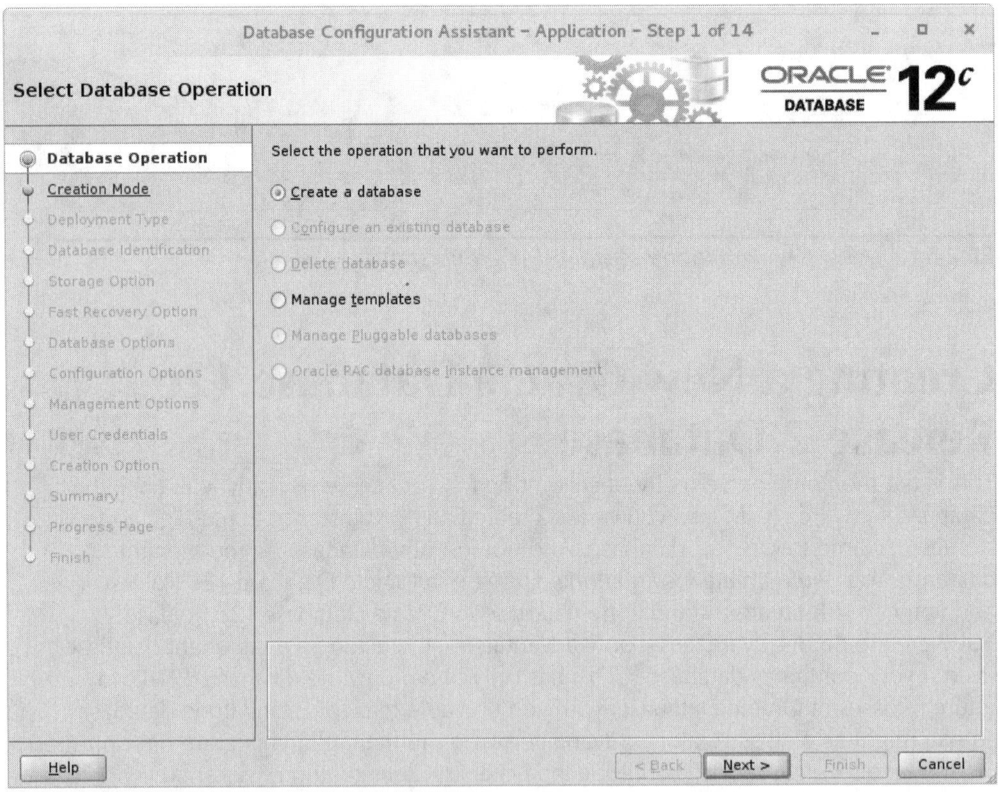

**FIGURE 2-12.** *Creating a new database*

create a container database; I am creating the first pluggable database (PDB) as DEV01, although I could create an empty CDB and create the PDBs later. The DBCA tool automatically recognizes that ASM is installed and will put the data files in the DATA disk group and put all recovery-related files in the RECO disk group. In Figure 2-13, it seems like there are going to be a lot of steps (this is step 2 of 14), but if you choose "Typical configuration," most of the intermediate steps are skipped.

Clicking Next provides the summary of what the new database will look like, as shown in Figure 2-14 for my configuration. Click Finish to proceed with database creation. Figure 2-15 shows a summary of the database that was created and where the SPFile is located for this database within ASM—remember that ASM will manage the storage for one or a thousand databases on any given server. Using ASM Flex, an ASM instance is not required on every database server.

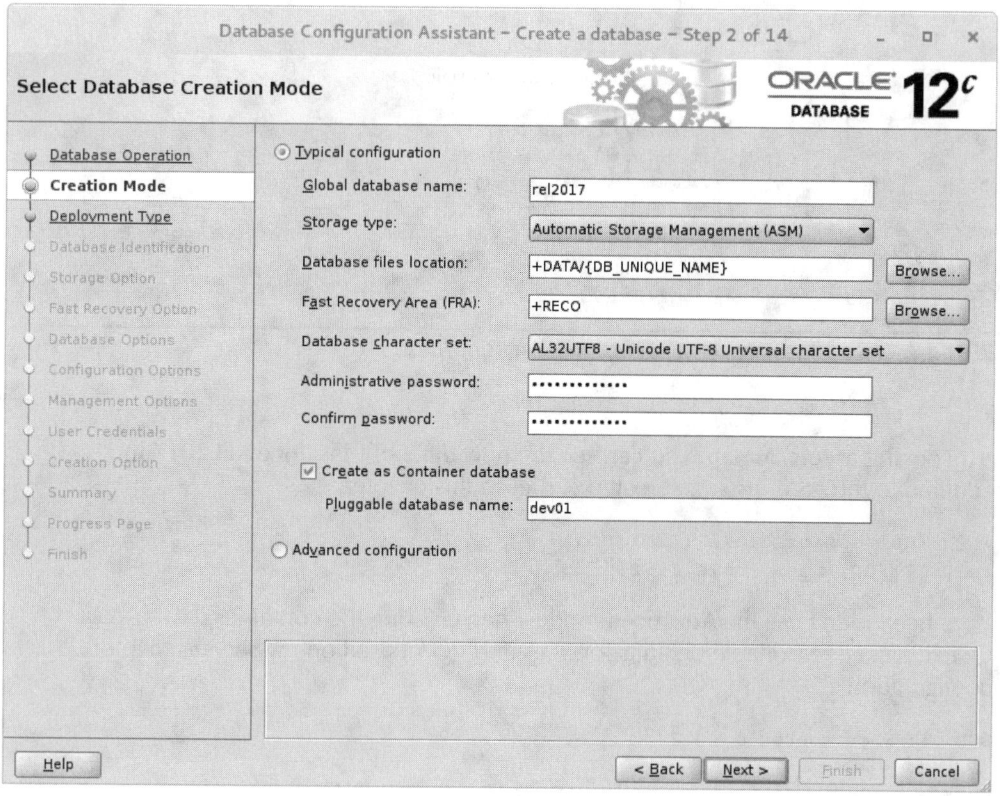

**FIGURE 2-13.** *Specifying database characteristics*

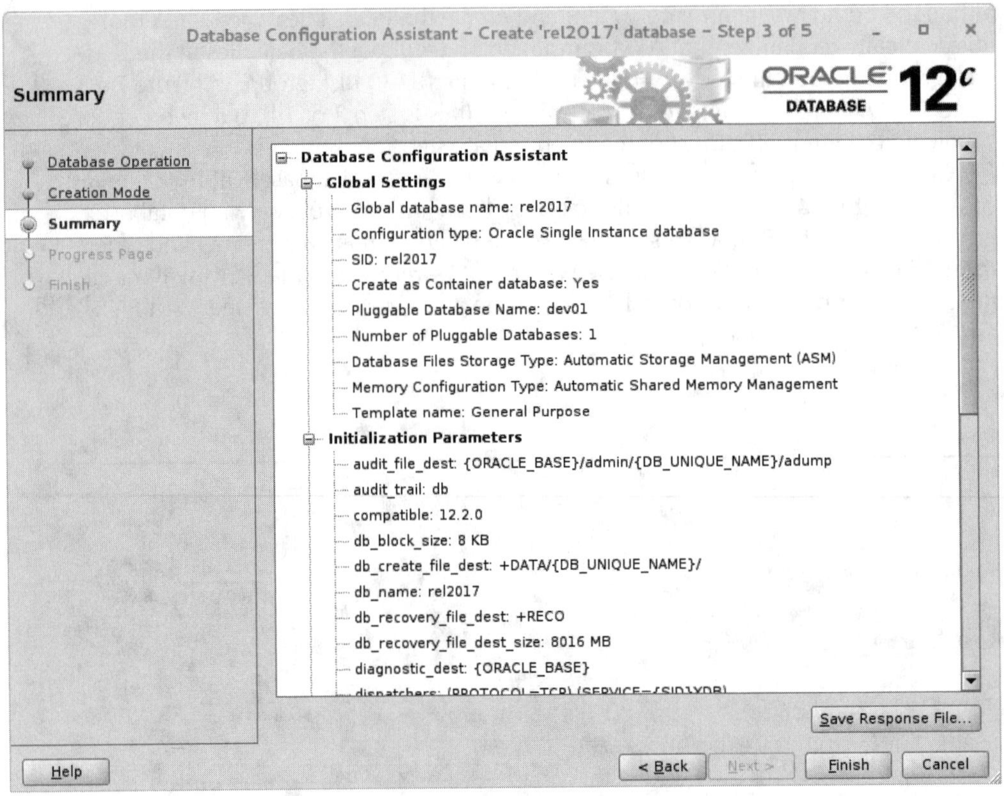

**FIGURE 2-14.** *Database creation preinstallation summary*

Looking at **/etc/oratab**, you can see the new database instance REL2017 in addition to the ASM instance created earlier in this chapter:

```
+ASM:/u01/app/oracle/12.2.0/grid:N
rel2017:/u01/app/oracle/12.2.0/db:N
```

Since I didn't use the Advanced mode when creating the container database, Oracle picked reasonable defaults for SGA and PGA based on my server's memory configuration:

```
SQL> show parameter sga_m

NAME                                 TYPE         VALUE
------------------------------------ -----------  -------------------------
sga_max_size                         big          integer 4752M
```

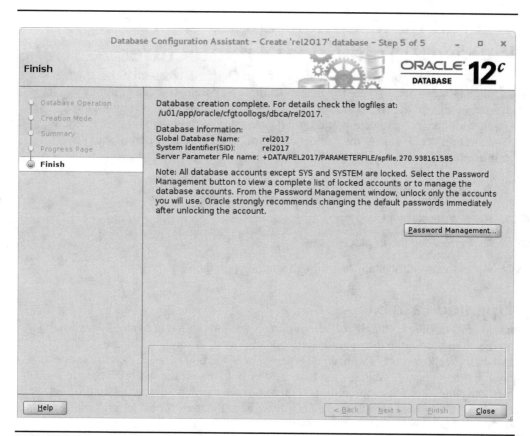

**FIGURE 2-15.** *Database creation summary*

```
sga_min_size                        big          integer 0

SQL> show parameter pga_agg

NAME                                TYPE         VALUE
----------------------------------- ------------ --------------------------
pga_aggregate_limit                 big          integer 3158M
pga_aggregate_target                big          integer 1579M
SQL>
```

# Upgrading to Oracle Database 12c Release 2: Traditional Architecture

In this section I am going to discuss upgrading an Oracle database that uses the traditional Oracle architecture to Oracle Database 12c Release 2. Later in this chapter, I will take the same approach to an Oracle database that is running the Oracle Multitenant architecture and provide an example of upgrading a multitenant database in place. Here are the subject areas you need to review before starting your upgrade:

- Upgrade paths
- Preparing for an upgrade
- Performing the in-place upgrade
- In the event of a failure, rolling back the upgrade

## Upgrade Paths

It's an unfortunate fact that if you are running a version of Oracle before 10g, you are going to have quite the upgrade path ahead of you. When upgrading to Oracle Database 12c Release 2, you have a choice of two upgrade paths: a direct upgrade or an indirect upgrade. This section first reviews both direct and indirect upgrade methods, then identifies some upgrade situations we won't be discussing in this chapter or this book, and wraps up by clarifying what the term "upgrade" encompasses in this chapter in relation to a "migration."

### Direct Upgrades

A *direct upgrade* refers to an upgrade in which you can use the upgrade tools, scripts, and utilities provided by Oracle to upgrade a database from a supported release level directly to Oracle Database 12c Release 2. No other tools or techniques are required. For example, upgrading from Oracle Database 12c Release 1 to Oracle Database 12c Release 2 usually involves a direct upgrade. Direct upgrades can be done either with the Oracle Database Upgrade Assistant (DBUA) tool or manually. We will discuss direct upgrades in much more detail later in this chapter, in the "Choose an Upgrade Method to Use" section.

## Indirect Upgrades

An *indirect upgrade* refers to an upgrade in which a direct upgrade is not supported from the Oracle Database release you are running to Oracle Database 12*c* Release 2. Examples of indirect upgrade methods include the following:

- Using a series of one or more direct upgrades that moves your database up to a version that Oracle Database 12*c* Release 2 supports for direct upgrade. For example, upgrading from Oracle7 to Oracle9*i*, then from Oracle9*i* to Oracle Database 11*g* Release 1, and then from Oracle Database 11*g* Release 1 to Oracle Database 12*c* Release 2.

- Using Oracle Data Pump or the Oracle Export and Import utilities to migrate your database from an older version to Oracle Database 12*c* Release 2.

- Using transportable tablespaces as an indirect upgrade path.

- Using a combination of database links and SQL commands, such as CREATE TABLE AS SELECT, to upgrade your database.

Before you can do any kind of upgrade, though, you need to do some serious preparation work, as described in the upcoming section "Preparing for an Upgrade."

## Upgrade Situations I Won't Be Discussing

The fact of the matter is that there are more ways to upgrade an Oracle database than those covered in this chapter, but the focus of this book is the new features in the database product. Therefore, I decided to limit the upgrade discussion to a single chapter so that I can devote the rest of the chapters to new features. The things I chose to leave out of this chapter are the following:

- Clusterware/RAC upgrades

- Upgrades using replication

- Upgrades using standby databases

You can find information on how to upgrade these configurations in the Oracle Database Upgrade Documentation or the documentation specific to the product that you want to use to perform the migration (for example, Oracle GoldenGate).

## Upgrades, Migrations, and Transporting Data

This chapter is titled "Installing or *Upgrading* to Oracle Database 12*c* Release 2," but it actually covers a number of different ways that you can take your existing data being managed by an earlier release of Oracle Database and ultimately have that data be managed by Oracle Database 12c Release 2. I use the word "upgrade" in a somewhat generic sense in this chapter to refer to all such operations, but it has a much more specific meaning. Generally, if you want your data to be managed by a newer release of Oracle Database, you may choose one of three processes:

- **Upgrade**   Move management of data from an earlier release of Oracle Database to a newer release without moving the data.

- **Migration**   Move management of data from an earlier release of Oracle Database to a newer release by logically moving the data (typically using Oracle Data Pump). *Migration* also refers to moving data from a non-Oracle database to an Oracle database, but that kind of migration is beyond the scope of this book.

- **Transport**   Move management of data from an earlier release of Oracle Database to a newer release through the use of the transportable tablespace mechanism.

In this chapter, then, I use the term "upgrade" generically to encompass all three processes, such as when I discuss the specific upgrade path using an upgrade method such as the DBUA or a manual upgrade.

## Preparing for an Upgrade

To quote Alexander Graham Bell, "Before anything else, preparation is the key to success." That certainly applies when upgrading your Oracle database from a previous release of Oracle to Oracle Database 12c Release 2. This section covers the various tasks that you need to perform when preparing for a successful Oracle Database upgrade:

- Read, and then read some more

- Testing

- Run the Pre-Upgrade Information Tool

- Check for compatibility issues

- Remove Oracle Enterprise Manager Database Control

- Back up the source database

- Choose an upgrade method to use

## Read, and Then Read Some More

Oracle Database 12*c* Release 2 comes with a plethora of documentation. As previously mentioned, you should not consider this chapter to be the essential guide to upgrading to Oracle Database 12*c* Release 2. Rather, this chapter is just a basic guide. A variety of factors can impact the upgrade process, and the best way to start your preparation for an upgrade is to read the Oracle documentation. In particular, you should read the *Oracle Database Upgrade Guide* for Release 2 and the installation documentation that pertains to your specific hardware.

This book will provide you with good insight into a number of new features in Oracle Database 12*c* Release 2, but there may be new features related to a particular component of the database you are using that are not covered in this book. A quick read of the new features section of the documentation related to the components you are using will round out your reading list and help you to put together a plan to upgrade your Oracle databases.

## Testing

The pre-upgrade testing process is a critical part of any successful upgrade plan. In fact, inadequate or improper testing is one of the most common major failures I've seen in upgrade projects over the years. I don't have any quantifiable facts behind this number, but I'd wager that of all the failed upgrade projects that I've seen, the root cause of some 75 percent of them has been something that was not done right in the testing phase.

With that reminder of the importance of pre-upgrade testing, let's look at a few key components of the pre-upgrade testing process:

- Testing and test plans
- Testing infrastructures

**Testing and Test Plans**   It is generally considered a best practice to put together test plans before you start your upgrade process. These plans should mandate testing of the database, the application itself, database and application performance, and data integrity issues. The plans should also specify to test backup and recovery, monitoring and alerting, and other infrastructure-related items to make sure they are compatible with Oracle Database 12*c* Release 2.

Testing connectivity is another item your plans should include. I've had more than one upgrade that encountered last-minute problems because one part of the middle tier was not compatible with the new release of Oracle. The middle tier can be so vast that it's often difficult to find all the components and ensure they are compatible. But, finding those components and ensuring compatibility before you have completed the upgrade is much better than waiting until after the production upgrade has completed.

I've seen cases where test upgrades went successfully, but the production middle tier included components that were not present in the test environment.

The bottom line is that you need to prepare for these contingencies in your planning and try to address as many of them as you can in planning. Also, document the problems you run into so that you, and everyone else, will have a record of these problems and the solution, in case the problem arises again. I don't know about you, but I'm exposed to loads of information in a month's time. I don't tend to remember everything, and even when I remember the big stuff, I often forget the details. The point is, keep good records, and keep them somewhere that's accessible to your co-workers so that they can benefit from your experiences.

**Testing Infrastructures**   To establish a successful test environment in which you can craft a process that repeatedly produces results that reflect the results that would appear in production, you need to address the following considerations:

- Make sure the hardware components are the same in the test and production environments.

- Make sure the operating system and its associated patch levels are the same between production and test environments, unless there is a good reason (such as comparison testing) for a difference.

- Make sure the networking configuration is the same between the test and production environments. This would include hardware, settings, switches, cabling, and all other aspects of the network.

- Make sure the Oracle configuration (including items such as Clusterware, the number of RAC nodes, the database version, and parameter settings) is the same across the test and production platforms unless a divergence is expected for testing.

- Review any parameters derived by system configuration information (for example, the number of CPUs or amount of memory) subject to change based on hardware differences. Make sure you understand those differences and how they might impact your test results.

- Ensure that data volumes are the same across the test and production platforms.

- Make sure the disk characteristics are the same between the test and production platforms, if at all possible. This would include the number of disks that the data is spread across, and the physical connections. For example, do both systems have the same number of host bus adapters (which can make a huge difference with respect to throughput)?

- Ensure that the transaction types that the application will execute are exercised in the test environment.

■ Ensure that the level of concurrency in the test environment is comparable to production.

■ Ensure that your change management process is sufficient to manage the overall enterprise configuration and in particular the production and test environments. It is important to make sure that any change to either configuration is tracked to ensure that test results are meaningful.

I've seen each of the preceding issues cause problems at one time or another because they weren't considered in the setup of the test environment. A test environment that does not even come close to replicating the production environment in any way is going to cause major problems. I also often see cases in which the testing methodology really does not represent the activity that will be occurring in production. Most frequently there is no volume/concurrency testing. That is to say, often the goal of the testing is to make sure that the right answers are being produced, in a reasonable amount of time, from a single process. Many times I've seen these "tested" processes fail when moved into production because tens if not hundreds of users started running them all at the same time.

Whole books have been written about how to do appropriate testing, so that's a topic beyond the scope of this book. Oracle provides a number of tools to help you with your testing. In particular, I recommend that you use Oracle Real Application Testing as you plan your Oracle Database 12*c* Release 2 upgrade. It will make your upgrade process much easier and provide a higher likelihood that your upgrade will be successful.

### Run the Pre-Upgrade Information Tool

The Pre-Upgrade Information Tool is designed to analyze your database and discover any issues that might cause a problem during an upgrade. Although the DBUA will run the tool and ask you to take action on any findings before it performs an upgrade, Oracle recommends that you run this tool manually before you start upgrading a database with the DBUA.

That being said, the old Pre-Upgrade Information Tool script has changed. The **preuprd.sql** and **utlupkg.sql** scripts have been replaced with a Jar file called **preupgrade.jar**. To run the Pre-Upgrade Information Tool, first set the ORACLE_SID for the database that you will be upgrading. The database also needs to be open. Then, use the JDK located in the ORACLE_HOME that you are upgrading from, and run the **preupgrade.jar** file contained in the ORACLE_HOME that you are going to upgrade to. Here is an example:

```
export OLD_ORACLE_HOME=/u01/app/oracle/12.1.0.2/db
export NEW_ORACLE_HOME=/u01/app/oracle/12.2.0.1/db
$OLD_ORACLE_HOME/jdk/bin/java -jar $NEW_ORACLE_HOME/rdbms/admin/preupgrade.jar
```

Note that you no longer need to copy the Pre-Upgrade Information Tool to the ORACLE_HOME of the database that you want to upgrade. The tool creates fixup scripts and its log files in the **$ORACLE_BASE/cfgtoollogs** directory of the database under a subdirectory called preupgrade. For example, if you were to run the tool on a database called ORCL, then the log files would be in **$ORACLE_BASE/cfgtoollogs /ORCL/preupgrade**. The files you will want to review include the following:

- **preupgrade.log**  Contains the results of the execution of the Pre-Upgrade Information Tool. Any conditions that need to be remedied are listed here.

- **preupgrade_fixups.sql**  Contains scripts that should be run before you upgrade the database either with the DBUA or manually. Note that the DBUA will run the **preupgrade_fixups.sql** script for you.

- **postupgrade_fixups.sql**  Contains scripts that should be run before you upgrade the database either with the DBUA or manually. Note that the DBUA will run the **preupgrade_fixups.sql** script for you.

If you are running the DBUA, keep in mind that it will run the Pre-Upgrade Information Tool for you and it will run the pre- and post-upgrade scripts. However, it's still a really good idea to run the tool manually before you upgrade a database and review the log files and the fixup scripts so that there are no surprises later when you're ready to upgrade your database.

### Check for Compatibility Issues

Compatibility issues frequently cause problems in upgrade projects. Often, some component is not compatible with the new Oracle Database release. You want to make sure that all new prerequisites for OS, hardware, and other component versions, settings, or certification issues are reviewed and any discrepancies are addressed. This section addresses the following compatibility issues:

- Infrastructure and application compatibility

- OS and hardware compatibility

- The database COMPATIBLE parameter

**Infrastructure and Application Compatibility**  When an upgrade project is delayed by a problem, the problem usually in not with the database upgrade process itself, but rather is a result of a compatibility issue with another component in the system. Therefore, before you upgrade your database to Oracle Database 12c Release 2, make sure Oracle Database 12c Release 2 is compatible with the other parts of your infrastructure. For example, check the following:

- Application support and/or certification for Oracle Database 12c Release 2

- Driver (such as ODBC or JDBC) support for Oracle Database 12c Release 2

- Infrastructure support for Oracle Database 12c Release 2, such as hardware-related version support (e.g., firmware), network compatibility, storage compatibility, and so on

**OS and Hardware Compatibility**   You need to check that your current operating system and hardware components are compatible with Oracle Database 12c Release 2. Install guides are available for each operating system platform that it supports. Make sure that you check this install guide for your OS to ensure that it is compatible with Oracle Database 12c Release 2. Also check to ensure that your system includes all patches and OS components (such as specific RPMs) that Oracle recommends be installed. You very likely will need to upgrade and patch your OS to install Oracle Database 12c Release 2. It's also possible that you will need to install new or updated libraries to install Oracle Database 12c Release 2. All of these prerequisites are listed in the Oracle-specific documentation that is associated with your database platform.

**The Database COMPATIBLE Parameter**   The COMPATIBLE parameter has two main purposes. The first is to control which features you can use in the Oracle database. The second, somewhat related to the first, has to do with your ability to back out of a migration done by DBUA or done manually, as discussed later in the chapter.

Generally, when you are migrating your database, I recommend that you keep COMPATIBLE set to the version of the source database until you are comfortable that the migration has been successful with respect to things like connectivity and application performance. Typically you will have this comfort level within a few days as you complete a couple of full application cycles: ETL, backups, batch reporting, and ad hoc reporting.

Rolling back the database upgrade (as discussed later in the chapter) should be a last-gasp affair. It is often indicative of a failure in the planning and testing previous to the production upgrade. Generally, if you find that you have a significant problem after upgrading, call Oracle Support and work with them to correct your problem. Don't panic and roll back the upgrade, as this makes finding a solution much more difficult.

Once you have migrated the database and tested it, go ahead and let it run in production mode with the COMPATIBLE parameter set to a value of 11.2.0 (the minimum required for an Oracle Database 12c Release 2 database) until you are convinced that everything is working well. Then, after several weeks of successful operation, start using your normal change-control process (meaning test it with gusto!) to change the COMPATIBLE parameter from 11.2.0 to 12.2.0.

### Remove Oracle Enterprise Manager Database Control

Oracle Enterprise Manager Database Control was replaced in Oracle Database 12*c* Release 1 by Oracle Enterprise Manager Database Express, but its desupport deserves mention here because more than a few readers likely will be skipping Oracle Database 12*c* Release 1 and moving right into Release 2. When you do an upgrade from a pre–Oracle Database 12*c* environment, you will find that Database Control is not in the Oracle Database 12*c* install base. In a nutshell, it's gone.

As a part of the upgrade process, Oracle removes the files in your database that are associated with Database Control. This can make the upgrade take longer, so I recommend you manually remove the files prior to the upgrade by running an Oracle-supplied script called **emremove.sql**, contained in the Oracle Database 12*c* Release 2 **$ORACLE_HOME/rdbms/admin** directory. In addition, in some cases you may need to remove the following files associated with Database Control. These files may or may not exist in your environment, depending on whether your database was previously upgraded.

- **$ORACLE_HOME/HOSTNAME_SID.upgrade**

- **$ORACLE_HOME/oc4j/j2ee/OC4J_DBConsole_HOSTNAME_SID**

If you are running Windows, you will want to remove the DB Console service associated with the database you are upgrading. This service is normally called **OracleDBConsole<SID>**. Oracle does provide a method of preserving and referencing historical DB Console information. See the *Oracle Database Upgrade Guide* for more information on this capability.

Oracle Database Express is a worthy replacement to Database Control—it has most if not all of the features you'd get if you opted to use Cloud Control to manage your database: managing users, managing storage, monitoring the server, and tuning SQL statements.

### Back Up the Source Database

One of the most critical actions you can take before upgrading to Oracle Database 12*c* Release 2 is to make sure the database is backed up. This should be a physical backup, and I strongly recommend that you use RMAN for this backup. To ensure you have a complete backup, you should back up the entire database (an online backup will do), back up all the needed archived redo logs, and back up the current control file.

**CAUTION**
*"Physical backup" means do not use Oracle Data Pump for your pre-upgrade backup! Oracle Data Pump is not a physical backup of a database. If you want to do an Oracle Data Pump export of the database, that might not be a bad idea, but it should not be your primary means to ensure you can recover your database after an upgrade failure.*

## Choose an Upgrade Method to Use

Direct and indirect upgrades were introduced earlier in the chapter, along with mention of the different kinds of upgrade methods and tools associated with direct and indirect upgrades. This section dives into the supported upgrade methods and tools in a bit more detail. It's important to select the best upgrade method for your particular situation. Sometimes the seemingly obvious choice might not be the best choice.

In this section we discuss the following upgrade methods:

- Direct upgrade using the Oracle Database Upgrade Assistant

- Direct upgrade using the manual upgrade method

- Indirect upgrade using the Oracle Data Pump utility

- Indirect upgrade using transportable tablespaces

- Indirect upgrade using the CREATE TABLE AS SELECT command

**NOTE**
*Whichever upgrade method you choose to use, make sure you carefully analyze your space needs and that you have enough space for the upgrade. A database upgrade can consume quite a bit of space between the install image of the software, the new ORACLE_HOME, the space required for the creation and maintenance of guaranteed restore points, additional archived redo log generation, and so on.*

**Upgrade Using the Oracle Database Upgrade Assistant**   Oracle introduced the Oracle Database Upgrade Assistant (DBUA) many versions ago, and over time it's gotten better and better. This tool makes the process of upgrading your existing

Oracle database very easy. You can use the DBUA tool when you are upgrading from the following versions of Oracle Database to Oracle Database 12c Release 2:

- Release 11.2.0.3 and later

- Releases 12.1.0.1 and 12.1.0.2

If you are using an earlier release, you need to do either of the following:

- Upgrade from that release to one of the releases in the previous list. For example, if you are running Oracle Database 11.2.0.2, you can upgrade to Oracle Database 11.2.0.3 first, and then use the DBUA to upgrade to Oracle Database 12c Release 2.

- Use a different method of upgrading to Oracle Database 12c Release 2. The methods that are supported if you are not at one of the releases in the previous list are Oracle Data Pump and the CREATE TABLE AS SELECT command (both of which are discussed later in this chapter).

You can determine which version your database is currently at by issuing the following query:

```
SQL> select * from v$version;
BANNER                                                             CON_ID
-------------------------------------------------------------- ----------
Oracle Database 12c Enterprise Edition Release 12.1.0.2.0 -
       64bit Production                                                 0
PL/SQL Release 12.1.0.2.0 - Production                                  0
CORE   12.1.0.2.0  Production                                           0
TNS for Linux: Version 12.1.0.2.0 - Production                          0
NLSRTL Version 12.1.0.2.0 - Production                                  0
```

In this case we are running Oracle Database 12c Release 12.1.0.2, which is supported by the DBUA, so we can use the DBUA to perform the upgrade. Note that if you are upgrading, the COMPATIBLE parameter must be set to 11.2.0 at a minimum. So, if you never reset the COMPATIBLE parameter after your last upgrade, you may need to do so now.

To start an upgrade, set your session to include the path of the new ORACLE_ HOME that you want to upgrade to, for example Oracle Database 12c Release 2. Then simply start the DBUA with the **dbua** command:

```
export PATH=/u01/app/oracle/12.2.0/db/bin:$PATH
dbua
```

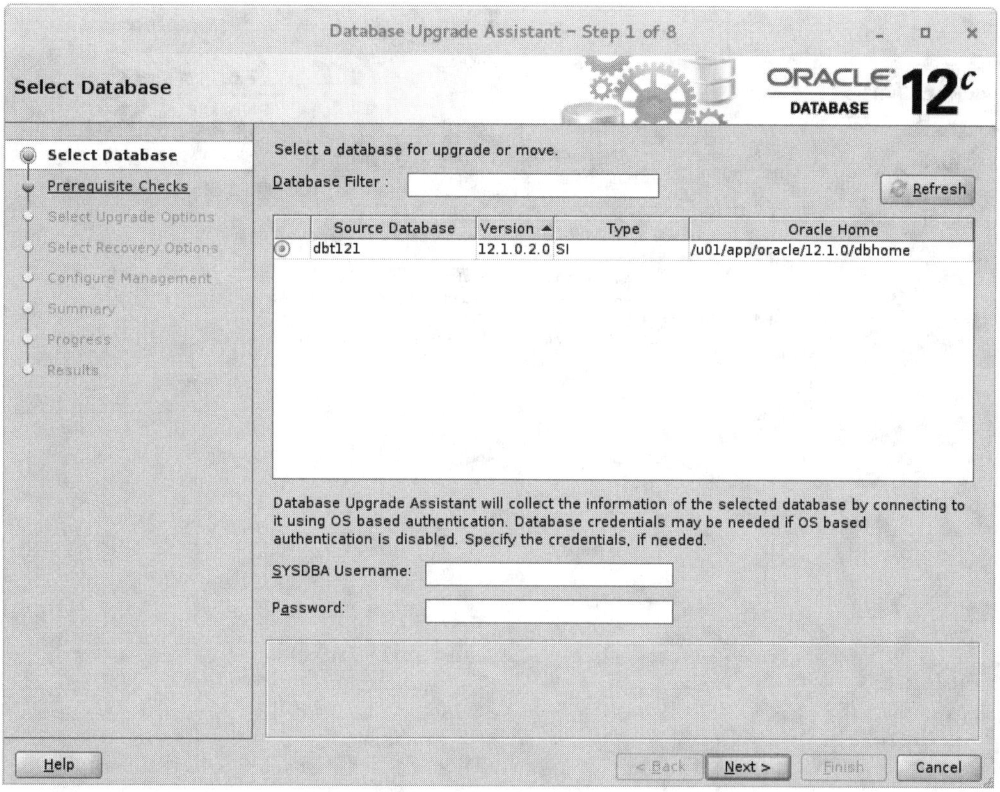

**FIGURE 2-16.**   *Selecting database to upgrade*

Once it's started, the DBUA first presents you with a list of databases you can
upgrade, as shown in Figure 2-16. If your database is not listed, make sure it's in
your **/etc/oratab** file. Once you have selected the database to upgrade, the DBUA
will run the Pre-Upgrade Information Tool for you and present its findings in the
Prerequisite Checks screen, shown in Figure 2-17. In some cases, the Prerequisite
Checks screen will actually offer to correct a condition for you. In other cases, if you
elect to correct the problems displayed, you will have to make those corrections
manually. You can also choose to ignore specific findings if you know they won't
really impact the upgrade.

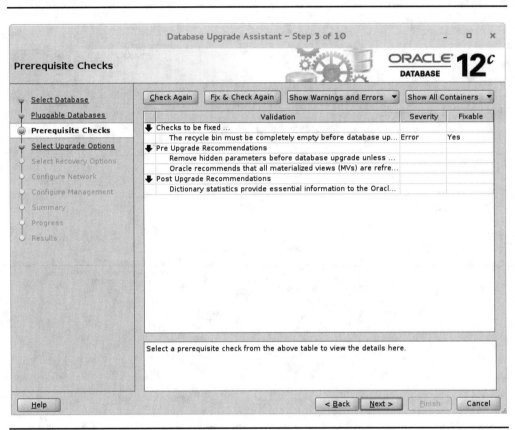

**FIGURE 2-17.** *Prerequisite Checks findings*

Once you click Next to proceed past the Prerequisite Checks screen, the DBUA presents the Select Upgrade Options screen to determine which options you want to enable with the upgrade. You can see some of these options in Figure 2-18.

Some of the options you have available to select from include

- Running the upgrade in parallel. This can speed up the upgrade process, assuming you have multiple CPUs. Oracle will determine the degree of parallelism for you (or it may decide to run the upgrade in serial).

- Recompile invalid object after the upgrade.

- Upgrade time zone data.

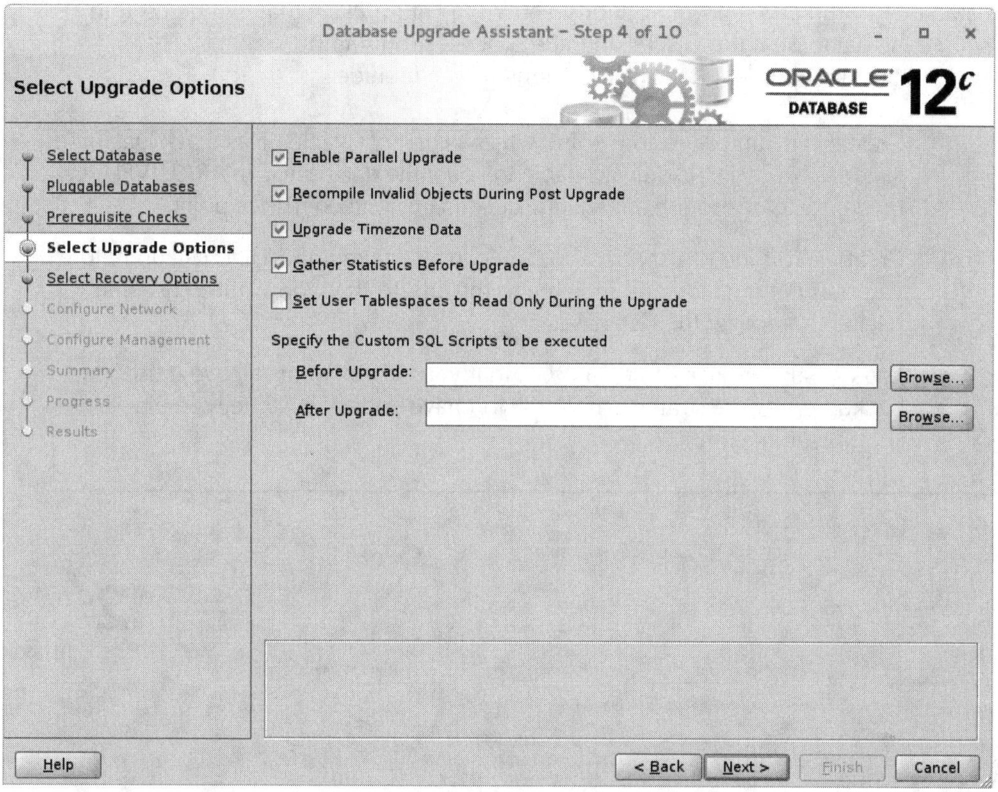

**FIGURE 2-18.**   *Upgrade options*

- Gather statistics before the upgrade of the database.

- Set user tablespaces to read-only status during the upgrade.

Personally, when I do an upgrade, I select all of these options. I recommend that you do the same unless you have a very specific reason not to do so. Along with the options you can select are the names of two scripts, pre- and post-SQL scripts, which can be run before and after an upgrade. Typically, you will not need to run any scripts before or after an upgrade.

Once you have selected the upgrade options, you will be presented with a list of database backup and recovery options, shown in Figure 2-19, that can be used to restore the database if the DBUA upgrade process should fail.

Options on the Select Recovery Options screen include

- Create a guaranteed restore point, which is part of Oracle's Flashback Database feature. This option is only available to you if the database is in ARCHIVELOG mode. You can also use a manually created guaranteed restore point.

- Create an offline RMAN backup. You can also take an RMAN backup before you start the upgrade and indicate to the DBUA that you want to use that backup to recover the database.

- You can also indicate to the DBUA that you do not want to have it use any backup or restore strategy, and that you have your own strategy in place should you need it.

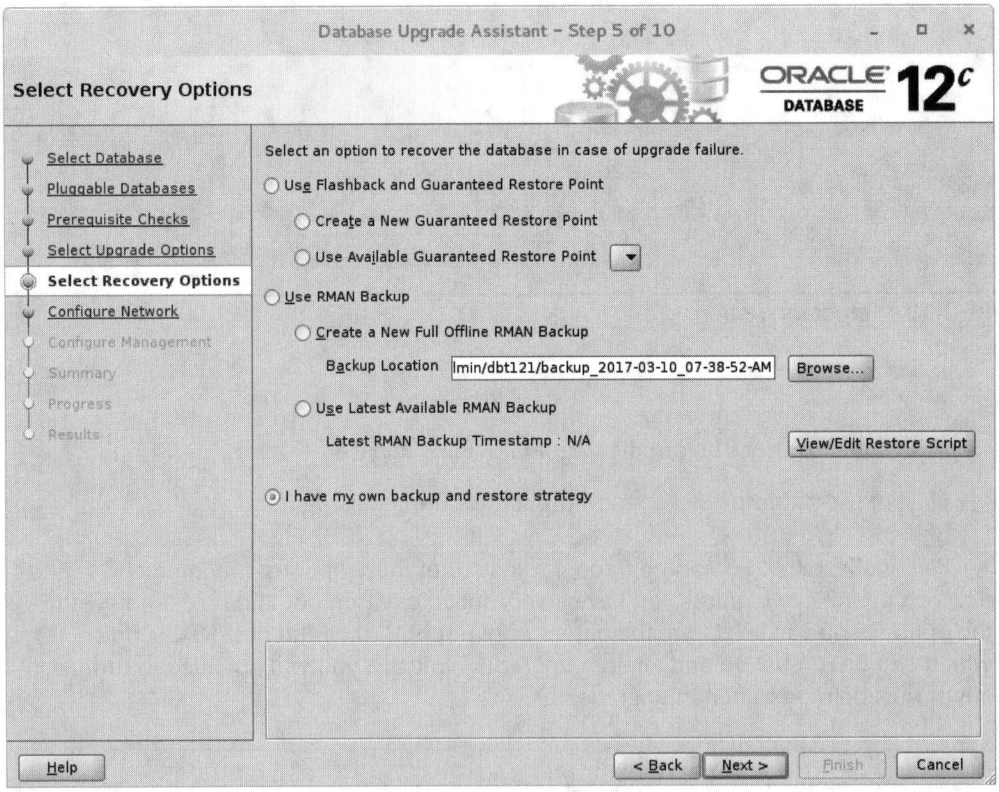

**FIGURE 2-19.** *Recovery options*

Once you have selected your recovery options, you will be asked if you want to upgrade an existing listener, if one exists that is not currently running Oracle Database 12c Release 2. You can select an existing listener from a list that is presented. Also, the DBUA provides the ability to create a new listener if you prefer.

The DBUA will also provide a way for you to configure Oracle Enterprise Manager Express, which is the replacement for Oracle Enterprise Manager Database Control. As previously mentioned, Oracle Enterprise Manager Express was introduced in Oracle Database 12c Release 1, and Database Control is no longer available on any Oracle Database 12c database. The DBUA also provides the ability to register the upgraded database with Oracle Enterprise Manager Cloud Control.

Once the interview questions are completed, you will be presented with a summary of the upgrade process that Oracle is about to start running, as shown in Figure 2-20. Start the upgrade by clicking Finish; an upgrade progress window will

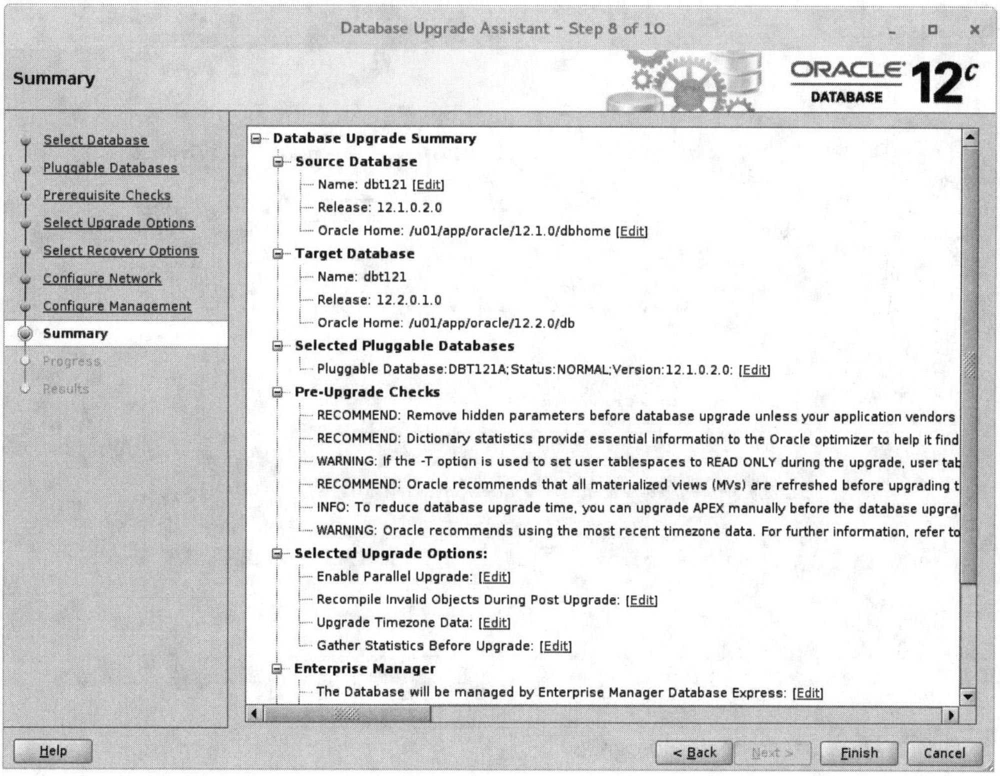

**FIGURE 2-20.**   *Upgrade database summary*

appear similar to Figure 2-21. Keep in mind that if you are running the upgrade with the parallel option enabled, you may see more than one of the steps with a status of In Progress at any one time.

You can stop the upgrade at any time. If you have chosen a restore method, then the DBUA will attempt to restore the database to the point and time of that restore point, or use RMAN to restore to a point in time before the upgrade started. You can also choose to stop the upgrade and not restore the database if that is your preference—depending on when you stop the upgrade, nothing has been changed on the original database yet, so you're safe to just start it up and figure out how to perform the upgrade again later.

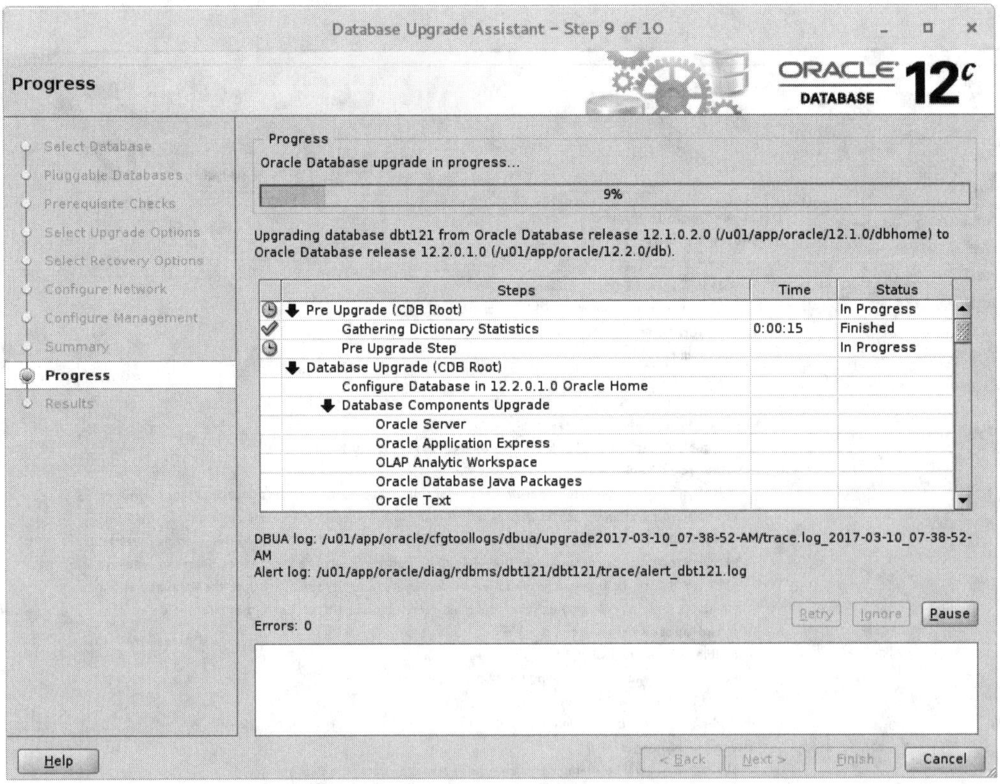

**FIGURE 2-21.** *Database upgrade progress*

You can monitor the upgrade progress from the log file indicated on the DBUA Progress screen. Very often I will use the Linux **tail -f** command to monitor the progress of the DBUA in the alert log or the log created by the DBUA itself.

Once the DBUA is complete, a Results screen of the actions taken, along with any problems or warnings, is displayed.

**Upgrade Using the Manual Upgrade Method**   The manual upgrade method is used to upgrade from an earlier Oracle Database release to Oracle Database 12*c* Release 2. The Oracle Database releases that support the manual upgrade method are the same as the Oracle Database releases that support upgrade via the DBUA (Release 11.2.0.3 and later and Releases 12.1.0.1 and 12.1.0.2). The manual upgrade method requires the execution of a number of scripts, and no GUI is available as in the DBUA method. The manual upgrade process can be a bit more error-prone since you have to manually execute the steps in the right order, which the DBUA does for you.

On the other hand, the manual upgrade method provides a bit more granularity to the upgrade process because you start and observe each step. When an error occurs, you can deal with it directly rather than depend on the software. Some DBAs prefer this "human" touch to upgrades, while others prefer to rely on the DBUA. In the past, the manual upgrade process provided some opportunity to recover from a mid-upgrade error, whereas the DBUA was almost an all-or-nothing approach. This has changed in the last few Oracle Database releases and the DBUA now provides many "restart" points that allow you to fix error situations and then restart the upgrade. At the end of the day, some DBAs will always prefer one method over the other. I generally prefer to use the DBUA for less critical databases and a manual upgrade for more critical databases, but that's just my preference. Your preference is what it boils down to most of the time when choosing which method to use.

To manually upgrade a database, you would follow these high-level steps:

1. Run the Pre-Upgrade Information Tool, which is described earlier in this chapter. Resolve any issues detected by the Pre-Upgrade Information Tool.

2. Back up the database before you start the upgrade process. I also recommend setting a guaranteed restore point.

3. Shut down the database normally and then exit SQL*Plus.

4. Modify the **/etc/oratab** file to reflect the new ORACLE_HOME for the database you will be upgrading. Make sure that you then set the environment (ORACLE_HOME, PATH, etc.) to point to the new ORACLE_HOME directory location. Make sure that ORACLE_SID points to the name of the database you will be upgrading.

5. Change to the **rdbms/admin** directory of the new ORACLE_HOME.

6. Start SQL\*Plus. Make sure you are running the new version of SQL\*Plus by checking the banner. Then, start the database in UPGRADE mode using the STARTUP UPGRADE command. Once the database has started in upgrade mode, exit SQL\*Plus.

7. Start the upgrade by doing one of the following:

   a. On Linux or Unix, run the **dbupgrade** script like this:

      ```
      ./dbupgrade
      ```

      The **dbupgrade** script is a new feature in Oracle Database 12*c* Release 2 that automates the startup of the parallel upgrade utility.

   b. On Windows, start the parallel upgrade utility manually by calling the **catctl** command as shown in this example:

      ```
      catctl catupgrd.sql -l
      ```

8. Once the upgrade script is complete, use the **catcon.pl** utility and run the **$ORACLE_HOME/rdbms/admin/utlrp.sql** script to recompile any objects that might be invalid:

   ```
   $ORACLE_HOME/perl/bin/perl catcon.pl -n 1 -e -b utlrp -d '''.''' utlrp.sql
   ```

9. Log into an account with DBA privileges with SQL\*Plus and run the **$ORACLE_HOME/rdbms/admin/postupgrade_fixups.sql** script while logged in as SYSDBA.

10. Use **catcon.pl** again and run the **$ORACLE_HOME/rdbms/admin/utlu122.sql** script. This script performs final upgrade activities that can occur while the database is not in UPGRADE mode. For example, if your ORACLE_HOME has had a Patch Set Update (PSU) applied, this script will apply any scripts that need to be run that are associated with that PSU:

    ```
    $ORACLE_HOME/perl/bin/perl catcon.pl -n 1 -e -b utlul122 -d '''.''' utlul122.sql
    ```

11. When the upgrade has completed, the database will be up and running and ready to be used.

12. I strongly advise that you make a backup of the database after the upgrade has been completed. Doing this before you allow users to log in is probably a good idea, but not always practical.

If you are running other Oracle software such as RAC, GoldenGate, and so on, you may need to run additional scripts, or configure additional components during the upgrade process. For example, if you are running RAC, you will need to update the Oracle Clusterware database configuration after the upgrade is complete by using the **srvctl upgrade database** command.

**Upgrade Using the Oracle Data Pump Utility**    If you are running an Oracle Database release that is not supported by the DBUA or the manual upgrade method, and you do not want to or cannot migrate that database to an Oracle Database release that supports these tools, then you can use Oracle Data Pump to perform an upgrade. Another case where you will need to use the Oracle Data Pump Utility is if you are moving your database between platforms with different endian byte configurations. For example, if you are moving your Oracle Database 11g database from a Sun SPARC platform to an Oracle Exadata platform, which have different endian byte formatting configurations, the only supported methods of upgrading across platforms are to use Oracle Data Pump or the CREATE TABLE AS SELECT command.

When you use Oracle Data Pump, you create the Oracle Database 12c Release 2 database first, and then you load the database metadata and data using Oracle Data Pump. The main drawback to using Oracle Data Pump over the previously described upgrade methods (DBUA and manual database upgrade) is that Oracle Data Pump is slower. You can use Oracle Data Pump features such as compression, direct network connection, and parallelism to improve performance of the export/import operations.

Another option available with Oracle Data Pump is to use its network import mode, which allows you to move the database between a source and target database over the network, without needing to create any Data Pump dump files (which means you'll need non-database storage—count on half the size of your database). Obviously, the larger the database, the more network throughput you will need to complete the migration in a timely fashion.

**Upgrade Using Transportable Tablespaces**    Using transportable tablespaces is a great option when upgrading a database. This option is particularly useful when you want to also move your database to new hardware as you upgrade it. Oracle also offers different variations on transporting data: you can transport individual tablespaces, transport sets of tablespaces, or transport the entire database.

If you decide to use this option, make sure to review the *Oracle Database Administrators Guide* with respect to limitations related to using transportable tablespaces as an upgrade option. For example, if you are using encrypted tablespaces, then you cannot transport them to a database platform with a different endian byte format. As another example, you have to check the compatibility of character sets between the databases you are transporting tablespaces from and to. You will also want to review the various Oracle documentation on the best way to transport the database tablespaces, including using Data Pump, RMAN, or a manual migration of the tablespace-related datafiles.

Database version compatibility is also an issue to consider when dealing with the different versions of transportable tablespace functionality. Table 2-2 provides a quick list of the minimum compatibility requirements that must be present for different transportable tablespace situations.

| Transport Case | Source Database (indicates COMPATIBLE parameter setting unless otherwise stated) | Target Database (indicates COMPATIBLE parameter setting unless otherwise stated) |
|---|---|---|
| Using Oracle full transportable export/import | >=12.0 | >=12.0 |
| Using Oracle full transportable export/import | >=11.2.0.3 (Data Pump VERSION parameter must be set to 12.0) | >=12.0 |
| Transporting a tablespace between databases on the same platform | >=8.0 | >=8.0 |
| Transporting a tablespace with different block sizes | >=9.0 | >=9.0 |
| Transporting tablespaces between databases on different platforms | >=10.0 | >=10.0 |
| Transporting tables between databases | >=11.1.0.6 (minimum COMPATIBLE setting for Oracle Database 12c database) | >=11.1.0.6 |
| Transportable tablespaces from backup files | Same version limitations as those listed above, except the source tablespace does not need to be made read-only. So, if you are transporting tablespaces across the same platform, the minimum version requirement is >= 8.0. | |

**TABLE 2-2.** *Source and Target Database COMPATIBLE Settings for Transportable Tablespaces*

**NOTE**
*The TRANSPORT TABLESPACE command was not available in RMAN until Oracle8i. I'd do a lot of testing if you plan on using any version of RMAN to transport tablespaces between any release of Oracle Database prior to Oracle Database 11g and make sure that you don't run into problems.*

As you can see, there are a lot of options, and some complexity, associated with the use of transportable tablespaces. On the other hand, in many cases using them is a very viable option for moving to Oracle Database 12c Release 2.

**Upgrade Using the CREATE TABLE AS SELECT Command**   The Oracle CREATE TABLE AS SELECT (CTAS) command is another supported method of migrating to Oracle Database 12c Release 2. Using this method, you create an Oracle Database link and then move the data over that database link from the old database to the new Oracle Database 12c Release 2 database.

This method has a few drawbacks that are readily apparent. First, you are dependent on your network bandwidth for movement of the data. Second, you have to create a CTAS statement for each table. Third, you have to re-create the various constraints and indexes and other supporting structures in the new database. As a result, this method is rarely used, as it can be quite time-consuming to write the scripts to re-create a given database in its entirety. Oracle Data Pump is preferable to the use of this method.

## The Last Word on Upgrading the Traditional Architecture

Usually, at this point I'd present another scenario using the DBUA and, perhaps, show some examples of a manual upgrade process. The truth is that the upgrade process has grown up now. The different ways you can move a database from an older release of Oracle Database to Oracle Database 12c Release 2 are numerous, and the best method of upgrading the database is dependent on a number of factors. Additionally, we still need to address upgrades in a multitenant environment, which offers its own degree of fun and excitement.

Still, I feel like I should give you my thoughts with respect to the question, "Which method of upgrading should I use?" It's a good question, and providing my own opinion is probably more useful to you than providing a long, drawn-out example or two that might not even apply to your situation.

In my opinion, if you can use the DBUA, you should. It has matured a great deal over the years. Upgrades can be complex, and having a guided method of performing the upgrade just makes the most sense to me. In the old days, if the DBUA failed, you had to restore your database and start over. Now, in most cases, you can simply restart the upgrade process in some cases, or just complete the upgrade manually if you experience a failure—no restore required. That makes the DBUA a winner in my book.

Obviously, there are upgrade situations where you can't use the DBUA. In these cases, I recommend that you do some quick analysis of your situation and use whichever method of upgrading (or migrating or transporting tablespaces) to Oracle Database 12c Release 2 offers you the most direct path from where you are to where you want to be. From a sheer time-savings point of view, using transportable tablespaces is likely the best option. If minimizing downtime is more important, using a combination of RMAN and transportable tablespaces may be the best option. If downtime is a real issue, then you will need to look at more complex migration techniques that involve things like using GoldenGate for replication.

One last comment. Oracle has announced the deprecation of the traditional Oracle Database architecture (non-multitenant). This means that, at some point in the future, Oracle will stop supporting the old architecture. That being said, it might be time to start strongly considering the Oracle Database Multitenant architecture, discussed later in this chapter.

# In the Event of Failure

Should your upgrade effort fail, there are a few different ways you can respond to the failure:

- Restore the partially upgraded database

- Correct the problem and restart the upgrade from the beginning

- Correct the problem and restart the upgrade from a specific phase that failed

Let's look at each of these options in a bit more detail.

## Restore the Partially Upgraded Database

One option if an upgrade fails is to restore the database using the backup you created before the upgrade, or restore it to the guaranteed restore point you created. You will also need to reset any changed environment variables, move any configuration files, and reverse out any other processes you followed when upgrading the database. You should use this option only as a last resort, in my opinion, but it is usually necessary if you have run into some problem during the upgrade that is not immediately solvable—perhaps some part of the upgrade process keeps stalling, or some incompatibility exists between the Oracle database and your server.

If you are running the DBUA and the upgrade fails, the DBUA may offer you an option to restore the database and the database environment. In this event, you can let the DBUA do all the work for you.

It is possible that the DBUA will not offer you an option to restore the database. For example, the DBUA may just stop running for some reason. Also, if you're doing a manual upgrade, the DBUA will not be able to manage your restore for you. In these cases, manual recovery may be the only way to start the recovery process. First, you would need to stop the DBUA (possibly by killing the process at the OS level if it's truly locked up). You would then need to reset the database environment back to the old ORACLE_HOME environment. This would include changing environment variables, making sure that the database parameter file and password file are in the correct place, making sure any **listener.ora** files are in the correct place, and so on. This is why it's important to back up not only the database before you do an upgrade, but also database-related files such as the parameter file, the password file, and other critical files.

Once you have restored the environment, you can then proceed to restore the database using either RMAN or the guaranteed restore point you created before you started the backup. There is really nothing special about the recovery process after that point—it's like any other database restore.

### Correct the Problem and Restart the Upgrade from the Beginning

Oracle Database 12c Release 2 provides the ability to restart an upgrade after it has failed in most cases. This functionality is available if you started the upgrade using either the DBUA or the manual upgrade method. This functionality requires that you complete the upgrade manually, because the DBUA interface does not allow for a restart of a failed upgrade from that interface.

Restarting the upgrade process from the beginning essentially requires that you shut down the database (if it's not already shut down) and issue the STARTUP UPGRADE command. Then, you simply follow the manual upgrade steps previously discussed in the "Upgrade Using the Manual Upgrade Method" section from the point at which you issue the STARTUP UPGRADE command, completing the upgrade. It's not too difficult, really.

### Correct the Problem and Restart the Upgrade from a Specific Phase that Failed

Oracle Database 12c Release 2 offers a new feature that allows you to restart a migration at various points in the overall migration process. As with restarting the entire upgrade process, restarting an upgrade from a specific point in the upgrade process is a manual process. The DBUA does not support restarting of upgrades through its interface. To restart the upgrade process from a specific point in the upgrade workflow, do the following:

1. Review the DBUA log files. The upgrade is divided into phases, and one or more phases may be logged in a given log file.

2. Look in the last log file for the first occurrence of the words "error occurred in phase" (obviously, this syntax might change at some point). When you find the first occurrence of this phrase, you should find a statement that indicates in which phase the process failed. For example, you might see this statement that indicates the error occurred in phase 20:

   ```
   catupgrd1.log error occurred in phase 20:
   ```

3. Once the failed phase has completed, **dbupgrade** will return to the OS prompt. Check the logs to find out what the issue is, and fix the issue. After that, you can then continue the upgrade by restarting the upgrade at the failed phase. To restart the upgrade, issue the **dbupgrade** command using the **–p** parameter. The **–p** parameter starts the upgrade at the step indicated and will not repeat a successful step. In our current example, since the failed phase was phase 20, we would indicate that stage as the stage to restart the upgrade at:

   ```
   dbupgrade -p 20 catupgrd.sql
   ```

   Oracle will then execute all of the remaining phases of the upgrade until the upgrade is complete (or it fails on some other step). Once the upgrade is completed, simply follow the remaining manual upgrade steps after the step that has you run the **dbupgrade** script.

# Upgrading to Oracle Database 12*c* Release 2: Multitenant Architecture

Oracle released the Multitenant database architecture in Oracle Database 12*c* Release 1. We are not going to spend a great deal of time discussing the basic principles of multitenant databases here. Suffice it to say that a multitenant database is an architecture that enables a single instance, called a container database (CDB), to manage one, but usually many instances, individually called pluggable databases (PDBs). Oracle Database 12*c* Release 2 provides a number of new features with respect to multitenant databases, which we will cover in Chapter 3.

In this section we are going to cover upgrading an existing multitenant database to Oracle Database 12*c* Release 2.

- Upgrading to Oracle Database 12*c* Release 2 for Multitenant

- In the event of a failure

# Upgrade Methods for Multitenant Databases in Oracle Database 12*c* Release 2

Just as there are many ways you can upgrade a non-multitenant database, there are many ways to upgrade a multitenant database. The most common methods are as follows:

- Upgrading the entire CDB and all of its PDBs using the DBUA

- Manually upgrading the entire CDB and all of its PDBs

- Upgrading specific PDBs by manually unplugging PDBs from their current CDB and plugging them into a CDB running the release of Oracle Database to which you want to upgrade

We will discuss each of these upgrade methods in more detail next. Other, less-common methods exist, such as using Data Pump or transportable tablespaces, but we won't discuss them here.

## Upgrading a CDB and Its PDBs with the DBUA

The overall look and feel of the DBUA when doing a multitenant upgrade is not much different from when you are upgrading a non-multitenant database, but there are a couple of differences. First, there is an additional screen that provides the ability to pick and choose which PDBs you want to upgrade and which ones you do not want to upgrade. Second, when you choose to do a parallel upgrade, this will also result in PDBs being upgraded in parallel.

Beyond those two differences, you still can do the same things with DBUA that you'd do during a non-CDB upgrade, such as upgrading the time zone files and keeping the user tablespaces available in read-only mode while the upgrade is running. Refer back to Figure 2-18 for the available options you can include during a multitenant upgrade.

When you start an upgrade with the DBUA, Oracle first upgrades the root container (CDB$ROOT) of the CDB. You have the option to leave the root container in UPGRADE mode until after all the PDBs are upgraded, or you can open the root container in READ WRITE mode after it has been upgraded and then upgrade some or all of the PDBs. When you choose to open the root container after its upgrade is complete, you can subsequently open and use PDBs after they have been upgraded. If you choose to wait to open the root container until after the PDBs have all been upgraded, then you will not be able to use any of the PDBs until the entire upgrade is complete.

Once the root container is upgraded, the DBUA proceeds to upgrade the remaining PDBs in the database. You can choose to have the DBUA upgrade PDBs in parallel or one at a time. Once the DBUA is finished, it will leave the upgraded CDB open in READ WRITE mode. It will also leave all upgraded PDBs open in READ WRITE mode if you chose to upgrade them. Any PDB that you chose to not upgrade will not be open and cannot be opened until it has been upgraded.

### Upgrading a CDB and Its PDBs Manually

The process of upgrading a multitenant database involves using the same basic steps that you use when upgrading a non-multitenant database, with a few additions. Here are the basic steps involved in a manual upgrade of a CDB and all of its PDBs:

1. Run the Pre-Upgrade Information Tool, as discussed earlier in this chapter. Resolve any issues detected by the Pre-Upgrade Information Tool.

2. Back up the database before you start the upgrade process. I also recommend setting a guaranteed restore point.

3. Shut down the database normally and then exit SQL*Plus.

4. Modify the **/etc/oratab** to reflect the new ORACLE_HOME for the database you will be upgrading. Make sure that you then set the environment (ORACLE_HOME, PATH, etc.) to point to the new ORACLE_HOME directory location. Make sure that ORACLE_SID points to the name of the database you will be upgrading.

5. Change to the **rdbms/admin** directory of the new ORACLE_HOME.

6. Start SQL*Plus. Make sure you are running the new version of SQL*Plus by checking the banner. Then, start the database in UPGRADE mode using the STARTUP UPGRADE command.

7. Open all of the PDBs in the CDB by using the ALTER PLUGGABLE DATABASE ALL OPEN UPGRADE command. You can check the status of the PDBs with the SHOW PDBS command from SQL*Plus. They should all show a status of MIGRATE. Once the database has started in UPGRADE mode, exit SQL*Plus.

8. Start the upgrade by doing one of the following:

    a. On Linux or Unix, run the **dbupgrade** script like this:

    ```
    dbupgrade
    ```

    The **dbupgrade** script is a new feature in Oracle Database 12*c* Release 2 that automates the startup of the parallel upgrade utility.

    b. On Windows, start the parallel upgrade utility manually by calling the **catctl** command as shown in this example:

    ```
    catctl catupgrd.sql -l
    ```

When you upgrade a PDB with the **dbupgrade** script or **catctl** command, Oracle first upgrades the root container of the CDB, then upgrades the seed database (PDB$SEED) of the CDB, and finally upgrades the individual PDBs in parallel. Oracle calculates the degree of parallelism to be used based on the number of CPUs divided by 2. You can pass parameters into the **dbupgrade** script and **catctl** commands to control the degree of parallelism or even force the database PDBs to be upgraded in a serial manner.

Note that Oracle does support partial upgrades of PDBs. Any PDBs that are not upgraded will not be able to be opened until they are upgraded later. Also note that you can choose to just upgrade the root and seed containers of the CDB. After they are upgraded, you can upgrade the PDBs of that CDB by unplugging them from the CDB and then plugging them back in again.

9.  After the upgrade script has completed, log back into the CDB and open all of the PDBs with the ALTER PLUGGABLE DATABASE ALL OPEN command.

10. Once the upgrade script is complete, use the **catcon.pl** utility and run the **$ORACLE_HOME/rdbms/admin/utlrp.sql** script to recompile any objects that might be invalid:

```
$ORACLE_HOME/perl/bin/perl catcon.pl -n 1 -e -b utlrp -d '''.''' utlrp.sql
```

11. Run the **$ORACLE_HOME/rdbms/admin/postupgrade_fixups.sql** script while logged in as SYSDBA using SQL*Plus, or you can use the **catcon.pl** script.

12. Use the **catcon.pl** utility to run the **$ORACLE_HOME/rdbms/admin/utlu122 .sql** script. This script performs final upgrade activities that can occur while the database is not in UPGRADE mode. For example, if your ORACLE_HOME has had a PSU applied, this script will apply any scripts that need to be run that are associated with that PSU:

```
$ORACLE_HOME/perl/bin/perl catcon.pl -n 1 -e -b utlu122s -d '''.''' utl122s.sql
```

13. When the upgrade has completed, the database will be up and running and ready to be used.

14. I strongly advise that you make a backup of the database after the upgrade has been completed.

As with manual upgrades of non-multitenant databases, be aware that if you are running other Oracle products, you may need to run additional scripts to complete the upgrade to Oracle Database 12c Release 2.

**NOTE**
*Oracle provides functionality that allows you to prioritize the order in which PDBs get upgraded. This is documented in the* Oracle Database Upgrade Guide.

## Manually Upgrading a CDB and All PDBs Using the Unplug/Plug Method

The previous two methods of upgrading a CDB and its PDBs enable you to upgrade the PDBs in parallel. You can also choose to use the unplug/plug method to upgrade a PDB. The unplug/plug method is a serial method of upgrading PDBs. The unplug/plug method provides the ability to

1.  Unplug PDBs from a CDB at the release of Oracle Database you want to upgrade from.

2.  Plug the PDBs into a CDB at the release of Oracle Database you want to upgrade to.

When using the unplug/plug method, you would typically create a new CDB using the release of Oracle Database you wish to upgrade to. You would then unplug the PDB from its current CDB. You would then plug the PDB into the new CDB and apply the required scripts to upgrade the PDB. I would suggest doing just one PDB first, resolving any issues, then using the unplug/plug method on the rest at the same time.

The following sections provide the high-level steps you would take assuming you are going to be moving PDBs from an Oracle Database 12c Release 1 database to an Oracle Database 12c Release 2 database. The exact steps may vary based on a number of conditions. First, we will look at the steps related to unplugging the PDB from the old ORACLE_HOME CDB. We will then look at plugging the PDB into the new ORACLE_HOME CDB. Finally, we will look at the steps involved in completing the upgrade of the PDB you just plugged in.

**Unplugging the PDB to Be Upgraded from the Old Database**    The first step in the unplug/plug upgrade process is to unplug the PDB you wish to upgrade. The following steps typically are used to perform this task:

1.  Use the ALTER SESSION SET CONTAINER command to point your session to the correct PDB.

2.  From the old ORACLE_HOME directory structure, run the Pre-Upgrade Information Tool on the PDB to be unplugged and upgraded.

3. Run the **preupgrade_fixups.sql** script on the source database. Review the results and take any action as required.

4. Close the PDB with the ALTER PLUGGABLE DATABASE CLOSE command.

5. Unplug the PDB with the ALTER PLUGGABLE DATABASE UNPLUG INTO command, passing the location of the resulting XML file that will get created.

6. Drop the PDB with the DROP PLUGGABLE DATABASE command using the KEEP DATAFILES option.

Note that these steps assume that you do *not* need to move the datafiles of the PDB (as indicated by the KEEP DATAFILES option in step 6). If you want to move the datafiles to a completely different server, the process will be different—you'll use the **cp** command within the **asmcmd** interface to copy the datafiles to an OS file system accessible by the other server, then use the **cp** command within the **asmcmd** interface on the destination ASM instance to copy the files into the new disk group before plugging the PDB into the upgraded database.

**Plugging the PDB into the New Database**   The second step in the unplug/plug upgrade process is to plug the PDB you want to upgrade into the CDB running the new version of the Oracle Database software. The following steps typically are used to perform this task:

1. Connect to the new CDB.

2. Plug in the PDB you wish to upgrade using the CREATE PLUGGABLE DATABASE USING command, passing the XML file that was created in the first step when you unplugged the PDB.

**Upgrading the Newly Plugged-in PDB**   Finally, you need to upgrade the PDB. Some upgrade steps occur automatically when you plug the PDB into the new CDB. However, you still have to perform the following steps:

1. Run the **catupgrd.sql** script via the **$ORACLE_HOME/rdbms/admin/catctl.pl** script. This upgrades the PDB. Pass the **catctl.pl** script the **–c** parameter, followed by the name of the PDB that you are upgrading. This name should be in capital letters.

2. Log into the container database where the new PDB resides using a SYSDBA account. Use the ALTER SESSION SET CONTAINER command to make the container you are upgrading the current container.

3. Start the container using the STARTUP command.

4. Using the **catcon.pl** script, run the **postupgrade_fixups.sql** script that was created by the Pre-Upgrade Information Tool earlier.

5. Using the **catcon.pl** script, run the **utlrp.sql** script to make sure any invalid objects are recompiled.

This will complete the upgrade of the PDB and it should be ready for use. You should back up the PDB after using this method of upgrading it.

## In the Event of Failure

Recovering from a failed upgrade of a container database follows the same process that you would follow with a non-multitenant database, with a few exceptions. For example, each PDB is upgraded in turn, and one or more of the PDBs may have an issue that prevents the upgrade of the problematic PDB and all remaining PDBs.

After fixing the reason for the PDB upgrade failure, restart the database upgrade using the **dbupgrade** utility along with the **–p** parameter *and* the **–c** parameter, followed by the step that the previous upgrade failed on. For example, to restart a failed upgrade on phase 20 with a PDB named DEV01, the command would look like this:

```
dbupgrade -p 20 -c 'DEV02' catupgrd.sql
```

# Going...Going...Gone: Deprecated and Desupported Features

As always, Oracle Database new releases move some features into the deprecated category and some into the desupported category. *Deprecated* means that the feature is no longer being enhanced and, at some point in time, will no longer be available in Oracle Database. It's a warning that the feature is on the road to being desupported. *Desupported* means Oracle is no longer fixing bugs in the feature and that the feature may well just disappear (if it has not already). It's the tolling of the bell that indicates, if you're still using the feature, you probably waited too long.

This section discusses the deprecated and desupported features in Oracle Database 12c Release 2. We will then review parameters that have been deprecated, parameters that no longer are supported, and one parameter that has had a default value change.

## Features Deprecated in Oracle Database 12*c* Release 2

The following features have been deprecated in Oracle Database 12*c* Release 2:

- The DBMS_JOBS package.

- Direct file system placement for Oracle Cluster Registry (OCR) and voting files. The upshot of this is that you will have to use Oracle Automatic Storage Management (ASM) once this feature becomes desupported.

- Intelligent Data Placement for ASM disks.

- The **oracle.jdbc.OracleConnection.unwrap()** and **oracle.jdbc.rowset** packages.

- **oracle.sql** extensions. Replace with standard Java types or use the **oracle .jdbc** extensions.

- The V$MANAGED_STANDBY view, in favor of the V$DATAGUARD_ PROCESS view.

- Some XML DB features and functions.

## Features Desupported in Oracle Database 12*c* Release 2

The following features are desupported in Oracle Database 12*c* Release 2 and are no longer available for use in most cases:

- Advanced Replication.

- JPublisher.

- Oracle Data Provider for .NET APIs for Transaction Guard.

- SQLJ support inside of the database.

- Some XML DB features. Please reference the *Oracle Database Upgrade Guide* for a complete list of desupported XML DB features.

## Deprecated Parameters in Oracle Database 12*c* Release 2

The following parameters are deprecated beginning with Oracle Database 12*c* Release 2:

- **O7_DICTIONARY_ACCESSIBILITY**  This parameter controls accessibility to the Oracle Database data dictionary. Oracle Database version 7 allowed for somewhat looser access standards to the data dictionary. This parameter allowed those looser access standards to be maintained when Oracle increased the security around access to the data dictionary.

- **PARALLEL_ADAPTIVE_MULTI_USER**  You should migrate to using parallel statement queuing instead of using this parameter.

- **UTL_FILE_DIR**  Oracle recommends converting to the use of directory objects (created with the CREATE DIRECTORY command) instead of using the UTL_FILE_DIR parameter.

- **UNIFIED_AUDIT_SGA_QUEUE_SIZE**  This parameter can still be set but it will be ignored—the queue size for the unified audit trail is automatically managed.

You can also run the following query to get the full list of deprecated parameters from the database itself:

```
select name from v$parameter where isdeprecated='TRUE' order by name;
```

Of special note is that the SEC_CASE_SENSITIVE_LOGON parameter is deprecated in Oracle Database 12*c* Release 2. This is because standards-based verifiers (SHA-1 and SHA-512) do not support case-sensitive password matching. Even though this parameter is deprecated, Oracle still suggests in the *Oracle Database Security Guide* that you enable this parameter and make your passwords case sensitive.

## Desupported Parameters in Oracle Database 12*c* Release 2

The following parameters are desupported in Oracle Database 12*c* Release 2. All of these parameters have previously been deprecated by Oracle. If you try to start an Oracle Database 12*c* Release 2 database with any of these parameters in use, the instance will fail to start.

- GLOBAL_CONTEXT_POOL_SIZE
- MAX_ENABLED_ROLES

- PARALLEL_AUTOMATIC_TUNING

- PARALLEL_IO_CAP_ENABLED

- PARALLEL_SERVER

- PARALLEL_SERVER_INSTANCES

# Summary

In this chapter we have covered a number of different topics related to Oracle Database 12c Release 2. I discussed the upgrade process using the Database Upgrade Assistant (DBUA), upgrading both multitenant databases and databases not using the multitenant architecture. When you can't use DBUA to upgrade or migrate a database, you can use other Oracle tools such as Oracle Data Pump or perform a manual upgrade. If something goes wrong during the upgrade, it's even easier to fix the issue and pick up where you left off.

Every database release has new initialization parameters and a number of parameters that are deprecated or desupported—Oracle Database 12c Release 2 is no exception. I pointed out a few that you may still be using and those that are critical to the security of your database.

Now that you have a new Oracle 12c Release 2 database ready to go, or you upgraded from a previous release, we're ready to look at how to leverage the new features. The next chapter identifies the new features of Oracle Multitenant and in particular how those new features dramatically improve your database's availability in a multitenant environment.

# CHAPTER
## 3

Oracle Database 12c
Release 2 Multitenant
New Features

Oracle Database 12*c* Release 1 introduced a radically different database architecture in the form of Oracle Multitenant. In this new architecture, Oracle provides the ability to store multiple databases called *pluggable databases (PDBs)* within the management infrastructure of a single Oracle Database instance called a *container database (CDB)*, or even within multiple database instances in the case of Oracle Real Application Clusters (RAC).

Oracle Database 12*c* Release 2 adds several new features related to Multitenant databases, which we will discuss in this chapter. Also, Oracle has announced that the old Oracle database architecture has been deprecated. What this means is that as time goes on, we are more likely to see new features that will work only with the new multitenant architecture. So, now is a good time to start becoming familiar with Oracle Multitenant.

We discuss Multitenant database new features in several other chapters in this book. For example, Chapter 2 discussed upgrading Multitenant databases. Chapter 4 introduces new features related to scalability and agility, and Chapter 6 covers new features related to backups and RMAN. Quite probably, most of the new features discussed in the next edition of this book will be related to PDBs in some way.

In this chapter we start with a review of some of the new features related to the creation of Oracle pluggable databases, as well as new cloning features—with every new release, more operations can be done while the PDB is online. There are new security features that are important to cover as well. Last, but not least, we'll cover performance enhancements to a container environment so that each PDB in a container will coexist more peacefully with the other PDBs in the CDB in terms of resource usage.

# New Features Related to Creating Pluggable Databases

New features related to creating (including cloning) pluggable databases include the following:

- Increase in how many PDBs a CDB can contain
- Parallel creation of PDBs
- Hot cloning of PDBs
- Refreshable read-only PDBs
- Creating UNDO tablespaces in individual PDBs
- Creating a PDB with a default tablespace
- Fine-grained PDB memory usage

- Support for PDBs with a different character set from that of the host CDB

- Changes in PDB support for time zones

That's a lot to cover, so let's get started!

# Support for Thousands of PDBs for Each Container Database

In the first release of Oracle Database 12*c*, you could create a maximum of 252 PDBs within a CDB. Oracle likely thought that was more than enough PDBs per CDB at the time. However, I can think of many cases where more than 252 PDBs might be helpful, and apparently Oracle agrees. In Oracle Database 12*c* Release 2, you can now create 4,096 individual PDBs within a CDB. I have no doubt someone will be bumping up against that limit any day now!

# Parallel PDB Creation

When you create a new PDB, using PDB$SEED as your source, you can now choose to parallelize the creation of that PDB. You do so by using the new PARALLEL clause of the CREATE PLUGGABLE DATABASE command, as shown in this example:

```
create pluggable database dw2 from seed parallel 4;
```

If you don't indicate a degree of parallelism by using the PARALLEL clause, then Oracle will decide one for you, even if you don't use the PARALLEL clause. If you don't want to have the PDB created in parallel, you can force it to be created in serial mode by using the PARALLEL parameter with a value of 1.

# Hot and Cold Cloning a PDB

You can now create a PDB from another PDB while the source PDB is still in READ WRITE mode. To do so, the CDB must be in ARCHIVELOG mode. You can also incrementally refresh a PDB that was opened READ ONLY. This fine-grained UNDO for PDBs also enables flashback features at the PDB level. All three of those features require setting up local undo mode. As long as these requirements are met, no additional parameters are required when issuing the CREATE PLUGGABLE DATABASE command.

## Configuring CDB Local Undo Mode

Oracle Database 12*c* Release 2 now offers the capability for PDBs to use their own UNDO tablespaces as opposed to the UNDO tablespace of the entire CDB. You can define the UNDO tablespace at the time you create the PDB or you can modify an existing PDB to start using local undo mode (this requires restarting the entire CDB). Additionally, when you create a PDB using the Database Configuration Assistant (DBCA), it will create a local UNDO tablespace for the new PDB, and enable local undo mode for that PDB by default.

To use local undo mode, you must enable it on the CDB. For an existing CDB, you can do this through the following steps:

1. Shut down the CDB.

2. Restart the CDB in upgrade mode with the STARTUP UPGRADE command.

3. While connected to the root container, issue the command ALTER DATABASE LOCAL UNDO ON.

4. Shut down and restart the CDB.

After restarting the database, you can tell that it's in local undo mode by querying the DATABASE_PROPERTIES view and searching the PROPERTY_NAME column for the value LOCAL_UNDO_ENABLED. If local undo mode is enabled, then the PROPERTY_VALUE column returns TRUE; otherwise it returns FALSE. The following example shows a query of the view and confirms that the database is in local undo mode:

```
select property_name, property_value
from   database_properties
where  property_name = 'LOCAL_UNDO_ENABLED';
PROPERTY_NAME          PROPERTY_VALUE
-------------------- --------------------
LOCAL_UNDO_ENABLED     TRUE
```

After the CDB is put in local undo mode, each PDB will have a new UNDO tablespace created when it is first opened, and the UNDO_TABLESPACE parameter will be set to the value of that new UNDO tablespace. (Note that the creation of the new UNDO tablespace in the PDB may cause the reopening of the PDB to take a bit longer the first time.)

Another way to confirm that local undo tablespaces have been created is to look in V$DATAFILE:

```
select con_id, file#, name
from v$datafile
order by con_id,file#;

CON_ID  FILE#   NAME
------- ------- ---------------------------------------------------------------
      1       1 +DATA/DB12CR2/DATAFILE/system.257.934060289
      1       3 +DATA/DB12CR2/DATAFILE/sysaux.258.934060323
      1       4 +DATA/DB12CR2/DATAFILE/undotbs1.259.934060349
      1       7 +DATA/DB12CR2/DATAFILE/users.260.934060349
```

```
2      5  +DATA/DB12CR2/3817ED.../DATAFILE/system.272.934060415
2      6  +DATA/DB12CR2/3817ED.../DATAFILE/sysaux.271.934060415
2      8  +DATA/DB12CR2/3817ED.../DATAFILE/undotbs1.270.934060415
3      9  +DATA/DB12CR2/46CF8E.../DATAFILE/system.275.934060653
3     10  +DATA/DB12CR2/46CF8E.../DATAFILE/sysaux.276.934060653
3     11  +DATA/DB12CR2/46CF8E.../DATAFILE/undotbs1.277.934060653
3     12  +DATA/DB12CR2/46CF8E.../DATAFILE/users.279.934060667
3     15  +DATA/DB12CR2/46CF8E.../DATAFILE/users2.281.934629025
3     16  +DATA/DB12CR2/46CF8E.../DATAFILE/users2.280.934659259

13 rows selected.
```

The container itself has its own undo tablespace as well as both the seed database and the single PDB in this CDB.

It is possible that this new local undo tablespace will not be sized correctly, or you may wish to create the local undo tablespace in a different location. Once the CDB is in local undo mode, you can connect to a PDB and create its own custom undo tablespace. Once it is created, simply change the UNDO_TABLESPACE parameter to point to the new UNDO tablespace. Once you have done that, and once the old UNDO tablespace is no longer in use, you can drop the old UNDO tablespace that was created.

```
create bigfile undo tablespace loc_undo
    datafile size 10g
    autoextend on
    next 10g maxsize 500g;
alter system set undo_tablespace=loc_undo;
```

You can reverse this process to take a CDB out of local undo mode. When you take the CDB out of local undo mode and put it back into shared undo mode, the UNDO tablespaces in the PDBs will not be used. Also, Oracle does not automatically drop the local UNDO tablespaces when the CDB is taken out of local undo mode. The DBA must drop these tablespaces in the individual PDBs in separate operations.

## Creating a PDB with a Default Tablespace

In Oracle Database 12c Release 1, you can define the default tablespace of a PDB when creating the PDB only if you are cloning it from the PDB$SEED container. To do so, you simply use the DEFAULT TABLESPACE clause as a part of the CREATE PLUGGABLE DATABASE command, which enables you to define the name, datafile location, and size of the datafile associated with that temporary tablespace. If you don't define a datafile, Oracle creates one for you.

However, in Release 1, if you are creating a PDB through any other method, then you cannot define the default tablespace for the PDB being created. For example, if you are creating a PDB using another user-created PDB as the source, you can't use the DEFAULT TABLESPACE clause. Instead, you have to connect to the new PDB once it has been created and then create the new tablespace that you want to use as the default tablespace. Then, you need to create a temporary tablespace for that PDB.

In Oracle Database 12c Release 2, you can now use the DEFAULT TABLESPACE clause within the CREATE PLUGGABLE DATABASE command when creating any PDB. Cloning the PDB from PDB$SEED really has not changed much in this respect. There is one additional requirement if you are cloning the PDB using any method other than cloning from PDB$SEED: the tablespace you will define as the default tablespace must already exist in the source database that the PDB will be cloned from.

For example, assume we have a PDB called DB12CR2NF and we wish to create a new PDB called TESTPDB using the DB12CR2NF PDB as the source. Further assume that we want to define a tablespace called DEFAULT_TBS as the default tablespace for the new PDB. To do this, first we would create the DEFAULT_TBS tablespace in the DB12CR2NF PDB (which will be the source PDB):

```
sqlplus rjb/rjb@localhost:1521/db12cR2nf as sysdba
 SQL> create tablespace default_tbs datafile size 100g;
Tablespace created.
```

Now, we connect to the CDB root and simply issue the CREATE PLUGGABLE DATABASE command, including the DEFAULT TABLESPACE clause that will cause the DEFAULT_TBS tablespace to be used as the default tablespace:

```
connect / as sysdba
create pluggable database testpdb from db12cr2nf
default tablespace default_tbs;
```

We can see the impact of this by logging into the TESTPDB PDB, opening it, creating a user, and then querying the data dictionary to see the user's default tablespace assignment:

```
alter pluggable database testpdb open;
alter session set container=testpdb;
create user testing identified by test;
select username, default_tablespace from dba_users where username='TESTING';

USERNAME                        DEFAULT_TABLESPACE
------------------------------  ------------------------------
TESTING                         DEFAULT_TBS
```

## Support for Different Character Sets in PDBs

When Oracle Multitenant was first released, a PDB had to be defined with the same character set as the CDB that owned it. This caused problems if you wanted to consolidate databases into a CDB if they did not share the same character set.

Oracle Database 12.2 relaxes the rules related to the compatibility of character sets in the PDBs contained in a given CDB. Now, for each PDB being plugged into a CDB, you must consider the combinations of database character sets and NLS character sets to determine if the plug-in of the PDB will be successful, or if you must convert the character set of the PDB to be able to use it.

Table 3-1 lists the different actions that will occur when you plug in a PDB, based on the character sets in use in both the PDB and the CDB.

| CDB Character Set | CDB NLS Character Set | PDB Character Set | PDB NLS Character Set | Plug-In Restricted | PDB Converted |
|---|---|---|---|---|---|
| Any | Any | Same as CDB | Same as CDB | No | No |
| Any | AL16UTF8 | Same as CDB | Any | No | No |
| Any | Not AL16UTF8 | Same as CDB | Not same as CDB | Yes, until character set is migrated. | No |
| AL32UTF8 | Any | Any | Same as CDB | No | No |
| AL32UTF8 | AL16UTF8 | Any | Any | No | No |
| AL32UTF8 | Not AL16UTF8 | Any | Not same as CDB | Yes, until character set is migrated. | No |
| Compatible Character Set with PDB | Any | Compatible Character Set with CDB | Same as CDB | No | Yes |
| Compatible Character Set with PDB | AL16UTF8 | Compatible Character Set with CDB | Any | No | Yes |
| Compatible Character Set with PDB | Not AL16UTF8 | Compatible Character Set with CDB | Not same as CDB | Yes, until character set is migrated. | No |
| Incompatible Character Set with PDB | Any | Incompatible Character Set with CDB | Any | Yes. Must migrate character set of PDB to be compatible with CDB. | No |

**TABLE 3-1.**   *PDB to CDB Character Set Compatibility*

In Table 3-1, when we talk about a character set being compatible, we mean that it must be *plug-in compatible*. This means that the character set in the PDB is a binary subset (proper subset) of the character set of the CDB that it's being plugged into. You can find the list of compatible character sets in the *Database Globalization Support Guide*, which is part of the Oracle Documentation Set for Oracle Database 12*c* Release 2.

One thing that is clear from Table 3-1 is that it's a really good idea to create any CDB using the AL32UTF8 character set. You should also always use the AL16UTF8 character set as the NLS character set for the CDB. In doing so, you will make the migration of PDBs into the CDB a much easier process.

Even when Oracle plugs in a PDB without an error message, and even converts the character set of the database, this does not mean that you are home free. Some character set conversions can still be problematic. For example, CHAR or VARCHAR2 column data may all of a sudden exceed the declared column lengths during the conversion. For these reasons, Oracle recommends upgrading the character set of the database or PDB before plugging it into a CDB.

Note that many of the Oracle utilities (such as LogMiner) and database features (such as standby databases) will also support the mixing of character sets between a CDB and a PDB. This support enables extended features such as rolling upgrades of the Oracle database.

## PDB Support for Different Database Time Zones

In Oracle Database 12*c* Release 2, you can now permanently set the time zone for any PDB to be different from that of the CDB by using the ALTER PLUGGABLE DATABASE command with the SET TIME_ZONE clause. To change the time zone of a PDB, you must be connected to the PDB. Once you have changed the time zone setting, you must restart the PDB. You can then see that the new time zone has been set properly by calling the DBTIMEZONE function. Here is an example that sets the time zone to GMT minus 6 hours:

```
select dbtimezone from dual;

DBTIME
------
+00:00

alter pluggable database set time_zone='-06:00';
shutdown
startup
select dbtimezone from dual;

DBTIME
------
-06:00
```

When you change the time zone for a PDB, it does not actually change any data. Therefore, you cannot change the time zone setting for a PDB if it has any columns with a type of TIMESTAMP WITH LOCAL TIME ZONE.

## PDB Support for Different Database Time Zone Files

You can now analyze the potential impact of upgrading to new time zone files for an individual PDB and then upgrade that PDB to use new time zone files, independent of the time zone file of the CDB. For example, you can run the DBMS_DST.BEGIN_UPGRADE command from within a PDB to upgrade its primary time zone setting as shown here:

```
SQL> show con_name

CON_NAME
-------------------------------
TESTTWO

exec dbms_dst.begin_upgrade(26);
select property_name, substr(property_value, 1, 30) value
from database_properties
where property_name like 'DST_%'
order by property_name;

PROPERTY_NAME                    VALUE
-------------------------------  -------------------------------
DST_PRIMARY_TT_VERSION           26
DST_SECONDARY_TT_VERSION         25
DST_UPGRADE_STATE                UPGRADE
```

**NOTE**
*Oracle Support Document 1509653.1 provides a great deal of detail on upgrading time zone files in a database. The information in that document also applies to upgrading time zone files for a PDB.*

# Moving, Copying, and Migrating PDBs

One of the reasons you use PDBs is to be able to unplug them, relocate them, and plug them into another CDB on the same or a different server. Oracle Database 12*c* Release 2 gives you several new options for PDB relocation and cloning such as moving a PDB to a different hardware and OS platform as well as using a PDB archive file to more efficiently unplug, package, and move a PDB as a single compressed file.

## Cloning a PDB in READ WRITE Mode

In Oracle Database 12c Release 1, you could easily clone one PDB to another, either within the same CDB or to another CDB on the same or different server, but the source PDB had to be opened READ ONLY. To allow cloning while the source PDB is open in READ WRITE mode, Oracle uses the current system change number (SCN) and undo data to ensure that a logically consistent copy of the PDB will be created in the target CDB.

In this example, you want to make a copy of a PDB called TESTPDB and call it TESTPDB_CLONE while TESTPDB is still open as READ WRITE. First, verify TESTPDB's open mode:

```
select con_id,name,open_mode
from v$pdbs;

CON_ID  NAME                 OPEN_MODE
-------  -------------------- ----------
     2  PDB$SEED             READ ONLY
     3  DB12CR2NF            READ WRITE
     4  TESTPDB              READ WRITE
```

Next, clone the PDB live:

```
create pluggable database testpdb_clone from testpdb;
Pluggable database TESTPDB_CLONE created.
```

Open the new PDB and verify status:

```
alter pluggable database testpdb_clone open read write;
Pluggable database TESTPDB_CLONE altered.
select con_id,name,open_mode
from v$pdbs;

CON_ID  NAME                 OPEN_MODE
-------  -------------------- ----------
     2  PDB$SEED             READ ONLY
     3  DB12CR2NF            READ WRITE
     4  TESTPDB              READ WRITE
     5  TESTPDB_CLONE        READ WRITE
```

Ideally, you want to minimize the amount of DML happening on the source PDB to speed up the completion of the cloning operation, but often you don't have that luxury in a production system that needs to be cloned during peak activity.

## Incrementally Refreshing a Read-Only PDB

Whatever method you use to clone a PDB, it's going to be a point-in-time snapshot of the source PDB, and in Oracle Database 12c Release 1, to refresh the clone you have to do a full copy of the source PDB. This can be a resource-intensive process if the source PDB is large and the clone needs to be refreshed on a frequent basis. Oracle Database 12*c* Release 2 makes this process less painful by supporting *PDB refresh*.

The refresh mode of the PDB is specified when the PDB is created. Here are the three refresh modes you can specify as part of the CREATE PLUGGABLE DATABASE . . . FROM command:

- **REFRESH MODE NONE (default)**   The PDB will not be refreshable.

- **REFRESH MODE MANUAL**   The PDB can be refreshed on demand.

- **REFRESH MODE EVERY *num_minutes* MINUTES**   The PDB is refreshed automatically every *num_minutes* minutes.

There are a few restrictions on incremental PDB refresh, and most of these make sense:

- A refreshable (manual or automatic) PDB can only be opened READ ONLY.

- The clone PDB must be closed during a refresh.

- The source and clone PDBs must be in different CDBs.

- If a PDB clone is open during a scheduled refresh, the refresh is attempted again at the next scheduled refresh time.

You can use ALTER PLUGGABLE DATABASE to change the refresh type from MANUAL to EVERY . . . MINUTES and vice versa. If you no longer want a clone to be refreshable, you can change it to NONE. However, you can't change it back without dropping and re-creating the clone as refreshable.

Some of these seem like features that are not fully implemented, but consider the restriction on the PDB always being in READ ONLY mode. What if the cloned PDB had a few table rows changed? It doesn't make sense that the changes would be propagated back to the source PDB. Even more importantly, what if the changes made to the clone conflicted with a recent change to the source PDB at refresh time? What if a table in the PDB clone was dropped? How would those conflicts be resolved? That kind of functionality is well outside of the use cases that incrementally updated PDBs were designed for.

## Flashback a PDB

Many of Oracle's Flashback features have been available for several releases of Oracle Database, and even Flashback Database was available in Oracle Database 11*g*.

However, in Oracle Database 12*c* Release 1, you could use Flashback Database only at the CDB level. In other words, if you needed to flash back a PDB to a previous point in time (SCN), all PDBs in the same CDB would be flashed back to the same SCN. This is clearly not very granular and is highly undesirable when you find out that your PDB has to be rolled back to yesterday because someone else's PDB lost a few tables and the only way to get them back is to flash back to the time before the tables were dropped.

Using Flashback Database, you create normal or guaranteed restore points (SCNs) at the PDB level independent of any other PDB. To perform flashback on a PDB, it must first be closed:

```
alter pluggable database qa_rel2 close;
```

You can perform the flashback itself by referencing an SCN or a restore point, as in these examples:

```
flashback pluggable database qa_rel2 to scn 38989823;
flashback pluggable database qa_rel2 to restore point tuesday;
```

As with any other incomplete recovery operation, you will have to open the PDB with the RESETLOGS option:

```
alter pluggable database qa_rel2 open resetlogs;
```

Flashback Database for PDBs is faster and less error prone when local undo is enabled for a CDB, but still possible without local undo. However, when flashing back, RMAN must create an auxiliary instance to perform the flashback, which could temporarily cause problems with disk space since some tablespaces must be restored to the fast recovery area to finish the flashback operation.

# Relocating a PDB

You can now use the CREATE PLUGGABLE DATABASE command to *move* a PDB between two CDBs while both CDBs are online with a minimal outage during which incremental redo is applied. To relocate a PDB, you include the FROM and RELOCATE clauses in the CREATE PLUGGABLE DATABASE command. These clauses indicate which PDB you wish to relocate and that it will be *moved*, not *copied*, to the current CDB. Oracle then moves the PDB, and its associated database files, for you automatically. While the PDB is being relocated, you can still query the source database. Any DML or DDL operations are queued during the relocation process, and they will be executed on the relocated PDB once the relocation is complete.

You can choose to relocate a PDB by issuing the CREATE PLUGGABLE DATABASE command on either the source CDB or target CDB. Relocating a PDB requires that a database link be created between the two databases.

If you are relocating the PDB from the source CDB, then you need to create a database link from the source CDB to the target CDB, connecting to the root container of the target CDB. If you are relocating the PDB while connected to the target CDB, then you need to create the database link from the target CDB to the source CDB. That link needs to connect either to the root of the source CDB or to the source PDB being relocated itself.

**NOTE**
*Relocation of PDBs is one way of moving PDBs into application containers. We discuss application containers in Chapter 4.*

After the PDB is relocated, Oracle drops all connections to the old PDB and then removes the source PDB. This is the default method and is known as *normal availability*. You can also declare the use of this method outright when issuing the CREATE PLUGGABLE DATABASE command by using the parameter AVAILABILITY NORMAL. Alternatively, you can choose to have Oracle actually redirect all connections for you, and move the PDB service, as a part of the relocation process. This is known as *maximum availability*. To indicate you want to use the maximum availability method, use the AVAILABILITY MAX parameter of the CREATE PLUGGABLE DATABASE command.

Several requirements must be met before you can relocate a PDB:

- The user issuing the CREATE PLUGGABLE DATABASE command must have the privileges to execute that command and must be connected to the root of the CDB.

- The source CDB and target CDB must be configured for local undo mode.

- The source PDB can be open in READ WRITE mode during the relocation only if the target database is in ARCHIVELOG mode; otherwise, the source PDB must be in READ ONLY mode.

- The source and target platforms must have the same endianness byte format and must have the same set of database options installed.

- The character set of the target CDB must be compatible with, or the same as, the character set of the source PDB (see Table 3-1 earlier in the chapter).

In this example, a new PDB called NEWPDB in the PDBRELOCATE is created by moving TESTPDB from another CDB.

You run this on the target CDB:

```
create user c##rjb identified by password;
grant create session to c##rjb;
grant sysoper to c##rjb;
grant create pluggable database to c##rjb;
```

This is run on the source CDB:

```
create database link to_target connect to c##rjb
identified by rjbpasswd
using 'localhost/pdbrelocate';

select count(*) from user_objects@to_target; -- check connectivity

create pluggable database newpdb@to_target
from testpdb relocate availability max;
```

## Manually Transporting PDBs Across Platforms

If you can't use the PDB relocation feature just discussed (for example, if there are byte format issues or you want to move the entire CDB), there are several other methods you can use to transport PDBs across various platforms:

- Transport the entire CDB between two different platforms. This method has not changed between Oracle Database 12*c* Release 1 and Release 2 and thus won't be described in this chapter.

- Transport a PDB between two different platforms using a read-only PDB as the source. This method is covered in the previous section as an alternative when a read-write PDB can't be the source during the relocation because the target database is not in ARCHIVELOG mode.

- Transport a PDB between two different platforms using a closed PDB as the source. This method is new in Oracle Database 12*c* Release 2.

- Transport a PDB between two different platforms using incremental backups as the source. This method also is new in Oracle Database 12*c* Release 2.

- Transport tablespaces that belong to a PDB across different platforms. This method is supported in Oracle Database 12*c* Release 1, but the requirement that the platforms be of the same endian format has been removed in Release 2.

Let's look next at the two new methods introduced in Oracle Database 12*c* Release 2 and the change to the final method that enables higher availability.

### Transporting a PDB Between Two Platforms Using a Closed PDB as the Source

Oracle Database 12*c* Release 2 provides the ability to transport a PDB across platforms using a closed PDB as the source. To perform this movement you must follow these steps:

1. Connect to the root using a common user, or SYS, with SYSDBA or SYSBACKUP privileges.

2. If the PDB is not already closed, then close the PDB.

3. Use the BACKUP PLUGGABLE DATABASE command with the TO PLATFORM clause to back up the PDB with RMAN.

4. Move the backup sets that were created in the previous step to the destination platform.

5. To perform the restore, on the destination CDB connect to the root container as a common user, or SYS, using the SYSDBA or SYSBACKUP privilege.

6. Check the backup to ensure that the PDB you are transporting over is compatible with the destination CDB. To do this, use the DBMS_PDB. CHECK_PLUG_COMPATIBILITY procedure. The function will return TRUE value if the source PDB is compatible with the CDB you intend to plug it into.

7. If the source PDB is compatible, then use the RESTORE PLUGGABLE DATABASE command with the FOREIGN PLUGGABLE DATABASE clause to complete the movement of the PDB into the new CDB.

8. Open the PDB.

### Transporting a PDB Between Two Different Platforms Using Online Incremental Backups as the Source

Movement of larger databases, or mission-critical databases, often allows only a small, if any, window for an outage. Oracle Database 12*c* Release 2 addresses this issue by supporting an incremental backup and restore strategy for cross-platform movement of a PDB. This method does require one outage, but it should be significantly shorter than previously supported methods.

The procedure to move PDBs in this way is as follows:

1. Create the first backup of the PDB with the BACKUP PLUGGABLE DATABASE command, along with the FOR TRANSPORT option. Use the new ALLOW INCONSISTENT keyword and INCREMENTAL LEVEL 0 parameters of the BACKUP command to indicate that the backup is the base of an incremental backup.

2. Start to restore the level 0 incremental backup on the remote CDB. Since the level 0 backup might be quite large, it could take a long time for the restore operation to complete. To restore the level 0 backup, first log into the destination CDB and then use the RESTORE PLUGGABLE DATABASE FROM BACKUPSET command after you have copied the RMAN backupset files to storage accessible to the CDB you want to import the PDB into.

3. On the source database, make one or more incremental backups that can be used to update the destination CDB. To do this, use the BACKUP PLUGGABLE DATABASE command again with the FOR TRANSPORT option. As in step 1, use the ALLOW INCONSISTENT keyword, but this time use the INCREMENTAL LEVEL 1 keyword.

4. Apply the incremental backups on the CDB that you are moving the PDB over to by using the RMAN RECOVER FROM BACKUPSET command with FOREIGN DATAFILECOPY.

5. When you are ready to complete the transport of the PDB, close the PDB on the source system with the ALTER PLUGGABLE DATABASE CLOSE IMMEDIATE command.

6. Use the BACKUP FOR TRANSPORT RMAN command to make the final backup of the PDB to be applied in the CDB that you wish to plug the PDB into.

7. Use the RECOVER FROM BACKUPSET command to complete the recovery of the PDB.

8. Once the PDB recovery is complete on the target, you can open it using the ALTER PLUGGABLE DATABASE OPEN command.

## Transporting Tablespaces That Belong to a PDB Across Different Platforms

Oracle Database 12c Release 2 now allows you to transport tablespaces between PDBs regardless of endian byte format differences between the two platforms. All requirements related to transporting of tablespaces still exist (for example, they must be self-contained).

Oracle Database offers three different options with respect to transporting PDB tablespaces across platforms. Note that all of these options require that you put the source tablespace in READ ONLY mode before you convert it.

The first option is to connect to the PDB with RMAN (with the PDB being the target), put the tablespace(s) in READ ONLY mode, and then use the BACKUP TABLESPACE command along with the TO PLATFORM and DATAPUMP FORMAT options. When using this option, you use the RMAN RESTORE FROM BACKUPSET command while connected to the target PDB.

The other two options are to use either the RMAN CONVERT TABLESPACE command or CONVERT DATAFILE command, whichever would be more appropriate for your situation. Clearly, if you had a tablespace with many datafiles, then the CONVERT TABLESPACE command would be the preferred way of starting the conversion process. RMAN will convert the datafiles and will also create a Data Pump dump file that is required to complete the transport of the tablespace(s) or datafile(s).

In this situation, after using the RMAN CONVERT command, you would then copy the converted files and the Data Pump export file that RMAN created to the destination database server. Once the files are copied over, you simply connect to the PDB you want to plug the tablespace into with Data Pump. You then transport in the tablespace(s) in the same way you would if you were using a non-CDB database.

# Using PDB Archive Files when Unplugging a PDB

Moving a PDB to another CDB can require the movement of a number of different files, including an XML file that contains the metadata related to the PDB as well as all of the datafiles associated with that PDB. Managing all these files can get cumbersome. In Oracle Database 12*c* Release 2, Oracle simplifies this process a great deal through the creation of *PDB archive files*.

A PDB archive file is a collection of all the files required to move a PDB between CDBs. The contents of the PDB archive file are compressed and Oracle assigns a **.pdb** extension to the file that is generated. Let's first look at an example of creating a PDB archive file when we unplug a database and then look at an example of using the PDB archive file when we plug the PDB in again.

### Creating a PDB Archive File when Unplugging a PDB

You issue the ALTER PLUGGABLE DATABASE command along with the UNPLUG INTO clause to unplug a PDB from a CDB (after closing the PDB, of course). If you include a filename with an extension of **.pdb** in the UNPLUG INTO clause, then Oracle will create a PDB archive file. You can also still create the XML file, as in Oracle Database 12*c* Release 1, if you wish. Here is an example of unplugging a database and creating a PDB archive file:

```
alter pluggable database pdb_prd
unplug into '/u01/pdbexp/unplug/pdb_prd.pdb';
```

### Plugging In a PDB with a PDB Archive File

Oracle has made it easy to plug in a PDB with an archive file. You simply put the PDB archive filename with the **.pdb** file extension into your CREATE PLUGGABLE DATABASE command. Oracle will automatically detect that you are using a PDB archive file.

# PDB Security: Lockdown Profiles

Oracle includes enhanced security features with every release of Oracle. When the multitenant features were introduced in Oracle Database 12*c* Release 1, the security at the PDB level was not fine-grained enough for the CDB owner to restrict a PDB's DBA from performing some, but not all, administrative tasks at the PDB level that could have an adverse effect on the CDB as a whole.

As a result, there are new features in Oracle Database 12*c* Release 2 that allow the CDB's DBA to set system-level attributes for the PDB, such as configuring minimum and maximum amounts of memory that the PDB must have available (discussed later in this chapter).

As the administrator of the overall CDB, you may want to restrict the PDB DBA's ability to use the ALTER SYSTEM command. For example, you may not want to let the DBA configure memory-related settings, such as SGA_MAX_SIZE. On the other hand, you may well want to give the DBA a free hand to change settings such as CURSOR_SHARING, OPEN_CURSORS, and STATISTICS_LEVEL, all of which can be set at a PDB level. Prior to Oracle Database 12*c* Release 2, this raised a problem because the ALTER SYSTEM privilege was kind of an all-or-nothing affair, lacking the capability to fine-tune the nature of these grants. This is where lockdown profiles, new in Release 2, come into play.

*Lockdown profiles* provide the capability to restrict a number of operations in PDBs, including:

- The ALTER SYSTEM statement, and specific clauses of the ALTER SYSTEM statement.

- Common user object access.

- Context operations that involve datastore types FILE_DATASTORE or URL_DATASTORE.

- Operations that involve network access. For example, you can restrict usage of UTL_HTTP, UTL_SMTP, or UTL_TCP with respect to its ability to communicate outside of a PDB.

- XDB protocols.

A lockdown profile is created at the CDB level. However, a lockdown profile is enabled at the PDB level. This provides the ability to create and assign different lockdown profiles to PDBs as required. When a lockdown profile is created, it must be given a name that is unique within the namespace of the CDB. Oracle provides three lockdown profiles by default in Oracle Database 12*c* Release 2:

- **PRIVATE_DBAAS**   Least restrictive lockdown profile. This profile allows users to connect to PDBs but prevents the use of administrative features, such as the ALTER SYSTEM command. This profile also requires that each PDB must have the same database administrator. You might use this lockdown profile if you are providing Database as a Service (DBaaS) as part of a cloud deployment.

- **SAAS**   Moderately restrictive lockdown profile. This profile builds on the PRIVATE_DBAAS profile by adding a restriction with respect to the application that can connect to the database. You might use this lockdown profile if you are providing Software as a Service (SaaS) in your cloud deployment. For example, you may wish to only allow a single application to connect to the PDBs of the CDB.

- **PUBLIC_DBAAS**   Most restrictive lockdown profile. This profile allows for different DBAs, users, and applications in each PDB, but highly restricts the administrative and network activity that is allowed outside of a given PDB.

The DBA_LOCKDOWN_PROFILES view provides a list of all lockdown profiles and the rules associated with those profiles. To create a new lockdown profile, you must connect to the root of the CDB as an administrative user or a user with the CREATE LOCKDOWN PROFILE system privilege. You can then use the CREATE LOCKDOWN PROFILE command to create the lockdown profile. As an example, let's create a lockdown profile called NO_ALTER_SYSTEM:

```
create lockdown profile no_alter_system;
```

Notice that we did not define the restrictions of the lockdown profile when we created it. This is done through the use of the ALTER LOCKDOWN PROFILE command, which we will use next to restrict the use of the ALTER SYSTEM command completely, with one exception: we *will* allow the CURSOR_SHARING parameter to be altered.

The first of the following ALTER LOCKDOWN PROFILE statements locks down the ALTER SYSTEM command completely. The second statement then eases that restriction slightly by allowing the use of the ALTER SYSTEM SET CURSOR_SHARING command.

```
alter lockdown profile no_alter_system
    disable statement = ('ALTER SYSTEM') clause all;

alter lockdown profile no_alter_system
    enable statement = ('ALTER SYSTEM')
    clause=('SET') OPTION = ('cursor_sharing');
```

We can now query the DBA_LOCKDOWN_PROFILES view and see that our new profile has been created:

```
select profile_name, rule_type, rule, clause,
    clause_option, status
from dba_lockdown_profiles
where profile_name='NO_ALTER_SYSTEM';


PROFILE_NAME     RULE_TYPE   RULE            CLAUS CLAUSE_OPTION    STATUS
---------------  ----------  --------------- ----- ---------------  ----------
NO_ALTER_SYSTEM STATEMENT   ALTER SYSTEM                           DISABLE
NO_ALTER_SYSTEM STATEMENT   ALTER SYSTEM    SET   CURSOR_SHARING   ENABLE
```

Of course, all we have done at this point is create a lockdown profile. Now we need to actually assign it to one or more PDBs. The way we do that is to log into the PDB as an administrator, or a user that has the CREATE LOCKDOWN PROFILE privilege. Then we issue the ALTER SYSTEM command using the SET PDB_ LOCKDOWN option to enable the lockdown profile for that PDB.

In this example, we have a PDB called TESTPDB that we will connect to as a privileged user. We will then enable the NO_ALTER_SYSTEM profile that we just created in the CDB by using the ALTER SYSTEM command. Note that this command is dynamic in nature, so the lockdown profile has immediate effect.

```
$sqlplus sys/syspass@localhost/testpdb as sysdba
SQL> alter system set pdb_lockdown=NO_ALTER_SYSTEM;
System altered.
```

Now, let's test the lockdown restriction. We have a local PDB user we have created in the PDB called TESTDBA. We have granted the TESTDBA user the DBA role within the PDB. If the TESTDBA user tries to use the ALTER SESSION command to modify the CURSOR_SHARING parameter, we can see that command ends in success. However, if that DBA then tries to flush the shared pool, Oracle gets a bit cranky (as we would expect) since we have locked down the ALTER SYSTEM command.

```
$sqlplus testdba/testdba@localhost/testpdb
SQL> alter system set cursor_sharing=force;
System altered.
SQL> alter system flush shared_pool;
alter system flush shared_pool
*
ERROR at line 1:
ORA-01031: insufficient privileges
```

Note that this restriction impacts all privileged users in the PDB. Even if you connect to the PDB using a SYSDBA privileged user, they will still only be able to use the ALTER SYSTEM command to change the CURSOR_SHARING parameter. To be able to use other restricted ALTER SYSTEM commands within the PDB, you would first need to either modify the lockdown profile to allow for the use of the parameter you intended to use, or disable the lockdown profile in the PDB.

You can set the PDB_LOCKDOWN parameter from the CDB root to cause the lockdown profile to be globally associated with all PDBs. This would not restrict the use of the ALTER SYSTEM command at the CDB level (which, if you think about it, would tend to make unsetting the PDB_LOCKDOWN parameter a bit difficult).

# Multitenant Performance-Related New Features

Oracle Database 12*c* Release 2 offers some new performance-related features that are specific to PDBs. First is the ability to limit the SGA usage of a specific PDB at the PDB level. Second, Oracle Database Resource Manager has some new improvements related to PDBs:

■ Instance caging can be configured at the share level.

■ I/O rates can be controlled at the PDB level.

■ Resource plans can be configured at the PDB level.

## Controlling SGA Use at the PDB Level

Oracle Database 12*c* Release 2 provides the ability to fine-tune the SGA settings for individual PDBs within a given CDB. Using the SGA_TARGET parameter, you can set a hard limit on how much SGA space that a given PDB can consume. This helps to prioritize instance SGA memory usage by PDB, and can also be useful when you are providing a shared services environment as one attribute of the service you provide.

Oracle has the ability to dynamically adjust the SGA memory allocated across PDBs. This works well generally, but in some scenarios you may want to make sure that certain PDBs always have a minimum amount of memory allocated to them. To ensure that a PDB has a minimum amount of memory available to it, you can use the new SGA_MIN_SIZE parameter.

Building on this notion, it should also be noted that many of the memory-related parameters that were previously CDB-level parameters are also now configurable at the PDB level. These parameters include:

■ SGA_TARGET

■ DB_CACHE_SIZE

- DB_SHARED_POOL_SIZE

- PGA_AGGREGATE_LIMIT

- PGA_AGGREGATE_TARGET

You can still set these parameters at the CDB level (and in fact, you should), but the addition of being able to set them at the PDB level gives you additional control over individual PDBs. Here is an example where we look at the SGA_TARGET setting of a CDB, and then connect to a PDB and look at its SGA_TARGET setting:

```
sqlplus / as sysdba
SQL> show parameter sga_target
NAME                                 TYPE        VALUE
------------------------------------ ----------- -------------------------
sga_target                           big integer 4800M

alter session set container=pdbdev1;

SQL> show parameter sga_target
NAME                                 TYPE        VALUE
------------------------------------ ----------- -------------------------
sga_target                           big integer 0

SQL> show parameter sga_min_size
NAME                                 TYPE        VALUE
------------------------------------ ----------- -------------------------
sga_min_size                         big integer 0
```

Note that both SGA_TARGET and SGA_MIN_SIZE are currently set to 0. This means that they are not set for this PDB and that they will have their memory managed by the CDB without any constraint. Let's change these parameters to test this new feature.

First, we are going to change the parameter SGA_MIN_SIZE to make sure that the PDB always has a minimum amount of memory. We need to be aware that Oracle requires that the value of SGA_MIN_SIZE be set to some amount less than 50 percent of the value of SGA_TARGET—as set at the CDB level. As you can see from the previous output, we have 4800 MB assigned to the SGA of the CDB. So, we need to make sure we allocate something less than 2400 MB to the setting of SGA_MIN_SIZE. After analyzing the needs of the database, we decide to make sure that its SGA always has 1 GB available to it. So, while connected to the PDB, we set the value of SGA_MIN_SIZE to 1 GB:

```
SQL> alter system set sga_min_size=1g;
System altered.
SQL> show parameter sga_min_size
NAME                                 TYPE        VALUE
------------------------------------ ----------- -------------------------
sga_min_size                         big integer 1G
```

If we change to a different PDB, we see that the SGA_MIN_SIZE change affects only the PDB we were connected to:

```
SQL> alter session set container=pdbqa;
SQL> show parameter sga_min_size
NAME                                    TYPE        VALUE
--------------------------------------- ----------- -------------------------
sga_min_size                            big integer 0
```

You can also configure a SGA memory ceiling for each PDB by setting the SGA_TARGET parameter at the PDB level. Oracle still uses SGA_TARGET at the CDB level as an indicator of how much memory to allocate to the entire CDB.

When configuring the SGA_TARGET parameter for a PDB that has the parameter SGA_MIN_SIZE set, SGA_TARGET must be configured at a value that is 200 percent the size of SGA_MIN_SIZE. In this example, we reduce SGA_MIN_SIZE low enough to allow us to set SGA_TARGET to 3 GB:

```
SQL> alter system set sga_target=3g;
System altered.
SQL> alter system set sga_min_size=500m;
System altered.
```

Note that Oracle will let you set SGA_TARGET and SGA_MIN_SIZE values that are beyond the current memory setting of the CDB's SGA_TARGET size and won't generate an error. As with a CDB, by default any ALTER SYSTEM change at the PDB level is persistent through PDB and CDB restarts. You can use the SCOPE=MEMORY setting if you do not wish the change to persist through the next restart of the PDB.

You can see the current settings of the SGA_MIN_SIZE parameters across the CDB by using the V$SYSTEM_PARAMETER view (when connected to the root container):

```
select a.pdb_id, a.pdb_name, b.name, b.value
from dba_pdbs a, v$system_parameter b
where a.con_id=b.con_id
  and b.name like '%sga%'
order by pdb_id;
```

| PDB_ID | PDB_NAME | NAME | VALUE |
|--------|----------|------|-------|
| 2 | PDB$SEED | sga_target | 0 |
| 3 | PDBORCL | sga_target | 0 |
| 5 | TESTTWO | sga_min_size | 2411724800 |
| 5 | TESTTWO | sga_target | 0 |
| 6 | PDBDEV1 | sga_min_size | 1073741824 |
| 6 | PDBDEV1 | sga_target | 0 |
| 7 | PDBQA | sga_min_size | 524288000 |
| 7 | PDBQA | sga_target | 6442450944 |
| 8 | TESTSNAP | sga_target | 0 |

```
9 rows selected.
```

As you can see, the sum of our SGA target dwarfs the database SGA target value of 4800 MB. This is basically oversubscription, and although Oracle will not generate an error, it will not allow the combined settings of SGA_TARGET at the PDB level to exceed the setting of SGA_TARGET at the CDB level.

# Resource Manager Changes Related to CDBs and PDBs

In Oracle Database 12*c* Release 1, Resource Manager was already PDB-aware and able to manage resources across all PDBs in a CDB by using shares. Oracle Database 12*c* Release 2 adds more granularity and ease of management to PDB resource management.

Using *PDB Profile Directives*, you can create directives at the CDB level, then either assign them explicitly at the PDB level or designate a specific directive as the default for any new PDBs. In addition, you can control both CPU and I/O bandwidth at the PDB level using PDB instance caging and I/O throttling.

### PDB Profile Directives

Oracle now makes it easier to manage sets of PDBs with Resource Manager. You can assign a single profile at the CDB level that can then be assigned to PDBs when they are created. The new DBMS_RESOURCE_MANAGER.CREATE_CDB_PROFILE_DIRECTIVE procedure is used to create the default directive. For example, we can create a profile directive (this example assumes you have already created the appropriate plan) that limits the amount of CPU that a given PDB can use to 30 percent by creating this CDB profile directive while connected to the root container:

```
begin
   dbms_resource_manager.create_pending_area();
   dbms_resource_manager.create_cdb_profile_directive(
      plan                  => 'std_pdb_plan',
      profile               => 'yellow_profile',
      shares                => 1,
      utilization_limit     => 30);
   exec dbms_resource_manager.validate_pending_area();
   exec dbms_resource_manager.submit_pending_area();
end;
/
```

Notice that this directive is assigned to the profile named YELLOW_PROFILE, which we would have already created. You can create different CDB profile directives to provide for varying classes of service. For example, you could create profiles that indicate some relationship to a class of service that a customer has purchased: red, yellow, and green perhaps. Red might have a higher number of PDB shares and a higher utilization limit, while green's might be lower. Having created the CDB profile directives, when you create the PDB, you will need to set the parameter DB_PERFORMANCE_PROFILE to the name of the profile that you want to use in order for that profile to be activated with the PDB you have created.

There are default values assigned to PDBs when you have not defined a CDB profile directive. Currently, these defaults are a share of 1 and the UTILIZATION_LIMIT and PARALLEL_SERVER_LIMIT parameters are set to 1.

## Share-Based Instance Caging

In Oracle Database 12c Release 2 you can combine instance caging (set with the parameter CPU_COUNT) and the utilization limit within your resource plan to control CPU utilization of a PDB at a finer level. For example, if CPU_COUNT is set to 6 and you have set a utilization limit of 50 percent, then the PDB will be limited to a maximum of three CPUs.

## Limiting I/O Rates for PDBs

Resource Manager also provides the ability to control I/O rates of individual PDBs. This keeps one PDB from wreaking havoc on all of the other PDBs within a given CDB. Oracle Database 12c Release 2 provides two new database parameters to control PDB I/O operations:

- **MAX_IOPS**   Controls the number of I/O operations that are allowed per second for a given PDB. The default for this parameter is 0, which means it's disabled.

- **MAX_MBPS**   Controls the total number of I/O operations in megabytes per second for a given PDB. The default for this parameter is 0, which means it's disabled.

Each parameter can be set to different values for individual PDBs within a CDB, giving you very fine control over I/O resource utilization of individual PDBs. These parameters can also be very helpful in shared services environments to ensure that you can meet negotiated service-level agreements and that one PDB won't risk the response time of other customers' databases.

Here is an example of setting each of these new parameters in a PDB. The first example limits the maximum I/O operations per second (IOPS) to a value of 4000. The second example limits the maximum number of megabytes of I/O per second to 10.

```
alter system set max_iops=4000 scope=both;
alter system set max_mbps=10 scope=both;
```

By the way, don't worry that these limits will interrupt critical I/O operations—things like writing to the control file will continue as usual with the highest priority.

However, the I/O from these operations will add to the overall limit and thus can impact DML statements or SELECT statements.

The DBA_HIST_RSRC_PDB_METRIC view has been around since Oracle Database 12c Release 1 to provide some insight into PDB resource consumption. You can use this view to get some idea on how you might want to use the MAX_IOPS and MAX_MBPS parameters.

You can use the DBA_HIST_RSRC_PDB_METRIC view to calculate a reasonable I/O limit for a PDB. Consider the values in the following columns when calculating a limit: IOPS, IOMBPS, IOPS_THROTTLE_EXEMPT, and IOMBPS_THROTTLE_EXEMPT. The **rsmgr:io rate limit** wait event indicates that a limit was reached.

### PDB Resource Plans

Just as a CDB can have its own resource plan, Oracle Database 12c Release 2 provides the ability to create resource plans at the PDB level too. A PDB resource plan is used to manage the resources within a given PDB and is created and managed much like the resource plans you might have already used in non-CDB databases. You use the same procedures (for example, DBMS_RESOURCE_MANAGER .CREATE_PLAN_DIRECTIVE) to manage PDB resource plans that you already use to create and manage non-CDB resource plans.

PDB resource plans are subject to the overall CDB resource plan directives (see the PDB profile directives mentioned earlier in this section) related to PDB resource allocations. Therefore, if the CDB resource plan directive limits your PDB to 50 percent of CPU resources, a PDB directive that further restricts CPU by 50 percent will result in a maximum CPU usage of 25 percent for any session assigned to that directive.

PDB resource plans are subject to some restrictions:

- A PDB resource plan cannot have any subplans.

- A PDB resource plan can have up to eight consumer groups.

- Resource Manager does not support multilevel scheduling policies for PDB resource plans.

# Summary

Well, this has been a whole bucketful of information on Oracle Multitenant–related new features in Oracle Database 12c Release 2. Really, it feels like we have not even scratched the surface as there are many additional new features discussed in coming chapters that can be used with Oracle Multitenant as well. This is only Chapter 3 and I hope your head is not already at capacity from all the new things you have learned. I also hope you are starting to see the flashing signs telling you that, in the future, the really good stuff is going to revolve around Oracle Multitenant.

# CHAPTER
## 4

# Application Containers
# and Hints Thereof

This chapter introduces new features of Oracle Database 12c Release 2 related to a completely new feature called Oracle Application Containers. Although container databases (CDBs) aren't new, Oracle Database 12c Release 2 uses CDBs in a new way with application containers. A database that is scalable provides for easy distribution of resources that are needed to perform the work at hand—new features such as application containers and sharding are central to scalability in Oracle Database 12c Release 2. *Agility* refers to the flexibility of the database architecture to respond to all sorts of incremental and on-demand changes, and application containers facilitate a new level of agility.

The second part of this chapter revisits an enhancement to another feature introduced in Oracle Database 12c Release 1: cross-container queries. In Oracle Database 12c Release 2, you can add optimizer hints to cross-container queries, including application containers. With the addition of application containers, you can run queries across multiple pluggable databases (PDBs) within the application container, and allowing new hints in those queries makes your application container environment more scalable and agile.

# Application Containers

I had difficulty deciding in which chapter to cover application containers, the reason for which will become clear shortly. An *application container* is a component within a container database that provides an application-specific root container, an application seed, and one or more application-related PDBs (application PDBs). This provides a way to create a single logical container for a given application database. This offers exceptional scalability in that you can now partition off application PDBs into their own application containers, making it easier to manage the entire application.

An application container also offers additional isolation, which I consider more of a security-related feature. When you create an application container, you first create the root of that application container. The root of the application container is a child of the CDB's root container; you may have several application root containers in a CDB. However, all of the objects that are created within the application root container are only visible to that application root container and the application PDBs attached to that container. They are not visible to the root CDB, nor are they visible to other application containers or individual PDBs. Figure 4-1 provides an example of the relationship between the root CDB, an application container, and the PDBs attached to the root CDB and the application PDBs attached to the application container.

To create an application container from a PDB, you can use one of the following methods:

- Clone an existing PDB

- Clone an existing non-CDB

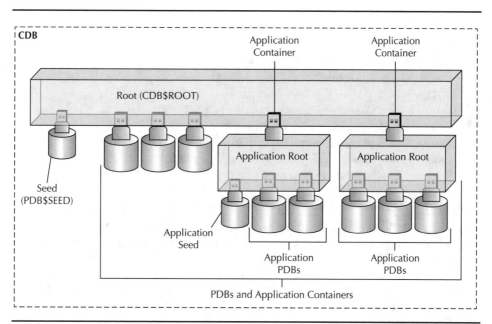

**FIGURE 4-1.** *The root CDB, application containers, and database PDBs*

- Relocate a PDB

- Plug in an unplugged PDB

But before we can use one of those methods, the CDB must exist and we must create the application container. I'll show how to do that in the next few sections.

## Creating the Application Container

For purposes of demonstration, we'll create an application container named HRAPP. The first requirement to create an application container is to connect to the CDB root as an administrative user. We'll use SYS (connecting as SYSDBA) in this example. Then, we will issue the CREATE PLUGGABLE DATABASE command, along with the AS APPLICATION CONTAINER clause, to create the application container. Because we are logging into the root of the CDB, Oracle will use the CDB seed as the source of the root of the application container that is going to be created. Here are the commands:

**NOTE**
*You need the CREATE PLUGGABLE DATABASE system privilege to use the CREATE PLUGGABLE DATABASE command.*

```
connect / as sysdba
create pluggable database hrapp
    as application container
    admin user rjb identified by rjb;
```

**NOTE**
*Version 13c of Oracle Enterprise Manager (OEM)
Cloud Control provides a graphical means of
creating, managing, and removing application
containers. We won't cover OEM in this chapter, but
Chapter 12 is devoted to OEM new features.*

If you are familiar with the CREATE PLUGGABLE DATABASE command
(introduced in the previous chapter), you know we could have customized the
command a great deal—we are keeping it simple here for the sake of brevity and to
focus on the topic at hand.

Once the command has completed, we have a new *application root container*
called HRAPP. Application root containers are much like a CDB within a CDB! We
can confirm the status of the application root container by querying the view DBA_
PDBS:

```
select pdb_id, pdb_name, application_root,
    application_pdb, application_seed,
    application_root_con_id from dba_pdbs;


PDB_ID  PDB_NAME  APP_ROOT  APP_PDB  APP_SEED  APP_ROOT_CON_ID
------  --------  --------  -------  --------  ---------------
3       DEV01     NO        NO       NO
2       PDB$SEED  NO        NO       NO
4       HRAPP     YES       NO       NO
```

Note that the APP_ROOT column is set to YES in the DBA_PDBS view. This indicates
that HRAPP is the root of an application container. There are no application containers
created yet, so the APP_ROOT_CON_ID column is empty for all PDBs.

When HRAPP is first created, it is not open, so we need to open it. In this example,
we change to the new HRAPP container, check its current status, and then start it up:

```
SQL> alter session set container=hrapp;
Session altered.
SQL> select open_mode from v$database;
OPEN_MODE
--------------------
MOUNTED
SQL> startup
Pluggable Database opened.
```

**NOTE**
*We could just have easily started the container using the ALTER PLUGGABLE DATABASE OPEN command from the root container.*

Now that HRAPP is created, the network services that support it have also been created. So, we can also connect to it via SQL*Plus:

```
[oracle@ol7base ~]$ sqlplus rjb/rjb@localhost:1521/hrapp
SQL*Plus: Release 12.2.0.1.0 Production on Thu Mar 16 09:06:56 2017
Copyright (c) 1982, 2016, Oracle.  All rights reserved.
Connected to:
Oracle Database 12c Enterprise Edition Release 12.2.0.1.0 - 64bit Production
SQL> show con_name
CON_NAME
------------------------------
HRAPP
SQL>
```

Finally, note that you can have many application root containers. However, you cannot create application root containers from any PDB other than the root PDB (CDB$ROOT). In other words, you cannot create an application container from within another application container. That makes sense since you can't create standard PDBs from within another PDB either—application root containers are much like standard PDBs (although they become CDBs from an application perspective).

**NOTE**
*Currently there is a 2 GB storage limitation on the application root. It is important, then, to control the tablespace space usage of the application root container. This limit does not apply to the application container seed or any PDBs created in the application container.*

# Creating the Application in the Application Root

We have created the application *root* container, but this root container is very different from the root of the CDB. Oracle tells you not to create objects in the root container of the CDB. In the case of application containers, Oracle very much does want you to create objects in the application root container of a CDB—but this is because an application root container is really more like a PDB. From an application perspective, the root container is more like a CDB since you can create application PDBs within the application root container. After you've looked at Figure 4-1 a few times and tried out these examples, your confusion will disappear!

Keep in mind that the purpose of an application root container is to store the collection of common database objects (and data). So, we need to install those objects somewhere, and that somewhere is the root of the application container.

For the purposes of this continuing example, I will create a schema and some objects in our HRAPP root container that are associated with an application we will call the HR application. We will create a common database user to own the objects and then we will create those objects in that common user's schema. Do keep in mind that the data model we are creating is very abbreviated and not designed to teach anything about database modeling, database normalization, or how to build a real HR schema or application! Here is the script we will use to set up the application root container:

```
sqlplus c##rjb/c##rjb@localhost:1521/hrapp
alter pluggable database hrapp open;
alter session set container=hrapp;
alter pluggable database application HR begin install '1.0';
create user hr identified by hr;
grant dba to hr;
create table hr.employee
    (emp_id   number primary key, lname   varchar2(30),
     fname  varchar2(30), date_hired date);
create table hr.company
    (co_id number primary key, address varchar2(30),
     city varchar2(30), state varchar2(30),   zip varchar2(10) );
create table hr.co_emp (emp_id number, co_id number);
alter table hr.co_emp add constraint pk_co_emp primary key (emp_id, co_id);
alter table hr.co_emp add constraint fk_emp_id foreign key (emp_id)
    references hr.employee;
alter table hr.co_emp add constraint fk_co_id foreign key (co_id)
    references hr.company;
insert into hr.employee values(1,'Bryla','Robert',sysdate);
insert into hr.company values (1,'200 West Prairie','Midwest Coast','WI',53713);
insert into hr.co_emp values (1,1);
commit;
alter pluggable database application HR end install '1.0';
```

> **NOTE**
> *To install an application into an application container, the user installing the application must be a common user with the ALTER PLUGGABLE DATABASE system privilege in the application root container.*

So, what have we done here? First, we opened the HRAPP PDB and then we switched to that container. We then created a normal (application) user and also some tables within the application root container. These objects are known as *application common objects* and will serve as a template that can be used for all application PDBs that we create within this application container (more on application PDBs in a moment). This application is version 1.0, which means you'll be able to create future versions in the same application root container, such as 1.1, 2.0, and so forth—with the added benefit that not all application users need to be on the same version at the same time. Or a user may never want to upgrade!

Note that we used the ALTER PLUGGABLE DATABASE command along with the BEGIN INSTALL option before we created the HR user or the objects within the user schema. This command instantiates the application (HR in this example) that these objects are associated with. When we issued this command, we gave the install a version number. This is how Oracle provides versioning to the objects in the application container.

After instantiating the application, we proceeded to create the HR user within the HRAPP application and then we created three tables in the HR schema and populated them with test data. Finally, we indicated to Oracle that we are done with the instantiation of the application objects by using the ALTER PLUGGABLE DATABASE command along with the END INSTALL option.

We have created application 1.0 of our database! Quite exciting!

What is the end game for all of this? Why create an application schema in the application root container? It's to make deployment of copies of this application schema easy to do. Many organizations routinely create and destroy databases for testing purposes. The application container gives you the ability to establish a "gold" copy of a database schema, and deploy it quickly and reliably. Application containers also provide a means of controlling the source schema, enabling you to keep it "pure."

The material covered in this section makes much more sense in the context of creating application PDBs. So, let's instantiate the application next!

## Creating an Application PDB

Application PDBs reside within the application root container. They are normal PDBs for the most part except that you can synchronize them with the common application objects in the application's root container. This provides a way for you to easily replicate a specific PDB over and over.

The rules for instantiating an application PDB are pretty simple. You must have the CREATE PLUGGABLE DATABASE system privilege, you must be connected to the root of the application container (use SHOW CON_NAME when in doubt), and the application container must be open.

So, let's go ahead and create an application PDB. First, we connect to the root of the application container HRAPP, and then we issue a CREATE PLUGGABLE DATABASE command:

```
alter session set container=hrapp;
create pluggable database rjbhr admin user rjb identified by rjb;
alter pluggable database rjbhr open;
```

This creates the pluggable database RJBHR within the application container HRAPP. We can query the DBA_PDBS view from the CDB root container to see this new container using the same query we ran earlier to check the type and state of each PDB:

```
select pdb_id, pdb_name, application_root,
    application_pdb, application_seed,
    application_root_con_id from dba_pdbs;
```

| PDB_ID | PDB_NAME | APP_ROOT | APP_PDB | APP_SEED | APP_ROOT_CON_ID |
|--------|----------|----------|---------|----------|-----------------|
| 3 | DEV01 | NO | NO | NO | |
| 2 | PDB$SEED | NO | NO | NO | |
| 4 | HRAPP | YES | NO | NO | |
| 5 | RJBHR | NO | YES | NO | 4 |

In the output, we now see a new PDB called RJBHR. We can see that it's an application PDB and that its parent container is HRAPP. Now, let's see if the schema and the schema objects that we added to the root of the application container are contained in the application PDB we just created:

```
alter session set container=rjbhr;
select owner, table_name
from dba_tables
where owner='HR';
no rows selected
```

What's the deal? These application common object things don't work? They will, but simply creating the PDB isn't enough to synchronize it with the application root container's objects. We need to perform one more step to get the application schema objects copied over: synchronize the PDB with the application root. We do so by issuing the ALTER PLUGGABLE DATABASE APPLICATION ALL SYNC command, from within the application PDB we want to synchronize, as shown here:

```
alter session set container=rjbhr;
alter pluggable database application all sync;
```

Now, let's look at what happens when we issue the previous query again:

```
alter session set container=rjbhr;
select owner, table_name
from dba_tables
where owner='HR';
```

| OWNER | TABLE_NAME |
|-------|------------|
| HR | EMPLOYEE |
| HR | COMPANY |
| HR | CO_EMP |

How cool is that? The objects associated with our "application" were cloned. You will notice though, if you do some further investigation, that if the tables in the application root container have data in them, that data is synchronized as well along with any constraints, indexes, and so forth on the tables. Now, let's query one of those tables:

```
alter session set container=rjbhr;
select * from hr.employee;

   EMP_ID LNAME                          FNAME                        DATE_HIRE
  ------- ------------------------------ ---------------------------- ---------
        1 Bryla                          Robert                       16-MAR-17
```

Even the "seed" data we created got moved over. Replication of the data is the default for an object when it is created in an application root. We can choose to replicate the seed data or not replicate it. To change the default behavior, you have two options. First, when you create the object, you can use the new SHARING parameter to control data sharing when you create the object in the application root container. The options are

- **METADATA**   Share metadata, *copy* data—data is unique to each container.

- **DATA**   Share metadata, share data—data is stored only in the application root container.

- **EXTENDED DATA**   Shares metadata, share data, but each application container can have its own data unique to that instantiation of the application.

- **NONE**   The table is not shared.

Here we show the creation of a table and indicate through the use of the SHARING parameter that we do not want to share the table outside of the application root container at all:

```
alter session set container=hrapp;
create table hr.pay_history sharing=none
   (paydate   date, paycheck_number number, emp_id number,
    gross_pay number, net_pay number);
insert into hr.pay_history values (sysdate, 1,1,100,10);
commit;
alter session set container=rjbhr;
alter pluggable database application all sync;
select * from hr.pay_history;

SQL Error: ORA-00942: table or view does not exist
```

Another option is to change the DEFAULT_SHARING database parameter at the PDB level. DEFAULT_SHARING is set to a default value of METADATA in all PDBs.

You could use the ALTER SYSTEM command and set the DEFAULT_SHARING parameter to METADATA in the HRAPP application root container if you wanted to have objects not share data by default when they are created. Note that the setting of SHARING=DATA at the object level overrides the setting of the DEFAULT_SHARING parameter at the PDB level, for example.

# Installing, Upgrading, and Patching the Application Container

As you saw earlier, to instantiate an application in an application root container, you must first use the ALTER PLUGGABLE DATABASE command with the APPLICATION BEGIN INSTALL option. Then, you finish it using the ALTER PLUGGABLE DATABASE command with the APPLICATION END INSTALL option. This probably gave you your first insight into the fact that Oracle helps you use version control to manage the application objects within the application root container.

Of course, you will need to make changes to the application root container objects from time to time, and you will want those changes to be propagated to the application PDBs that are created based on the application root container. Oracle enables you to do this in either of two ways: an upgrade or a patch.

You upgrade the application root container if you want to make major changes to your application schema (especially if you want to do things such as drop objects). You indicate that you are upgrading the application container by issuing the ALTER PLUGGABLE DATABASE BEGIN UPGRADE command, followed by the commands to create, modify, or remove the application objects that are associated with that upgrade. You then issue the ALTER PLUGGABLE DATABASE END UPGRADE command to complete the upgrade. Finally, you connect to each PDB and issue the ALTER PLUGGABLE DATABASE APPLICATION ALL SYNC command to complete the propagation of the changes to the PDBs.

**NOTE**
*A manual method is available to perform upgrades that will not cause changes to be propagated. You can find more details in the* Oracle Database Administrator's Guide.

Patching of an application container involves minor changes to the container. For example, when patching a container, you can create a new table, but you cannot drop a table. To drop a table, you must upgrade the container. Patching a container works in much the same way as upgrading. You start the patch with the ALTER PLUGGABLE DATABASE BEGIN PATCH statement, make your changes, and then complete the patching work with the ALTER PLUGGABLE DATABASE END PATCH statement.

The main difference between an upgrade and a patch is the amount of work Oracle has to do in the background when processing your changes. When upgrading, Oracle creates a clone of the application root (call it version 1.0), which will be in READ ONLY mode. The clone PDB appears in the DBA_PDBS view and is given a default name by the database when it's created. The creation of the clone takes additional time, so the ALTER PLUGGABLE DATABASE UPGRADE command takes longer to complete than the ALTER PLUGGABLE DATABASE PATCH command.

During an upgrade, application PDBs are ported over to the clone when the END UPGRADE command is issued, and the clone is open for activity. Thus, the application PDBs remain associated with the version 1.0 clone. During the move of the application PDBs to the version 1.0 clone, there are some momentary accessibility issues. These considerations are documented in the *Oracle Database Administrator's Guide*.

When the application PDBs are synchronized with the root CDB, they are ported over from the version 1.0 clone to the upgraded version 2.0 application root container. At that time, they will have access to the new application schema changes that were made. The clone will remain available in the application root container, and new PDBs can be attached to either the version 1.0 clone or the version 2.0 clone.

## Creating the Application Seed

Just like the root container of a CDB has a seed database, application root containers can optionally have a seed database. A seed database can speed up the creation of any application PDBs that you might choose to create. The application seed is created much like the application PDB.

The application seed starts out as a copy of the application root seed. To create the application root seed, connect to the application root container (not the root of the CDB) and issue a CREATE PLUGGABLE DATABASE command, using the AS SEED clause. Once the seed container is created, we need to synchronize it with the application root container, just as we did earlier with a new application PDB. Then, we close the seed container and open it in READ ONLY mode. Here are the commands that you would use to create the application seed:

```
connect c##rjb/c##rjb@hrapp as sysdba
create pluggable database as seed admin user rjb identified by rjb;
alter pluggable database hrapp$seed open;
alter session set container=hrapp$seed;
alter pluggable database application all sync;
alter pluggable database hrapp$seed close;
alter pluggable database hrapp$seed open read only;
alter pluggable database hrapp$seed save state;
```

Note that we didn't give this pluggable database a name. Oracle will always assign a default name to the application seed containers. The naming convention Oracle uses is to prefix the application seed with the name of the PDB, followed by a $ sign, and then end it with the word SEED. So, for the HRAPP application container, the seed database is HRAPP$SEED.

We can return to the root CDB and issue our query against DBA_PDBS again to see the new seed PDB that we created:

```
select pdb_id, pdb_name, application_root,
   application_pdb, application_seed,
   application_root_con_id from dba_pdbs;
```

| PDB_ID | PDB_NAME | APP_ROOT | APP_PDB | APP_SEED | APP_ROOT_CON_ID |
|--------|----------|----------|---------|----------|-----------------|
| 3 | DEV01 | NO | NO | NO | |
| 2 | PDB$SEED | NO | NO | NO | |
| 4 | HRAPP | YES | NO | NO | |
| 5 | RJBHR | NO | YES | NO | 4 |
| 6 | HRAPP$SEED | NO | YES | YES | 4 |

Note that we have added HRAPP$SEED and that the columns APPLICATION_PDB and APPLICATION_SEED are both marked YES now. This indicates that this PDB is the seed container within an application container. Also, note the APPLICATION_ROOT_CON_ID column is set to 4. This is the PDB_ID for the HRAPP container, which is the root container of the application container. Of course, this value will vary for different databases.

Now that the seed container is created, it will be constantly updated when changes are made to the root of the application container. That way, you don't need to resync a newly created PDB to get it synchronized with the application root container—the seed PDB is already synced up!

I hope this overview of application containers has given you enough information to pique your interest in learning more about this new feature in Oracle Database 12*c* Release 2. There are many more features and much more functionality to explore beyond the scope of this introduction, but I've given you a sufficient foundation to get started and discover what this powerful new feature can do for you and your application development teams!

# Using Hints in the Containers Query

In Oracle Database 12*c* Release 1, you could run queries against an aggregate of all tables with the same name owned by a CDB common user. One nice feature of Oracle Multitenant is that you can aggregate data across PDBs within a given CDB. For example, if each of your customers requires separate databases but you need to generate reports across all of your customers, you could create a PDB for each customer and then issue SQL queries across the entire set of PDBs. This is done using the FROM CONTAINERS clause in a SELECT statement.

Because of the expanded use cases that arose from the application containers feature in Oracle Database 12c Release 2, there is a new hint called CONTAINERS that you can use when running a query that has a FROM CONTAINERS clause. With the CONTAINERS hint specifying the DEFAULT_PDB_HINT argument, you can run a SELECT statement that will cross all of the containers of the database *and* use the embedded hint within each PDB. The following example indicates that the optimizer should not use parallel query as it processes this query across all of the containers in the CDB for the EMPLOYEES table:

```
select /*+ CONTAINERS(DEFAULT_PDB_HINT='no_parallel') */
count(*)
from containers (employees) where dept_id=30;
```

The context is important with that query. The syntax of the query is identical whether you're running it as a common user in a CDB or as a common user in an application container. In a CDB, the EMPLOYEES table must exist in the CDB root and all open PDBs. If you're in an application container, the query has to be run from the application root container and the table must exist in the application root container and all PDBs in the application container.

# Summary

This chapter covered one very extensive new feature and one extension to an existing feature, and those features are related. Using the Oracle Application Containers feature in Oracle Database 12c Release 2, you can create an application container that packages an application's tables and data into a PDB that is treated like a CDB for the purposes of sharing (cloning) those tables and data to different groups of users with the option of maintaining different versions of the application for those groups of users with Oracle's built-in version control. In an application container, you also have the option to keep the data only in the application root container, only in each application PDB, or both!

Because of the extended container database functionality provided by Oracle Application Containers in Oracle Database 12c Release 2, the options you can use when running a CONTAINERS query have also been extended. Not only can the CONTAINERS clause apply to the application root container and all of its PDBs, you can also use a CONTAINERS hint in a query using the CONTAINERS clause to specify a hint that is used for the recursive queries run against each PDB in the CDB or application root container.

# CHAPTER
## 5

# Administrative, High Availability, and Security New Features

I n addition to the significant performance improvements in Oracle Database 12c Release 2, there are also major improvements for the DBA who must administer the database and make sure that the database is available and secure for the users who need to leverage the high performance of Oracle Database 12c Release 2. A fast and feature-rich database is not of much use if the users cannot access the database, the database is down, or unauthorized users are accessing the database.

Redundancy at every level in the Oracle stack is key to high availability. Oracle Real Application Clusters (RAC) installations that are spread across widely dispersed geographic regions are easier to set up and manage. A key component of RAC, Automatic Storage Management (ASM), has been enhanced so that disk group rebalancing can be prioritized.

Last and certainly not least are improvements in database security. Transparent Data Encryption (TDE) for a single tablespace can happen online, and several new encryption algorithms have been added. Auditing of an application's or a user's SQL statements using Virtual Private Database (VPD) now includes not only the original SQL statement, but also the predicates in the WHERE clause that were generated by the VPD policy itself.

# Administration

With the demand for instant connectivity and global access to e-commerce websites, there is little tolerance for downtime. In Oracle Database 11g, many table and index operations were enhanced to allow for concurrent user access—even DML operations—while the table definition was changed online with minimal table unavailability at the end of the operation. In Oracle Database 12c Release 1, more table types could be redefined while staying online. In Oracle Database 12c Release 2, the list of online capabilities has been expanded even more to include more scenarios with partitioned tables.

## Online Table Redefinition

If you have a large production database, it will take a long time to perform any kind of operation on it, including adding or removing columns, adding or removing indexes, and so forth. Those operations need to happen while the table is online; however, things don't always go as expected. Your operation may run for hours or days...and fail right before it completes. Instead of starting the operation over, Oracle Database 12c Release 2 lets you pick up where you left off. In another scenario, you may complete the table redefinition only to find out that the group requesting the change didn't want the change after all. The new ROLLBACK procedure of DBMS_REDEFINITION lets you put the table back into its original state with minimal effort.

## Restarting Redefinition After a Failure

When you re-create or redefine a table online, many things can go wrong. You may run out of space, the database instance may crash, or the power may fail. In many cases, the DBMS_REDEFINITION package will let you pick up after you left off when the failure condition has been addressed.

In this example, I'll use a table called MY_SEGMENTS whose structure is similar to the data dictionary view DBA_SEGMENTS:

```
describe my_segments
```

```
Name                    Null? Type
--------------------    ----- -------------
OWNER                         VARCHAR2(128)
SEGMENT_NAME                  VARCHAR2(128)
PARTITION_NAME                VARCHAR2(128)
SEGMENT_TYPE                  VARCHAR2(18)
SEGMENT_SUBTYPE               VARCHAR2(10)
TABLESPACE_NAME               VARCHAR2(30)
HEADER_FILE                   NUMBER
HEADER_BLOCK                  NUMBER
BYTES                         NUMBER
BLOCKS                        NUMBER
EXTENTS                       NUMBER
INITIAL_EXTENT                NUMBER
NEXT_EXTENT                   NUMBER
MIN_EXTENTS                   NUMBER
MAX_EXTENTS                   NUMBER
MAX_SIZE                      NUMBER
RETENTION                     VARCHAR2(7)
MINRETENTION                  NUMBER
PCT_INCREASE                  NUMBER
FREELISTS                     NUMBER
FREELIST_GROUPS               NUMBER
RELATIVE_FNO                  NUMBER
BUFFER_POOL                   VARCHAR2(7)
FLASH_CACHE                   VARCHAR2(7)
CELL_FLASH_CACHE              VARCHAR2(7)
INMEMORY                      VARCHAR2(8)
INMEMORY_PRIORITY             VARCHAR2(8)
INMEMORY_DISTRIBUTE           VARCHAR2(15)
INMEMORY_DUPLICATE            VARCHAR2(13)
INMEMORY_COMPRESSION          VARCHAR2(17)
CELLMEMORY                    VARCHAR2(24)
```

Unfortunately, the usage of the MY_SEGMENTS table has gone beyond its original purpose, and the column BUFFER_POOL has new values and must have its length changed from VARCHAR2(7) to VARCHAR2(20). Also, due to space limitations in the

USERS tablespace, the new table must reside in the USERS2 tablespace. The following example shows how you can get your redefinition operation back on track when the unexpected happens.

To start out, I create the staging table as the target in the USERS2 tablespace:

```
create table my_segments_new
    tablespace users2
as
    select * from my_segments where 1=0;

alter table my_segments_new modify (buffer_pool varchar2(20));
```

Once the staging table is ready, I can initiate the conversion with the DBMS_REDEFINITION package:

```
begin
    dbms_redefinition.start_redef_table
    (
        uname => 'C##RJB',
        orig_table => 'MY_SEGMENTS',
        int_table => 'MY_SEGMENTS_NEW'
    );
end;
/

Error report -
ORA-12008: error in materialized view or zonemap refresh path
ORA-01653: unable to extend table C##RJB.MY_SEGMENTS_NEW by 1024
    in tablespace USERS2
ORA-06512: at "SYS.DBMS_REDEFINITION", line 109
ORA-06512: at "SYS.DBMS_REDEFINITION", line 3887
ORA-06512: at "SYS.DBMS_REDEFINITION", line 5127
```

The destination tablespace has run out of space. Check the view DBA_REDEFINITION_STATUS to confirm that this operation may be restarted where it left off:

```
select base_table_name,interim_object_name,
    operation,status,restartable,action
from dba_redefinition_status;

BASE_TABLE_NAME        INTERIM_OBJECT_NAME               OPERATION
  STATUS      RESTARTABLE       ACTION
-------------------- ------------------------------- --------------------
---------- --------------- -------------------------
MY_SEGMENTS            MY_SEGMENTS_NEW                   START_REDEF_TABLE
  Failure     Y                 Abort redefinition
```

Add more space to the destination tablespace as follows:

```
alter tablespace users2 add datafile size 500m autoextend off;
```

Rerun the SYNC_INTERIM_TABLE procedure and finish the redefinition process:

```
begin
    dbms_redefinition.sync_interim_table('C##RJB','MY_SEGMENTS','MY_SEGMENTS_NEW');
end;
/
```

## Rolling Back Redefinition

Even if your table redefinition is successful, you have the option to reverse the changes to the table. You may find that the performance of the table is suffering due to a data type change or you may find out that the user who requested the change didn't change the right column! Figure 5-1 shows the flow of tasks you will perform whether you decide to keep your changes or reverse them.

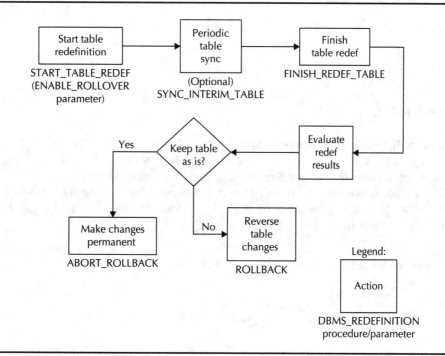

**FIGURE 5-1.** *Process flow for table redefinition*

**Starting the Table Redefinition** Most of the redefinition process you're already familiar with is the same when leveraging the rollback feature. You first create the interim table as you would during any redefinition effort, as in this example:

```
create table my_segments_new
    tablespace users2
as
    select * from my_segments where 1=0;
create unique index pk_seg2 on my_segments_new(pk_seg) tablespace users2;
alter table my_segments_new add constraint pk_seg2
    primary key(pk_seg) using index;
```

To start the redefinition, use the START_REDEF_TABLE, but add the ENABLE_ROLLBACK parameter like this:

```
begin
    dbms_redefinition.start_redef_table
    (
        uname => 'C##RJB',
        orig_table => 'MY_SEGMENTS',
        int_table => 'MY_SEGMENTS_NEW',
        enable_rollback => TRUE
    );
end;
/

PL/SQL procedure successfully completed.
```

As you might expect, to ensure backward compatibility, ENABLE_ROLLBACK defaults to FALSE.

**Periodically Syncing the Interim Table** Because DBMS_REDEFINITION.START_REDEF_TABLE is an online operation, it keeps the original table available for DML. If your redefinition operation takes a while, you might want to keep the interim table synced so that the final redefinition operation will take less time for the final full refresh. Continuing the previous example, you would use the following call to synchronize the redefinition operation:

```
begin
    dbms_redefinition.sync_interim_table
    (
    uname => 'C##RJB',
    orig_table => 'MY_SEGMENTS',
    int_table => 'MY_SEGMENTS_NEW'
    );
end;
/

PL/SQL procedure successfully completed.
```

**Finishing Table Redefinition**   To finish the redefinition process, run the FINISH_REDEF_TABLE procedure as follows. You use this procedure whether or not you have enabled rollback.

```
Begin
    dbms_redefinition.finish_redef_table
    (
    uname => 'C##RJB',
    orig_table => 'MY_SEGMENTS',
    int_table => 'MY_SEGMENTS_NEW',
    disable_rollback => false
    );
end;
/

PL/SQL procedure successfully completed.
```

The table is locked briefly during this procedure call. If you were absolutely sure that you wanted to keep the results of this redefinition, you could set the DISABLE_ROLLBACK parameter to TRUE—but in this example we're really not sure at this point, so read on!

**Accepting Table Changes**   Once your new table has been tested and validated, you can perform further cleanup by dropping the interim table, which was saved when you specified ENABLE_ROLLBACK => TRUE. Use the ABORT_ROLLBACK procedure. Using a procedure with the word "abort" in it usually means that something bad has happened, but in this case, you're aborting the possibility of rolling back the changes to the original table. After you've finished the redefinition process with FINISH_REDEF_TABLE, run this:

```
Begin
    dbms_redefinition.abort_rollback
    (
    uname => 'C##RJB',
    orig_table => 'MY_SEGMENTS',
    int_table => 'MY_SEGMENTS_NEW'
    );
end;
/
PL/SQL procedure successfully completed.
```

The materialized views are dropped, the interim table retains the structure of the original table, and the interim table is truncated.

**Rejecting Table Changes**   For whatever reason, the changes you made are not correct. To roll the changes back (and restore the original table to its original state), use the ROLLBACK procedure like this:

```
Begin
    dbms_redefinition.rollback
    (
     uname => 'C##RJB',
     orig_table => 'MY_SEGMENTS',
     int_table => 'MY_SEGMENTS_NEW'
    );
end;
/

PL/SQL procedure successfully completed.
```

The original table has been restored to its original state and the materialized views are dropped. The interim table is still populated, however, so you can drop or truncate it at this point.

**Assessing Redefinition Overhead**   What are the side effects of being able to roll back your table redefinition? Primarily disk space. Before you run the FINISH_REDEF_ TABLE procedure, the interim table will be at least as large as the table to be redefined:

```
select owner,segment_name,partition_name,bytes
from dba_segments
where owner='C##RJB' and segment_name like '%SEGMENTS%';
```

| OWNER | SEGMENT_NAME | PARTITION_NAME | BYTES |
| --- | --- | --- | --- |
| C##RJB | MY_SEGMENTS | | 776,994,816 |
| C##RJB | MY_SEGMENTS_NEW | | 838,860,800 |

Even after running FINISH_REDEF_TABLE, the table MY_SEGMENTS_NEW is still populated with the old version of the table, in case you still wanted to change your mind:

| OWNER | SEGMENT_NAME | PARTITION_NAME | BYTES |
| --- | --- | --- | --- |
| C##RJB | MY_SEGMENTS | | 805,306,368 |
| C##RJB | MY_SEGMENTS_NEW | | 784,334,848 |

Notice how the two tables have "switched roles"! As mentioned previously in this chapter, rolling back a redefinition leaves the interim table data intact, whereas aborting a rollback truncates the data in the interim table.

# Converting Nonpartitioned Tables to Partitioned Tables

It's often the case that when you create a table for a user or an application, you're not sure how big it will get or how long it will be needed. Before you know it, the table grows so large that the reports running against the table are getting noticeably slower every week. One of your astute developers notices that most of the reports need only a small subset of the table's rows and that partitioning the table will keep the table's performance manageable.

The catch, of course, is that the table is used for reporting and analysis 24×7 and you really can't afford to have downtime during the conversion of the table from nonpartitioned to partitioned. In Oracle Database 12c Release 2, the conversion is as easy as doing an ALTER TABLE . . . MODIFY on the table, specifying the partitioning scheme, and specifying the ONLINE keyword.

In this example, the table PART_OBJECTS has a good date column called CREATED for partitioning. Let's convert the table to partitioned while online:

```
alter table part_objects
modify
    partition by range(created) interval(numtodsinterval(1,'DAY'))
    (
        partition p0 values less than (to_date('2015-12-31','YYYY-MM-DD'))
    )
online;

Table PART_OBJECTS altered.
```

Looking at DBA_TAB_PARTITIONS, you can see that interval partitioning by day works well since the column CREATED is not nullable:

```
select table_owner,table_name,partition_name,high_value
from dba_tab_partitions
where table_owner='C##RJB';
```

| TABLE_OWNER | TABLE_NAME | PARTITION_NAME | HIGH_VALUE |
|---|---|---|---|
| C##RJB | PART_OBJECTS | P0 | TO_DATE(' 2015-12-31 |
| C##RJB | PART_OBJECTS | SYS_P418 | TO_DATE(' 2016-07-21 |
| C##RJB | PART_OBJECTS | SYS_P419 | TO_DATE(' 2017-01-24 |
| C##RJB | PART_OBJECTS | SYS_P420 | TO_DATE(' 2017-01-26 |
| C##RJB | PART_OBJECTS | SYS_P421 | TO_DATE(' 2017-01-25 |
| C##RJB | PART_OBJECTS | SYS_P422 | TO_DATE(' 2017-01-27 |
| C##RJB | PART_OBJECTS | SYS_P423 | TO_DATE(' 2017-01-31 |
| C##RJB | PART_OBJECTS | SYS_P424 | TO_DATE(' 2017-02-01 |
| C##RJB | PART_OBJECTS | SYS_P425 | TO_DATE(' 2017-01-28 |

```
C##RJB          PART_OBJECTS    SYS_P426        TO_DATE(' 2017-01-30
C##RJB          PART_OBJECTS    SYS_P427        TO_DATE(' 2017-01-29

11 rows selected.
```

Existing indexes on the table can be migrated as is or changed to partitioned indexes. Although you cannot change the indexed column list, you can change existing indexes to either local or global partitioned indexes. To manage the indexes in the migrated table, use the UPDATE INDEXES clause. The PART_OBJECTS table was indexed on the CREATED column, so adding the UPDATE INDEXES clause to the previous example re-creates that index as a LOCAL index:

```
alter table part_objects
modify
    partition by range(created) interval(numtodsinterval(1,'DAY'))
    (
        partition p0 values less than (to_date('2015-12-31','YYYY-MM-DD'))
    )
online
update indexes
(
 ie_created local
);
```

Remember that you don't need to specify much for a local partitioned index since it inherits the partitioning scheme of the table. If you do not specify the UPDATE INDEXES clause, any prefixed indexes are automatically converted to a local partitioned index.

## Creating a New Table with Partition Characteristics

You like using partitioned tables—it enhances performance, and partition maintenance operations make it easy to manage the table in parts or as a whole. However, even though the column definitions in your partitioned tables stay the same, other aspects of the partitioned table may change and cause issues when doing partition maintenance. This section will present an example of what I'm talking about and how to fix it with a new feature in Oracle Database 12*c* Release 2.

In the following scenario, my nightly ETL to the data warehouse uses a staging table that has the same structure as your partitioned fact table, and I do an EXCHANGE PARTITION every morning to refresh the live fact table. I had created the staging table yesterday like this:

```
create table part_objects_exch as select * from part_objects where 1=0;
```

During the ETL window, I populated PART_OBJECTS_EXCH. But when I tried to do the EXCHANGE early in the morning, I received an error:

```
alter table part_objects
    exchange partition for (to_date('2017-02-02','YYYY-MM-DD'))
    with table part_objects_exch;
Error report -
ORA-14096: tables in ALTER TABLE EXCHANGE PARTITION must have the same number of
columns
```

But how could it be accurate? I performed the CREATE TABLE command to copy every column as is, so the tables must have the same number of columns! Not exactly…it turns out that earlier in the day, the developer requested that the other DBA add a virtual column:

```
alter table part_objects
    add (neg_data_object_id generated always as (-data_object_id));
```

When running the Create Table As Select (CTAS) command, the virtual column was converted to a physical column. Thus, the new table I created doesn't have the same number and type of total columns as the partitioned table.

To fix this, you can use the new FOR EXCHANGE clause in your CREATE TABLE statement so that you copy all new or changed columns or attributes of the partitioned table, including hidden columns, unused columns, function-based indexes, and so forth. Here is how you can create your staging table to avoid the mismatch issues:

```
create table part_objects_exch
    for exchange with table part_objects;
```

Notice that you also no longer have to use the CTAS syntax to create the staging table. Load the PART_OBJECTS_EXCH table and try the exchange again:

```
alter table part_objects
    exchange partition for (to_date('2017-02-02','YYYY-MM-DD'))
    with table part_objects_exch;

Table PART_OBJECTS altered.
```

# High Availability

Another aspect of Oracle's high-availability infrastructure is at a much lower level: clustering and storage. With Real Application Clusters, you can scale your computing resources to meet your processing needs while keeping your availability high even if one or more nodes in the cluster go down. From a storage perspective, Automatic Storage Management will enhance performance by spreading out your I/O workload across multiple disks in your storage area network (SAN), or even by using sharding to move parts of your database storage geographically closer to where the subset of table data is needed.

# RAC and Grid Infrastructure

Most of the enhancements in Real Application Clusters are in the areas of manageability and monitoring (ASM, an integral component of RAC, is covered in the next section). The level and types of logging available to the DBA go beyond just error reporting to providing the status and level of cluster resource activity as well as enhancements to the Cluster Verification Utility (CVU).

## Cluster Resource Activity Log

The cluster resource activity log is an existing component of Oracle's Autonomous Health Framework. Previously, the emphasis was primarily on reporting error conditions. It's a fine line between an error condition and a problem waiting to happen—in other words, you can configure the cluster resource activity log to check and monitor file attributes. Why would you use file attribute monitoring? At the OS level, you have many key files and directories that need to be accessible either continuously or on a periodic basis. What if your Oracle background processes can't get to the OS directory where the alert log is stored? What if the permissions of a directory were changed to allow any user to read or create files in that directory?

To address this issue proactively, you can run the Oracle ORAchk (**orachk**) or EXAchk (**exachk**) utilities with the **-fileattr** option. When you install ORAchk, be sure to have the **expect** package installed first, then start the monitoring daemon:

```
# yum install expect
# ./orachk -d start
```

Once started, the daemon shows the current state of the monitored environment:

```
Checking Status of Oracle Software Stack - Clusterware, ASM, RDBMS
-------------------------------------------------------------------------
Oracle Stack Status
-------------------------------------------------------------------------
Host Name   CRS Installed  ASM HOME     RDBMS Installed  CRS UP    ASM UP
-------------------------------------------------------------------------
odb12cr2    No             Yes          Yes              No        Yes


RDBMS UP  DB Instance Name
-------------------------
Yes       db12cR2
```

To configure and check for changes to file attributes, you'll first specify any directories you want to monitor (in addition the default Grid home). In this example, you want to add the directory **/etc** to the list of monitored directories:

```
[root@odb12cR2 orachk]# ./orachk -fileattr start -includedir "/etc"
Sending commands to daemon (mypid 25767) args : -fileattr start -includedir /etc
CRS stack is running and CRS_HOME is not set. Do you want to set CRS_HOME to
  /u01/app/oracle/12.2.0/grid?[y/n] [y]y
Checking for prompts for oracle user on all nodes...
List of directories(recursive) for checking file attributes:
/u01/app/oracle/12.2.0/grid
/etc

. . . . . . . . . . . . . . . . . . . . . . . . . . . . . . . . . . . . .

orachk has taken snapshot of file attributes for above directories at:
 /u01/app/orachk/orachk_odb12cR2_20170202_080425/Snapshot_2017-02-02_08-04-25.txt
Terminated
[root@odb12cR2 orachk]#
```

At some point in time after that ORAchk was run, the Oracle DBA accidentally sets the permissions of **/etc/oratab** to 666 instead of the default 664:

```
[oracle@odb12cR2 orachk]$ cd /etc
[oracle@odb12cR2 etc]$ ls -l oratab
-rw-rw-r--. 1 oracle oinstall 820 Jan 23 21:11 oratab
[oracle@odb12cR2 etc]$ chmod 666 oratab
[oracle@odb12cR2 etc]$ ls -l oratab
-rw-rw-rw-. 1 oracle oinstall 820 Jan 23 21:11 oratab
[oracle@odb12cR2 etc]$
```

When you run **exachk** again, either on demand or on a schedule, you can find out if anything has changed recently:

```
[root@odb12cR2 orachk]# ./orachk -fileattr check -includedir "/etc" -fileattronly
Sending commands to daemon (mypid 999) args :
  -fileattr check -includedir /etc -fileattronly
CRS stack is running and CRS_HOME is not set.
  Do you want to set CRS_HOME to /u01/app/oracle/12.2.0/grid?[y/n] [y]y
Checking for prompts for oracle user on all nodes...
List of directories(recursive) for checking file attributes:
/u01/app/oracle/12.2.0/grid
/etc
Checking file attribute changes...
.

"/etc/oratab" is different:
Baseline :      0664     oracle   oinstall /etc/oratab
Current  :      0666     oracle   oinstall /etc/oratab
. . . . . . . . . . . . . . . . . . . . . . . . . . . . . . . . . . . . .
```

```
File attribute check report (html) -
    /u01/app/orachk/orachk_odb12cR2_20170202_083406.html
Terminated
[root@odb12cR2 orachk]#
```

Although this is not a fatal error by any means, you don't want to give every Linux user on this server the ability to change the contents of this file!

### Cluster Verification Utility

The Cluster Verification Utility (CVU) is a command-line utility that you run either on an ad hoc basis or during an install or upgrade via a GUI. When you initiate CVU, you can now save the output as an HTML file and each step in the CVU process provides more detailed status at each step of the check. In this example, you want to run a cluster health check, save the output as HTML, and put the results into the directory **/tmp**:

```
[oracle@odb12cR2 grid]$ ./runcluvfy.sh comp healthcheck -html -save -savedir /tmp
```

When the **runcluvfy.sh** command finishes, it will automatically open a web browser to display the results, as you can see in Figure 5-2.

## Automatic Storage Management

Enhancements to ASM include improved quota management and prioritized rebalancing in Flex ASM disk groups. I'll talk about both of those in the following sections and how they can help you from a management and performance perspective.

### Flex ASM Disk Group Quota Management

For local ASM disk groups, quota management is straightforward. However, with a Flex ASM disk group, controlling access is not enough given the global availability of Flex ASM disk groups: you need to limit the amount of disk space used with quotas. A *quota* is defined as an aggregate of disk space used by different databases. You can manage quota groups using SQL commands or within the **asmcmd** utility. To add the quota group QG01 to the disk group RECO_T01 and set the quota to 5 terabytes, you'd run this command:

```
alter diskgroup reco_t01
    add quotagroup qg01
    set 'quota'=5t;
```

To change the file group FG01 to use the QG01 quota group:

```
alter diskgroup reco_t01
    modify filegroup fg01
    set 'quota_group'='qg01';
```

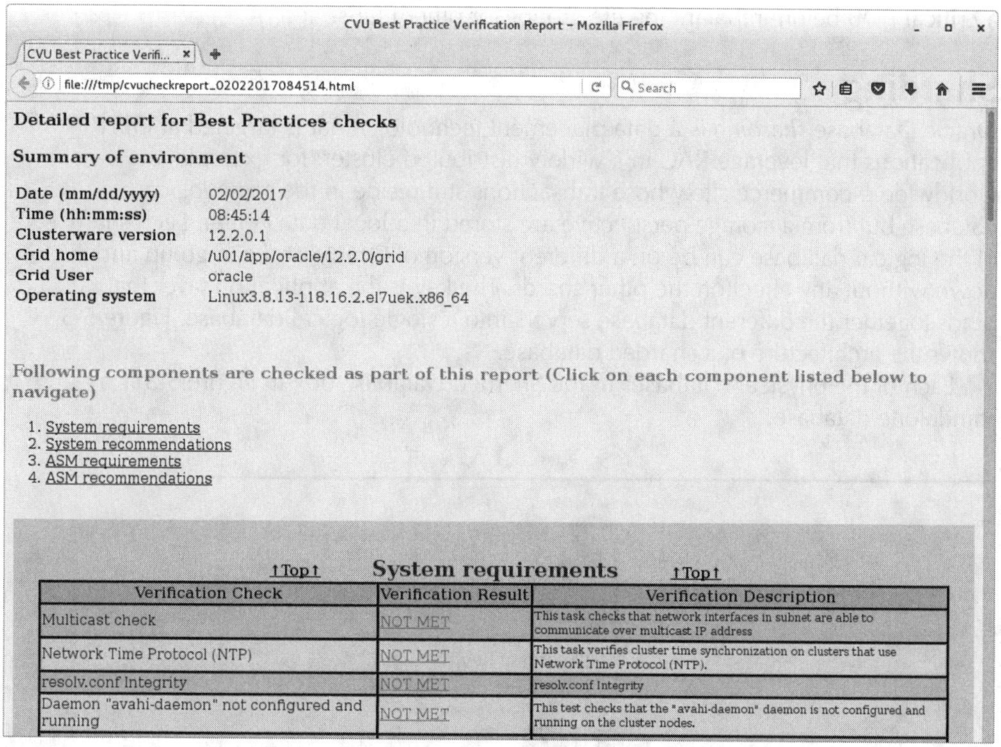

**FIGURE 5-2.** *HTML output from runcluvfy.sh*

The following are some other important rules regarding quota groups:

- A file group can belong to only one quota group at a time.

- A quota group cannot cross disk groups.

- The quota value is evaluated and enforced when a file is created or resized.

- A file group can be moved to another quota group even if the target quota group does not currently have enough quota for the file group.

## ASM Prioritized Rebalancing

In the previous two releases of Oracle Database, you have been able to control the rebalancing rate so as not to adversely affect ongoing application I/O performance. Rebalancing capabilities have been enhanced in Oracle Database 12c Release 2 so that a particular file set is rebalanced before others. This is especially useful in a pluggable database (PDB) environment so that you can rebalance a file group for a critical PDB before rebalancing file groups for other PDBs.

## Sharding

Oracle Database *sharding* is a data placement technology that is targeted at OLTP applications that leverage RAC in a widely distributed cluster: for example, a worldwide e-commerce site whose transactions still reside in the same *logical* database but from a storage perspective are stored in a local data center. Each shard of the logical database can be on a different version of Oracle and can go up and down without any effect on the other shards. The key is the application layer that binds together the different database servers into a single logical database. Figure 5-3 shows the architecture of a sharded database.

Each of the physical databases in the Sharded Database box in Figure 5-3 is a standalone database.

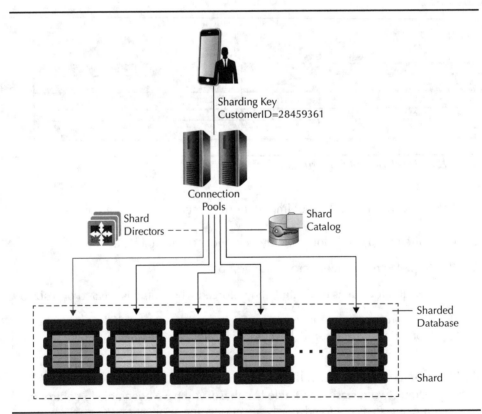

**FIGURE 5-3.** *Sharding architecture*

# Security

Overall there are over 40 new security features mentioned in the various books of the Oracle Database 12c Release 2 documentation and in the *Oracle Database New Features Guide, 12c Release 2 (12.2)*. The new security features you will most likely use immediately and most often will be presented in the following sections. Here are the features I'll cover:

- Encryption and redaction

- Database Vault

- Auditing

- Privilege analysis

- Separation of duties

- User and password management

- STIG (Security Technical Implementation Guides)

## Encryption and Redaction

In Oracle Database 12c Release 2, a dramatic improvement was made in securing the database with regard to encryption and redaction (E&R). But, before we get into these new features, let's take a moment to review the basic concept of E&R. *Encryption* touches the actual data by scrambling plaintext data into a meaningless and unrecognizable form. *Redaction*, on the other hand, does not affect the data. Redaction obscures the viewing of the data. Please take a short moment to fully understand the difference before moving on. By taking the time to grasp this simple concept of how encryption differs from redaction, the rest of this section will fall into place.

### Encryption

The need to secure data at rest is a best practice in many industries and is a requirement in several others. If you are working in a regulated arena such as healthcare, government, or financial industries, you are most likely *required* to use encryption. For those who are not working in one of those regulated industries, you should probably be using encryption anyway.

The new features related to Transparent Data Encryption (TDE) in Oracle Database 12c Release 2 allow for encryption, decryption, and rekeying of existing tablespaces online *without* downtime. Also, TDE in not just at the tablespace level anymore; now the entire database can be encrypted, decrypted, and rekeyed online *without* downtime. What is meant by the phrase "entire database"? Well, this includes the default database tablespaces SYSTEM, SYSAUX, and UNDO, all of which can now have TDE applied to them.

**NOTE**
*New encryption algorithms that are supported in Oracle Database 12c Release 2 include SEED and ARIA for South Korea and GOST for Russia.*

The ability to use TDE online for encryption, decryption, and rekeying opens up the opportunity to keep databases up and use fewer downtime windows. But, if you are in an organization that plans ahead or has a limited amount of available storage space, then use of offline conversion will interest you. In Oracle Database 12c Release 2, you can apply encryption to tablespaces offline and do so without additional storage space requirements. I'll demonstrate both methods in the next two sections.

**Leveraging Online Encryption**   Now it is time to see these new features of TDE in action. We will create a specific user with the SYSKM privilege in a pluggable database, PDB1, and work through examples of the previously mentioned new features.

In this example, log into the CDB as SYSDBA and then issue an ALTER SESSION command to move into the PDB. You can log into your test PDB directly if you prefer. I will create a tablespace, a user, and a couple of tables for the encryption examples in PDB1.

```
sqlplus / as sysdba
```

Once logged into the CDB, I run a query to confirm that the pluggable database is open and in the proper mode:

```
SQL> select con_id, name, open_mode from  v$pdbs;

CON_ID     NAME          OPEN_MODE
---------- ------------- ----------
2          PDB$SEED      READ ONLY
3          PDB1          READ WRITE
```

Then change your session to the pluggable database that you wish to use. In our case the pluggable database is PDB1.

```
SQL> alter session set container = PDB1;
Session altered.
```

I create a new tablespace next:

```
SQL> create tablespace test_encryption
    datafile '/u01/app/oracle/oradata/orcl12/pdb1/test_encryption01.dbf'
    size 1m autoextend on next 1m;

Tablespace created.
```

Next, I create a user and grant the proper privileges:

```
SQL> create user overwatch identified by seer
    default tablespace TEST_ENCRYPTION temporary tablespace temp;

User created.

SQL> grant dba to overwatch;

Grant succeeded.
```

Finally, I create a table and load some data, and then confirm the data is there:

```
create table overwatch.encrypt_me
    (col1 varchar2(200), col2 varchar2(200));
insert into overwatch.encrypt_me values ('Is this ', 'safe to use 1');
insert into overwatch.encrypt_me values ('Is this ', 'safe to use 2');
COMMIT;

set linesize 150
COL COL1 FORMAT A50
COL COL2 FORMAT A50
select * from overwatch.encrypt_me;
```

Now that I have created the TEST_ENCRYPTION tablespace and populated a table in that tablespace, I'll encrypt the entire tablespace online using the AES192 algorithm. But before we can encrypt the tablespace, we need to create a KEYSTORE, as the following steps illustrate.

Modify your **sqlnet.ora** file as follows and create the corresponding location on your file system:

```
ENCRYPTION_WALLET_LOCATION =
    (SOURCE =(METHOD = FILE)(METHOD_DATA =
    (DIRECTORY = /u01/app/oracle/admin/orcl12/encryption_keystore/)
```

Here is the command to run as **root** at the OS level:
**# mkdir -p /u01/app/oracle/admin/orcl12/encryption_keystore/**

Create and open a master encryption key as SYSDBA in the CDB:

```
administer key management create keystore    '/u01/app/oracle/admin/
orcl12/encryption_keystore/'
   identified by MyPassword123;
administer key management set keystore open
   identified by mypassword123 container=all;
administer key management set key
   identified by MyPassword123 with backup container=all;
```

Now that the setup is complete, I'll issue the actual command to execute the online encryption using the AES192 algorithm.

While still using the SYS account in the CDB, I run the following statements:

```
alter session set container = PDB1;
alter tablespace test_encryption encryption online
   using 'aes192' encrypt
   file_name_convert = ('test_encryption01.dbf', 'test_encrypted01.dbf');
Tablespace altered.
```

To confirm that the tablespace is now encrypted I'll use the following query:

```
select ddf.tablespace_name, ddf.file_name,
       vet.encryptedts, vet.encryptionalg, vt.con_id
from  dba_data_files ddf, v$tablespace vt,  v$encrypted_tablespaces vet
where ddf.tablespace_name = vt.name
and   vt.ts# = vet.ts#;

TABLESPACE_NAME FILE_NAME
--------------- -----------------------------------------------------------
TEST_ENCRYPTION /u01/app/oracle/oradata/orcl12/pdb1/test_encrypted01.dbf

ENCRYPTEDTS     ENCRYPT  CON_ID
--------------- -------- ------
YES             AES192   3
```

Now the TEST_ENCRYPTION tablespace is encrypted with the AES192 algorithm. But as normal, things change. A change request has arrived to alter the encryption algorithm to support the GOST encryption algorithm because we are now storing data of RUSSIAN origin. We can accomplish this by rekeying that tablespace (online!) and running the previous verification script:

```
alter tablespace test_encryption encryption
   using 'GOST256' rekey
   file_name_convert = ('test_encrypted01.dbf', 'test_encrypted_GOST.dbf');

Tablespace altered.
```

Our results should show the following after changing the encryption algorithm to GOST:

```
TABLESPACE_NAME FILE_NAME
--------------- -------------------------------------------------------------
TEST_ENCRYPTION /u01/app/oracle/oradata/orcl12/pdb1/test_encrypted_GOST.dbf

ENCRYPTEDTS     ENCRYPT CON_ID
--------------- ------- ------
YES             GOST256 3
```

Here are some important points to consider when using online tablespace encryption:

- There is a space requirement equal to the size of the tablespace being encrypted online. For a 100 GB tablespace, you will need at least 100 GB of additional file system storage space.

- If the online encryption is interrupted, it can be recovered with the FINISH clause of the ALTER TABLESPACE command.

- A redo log is generated for each online tablespace conversion.

- You cannot encrypt, decrypt, or rekey a temporary tablespace online.

- Temporary tablespaces need to be dropped and re-created with encryption.

For a complete list of other features and restrictions, please refer to "About Encryption Conversions for Existing Online Tablespaces" in the *Oracle Database Advanced Security Guide 12c Release 2 (12.2)*.

Now that I've showed how to use the new feature of online encryption for user-defined tablespaces I'll move on to offline encryption in the next section.

**Leveraging Offline Encryption** Why consider offline encryption? The simple answer is that offline encryption is an "in place" operation. As such, there is no additional storage needed when using offline encryption.

Offline encryption is a very straightforward operation. The steps are presented next with comments. To encrypt a PDB offline, you need to close it while keeping the root container (CDB$ROOT) open. Since this is an "in place" operation, taking a backup should be your first action and is highly recommended.

First, take the tablespace offline:

```
alter tablespace test_encryption offline normal;
```

Open the KEYSTORE:

```
administer key management
    set keystore open identified by MyPassword123 container=all;
```

Encrypt the tablespace offline:

```
alter tablespace test_encryption encryption offline encrypt;
```

Or you can choose to encrypt each datafile individually:

```
alter database datafile 'test_encryption_01.dbf' encrypt;
alter database datafile 'test_encryption_02.dbf' encrypt;
```

Bring the tablespace online:

```
alter tablespace test_encryption online;
```

**Choosing Between Online and Offline Encryption**   Here are some closing thoughts about encryption. Plan your success by determining ahead of time which method to use when encrypting tablespaces or the entire database. Online encryption is useful if you have enough extra storage space. Although the offline method needs downtime, it does not require the additional storage. The choice of encryption algorithms to use will, in most cases, be dictated by business and legal requirements. Plus, with the ability to now rekey online, changing encryption algorithms is much easier than before. In the next section I'll talk about new features related to encryption's close relative, redaction.

### Redaction

Encryption protects data at rest from attacks on the database files from the storage level. Redaction, on the other hand, changes the appearance of the data when presented to the application layer. One of the new features in Oracle Database 12c Release 2 is redaction with the ability to set the redacted column to a null value. This new feature is shown in the following example.

I'll continue to use the OVERWATCH schema in PDB1 for demonstrating the new redaction features. In the OVERWATCH schema, I create the table REDACT_ME with some data that will be redacted. The user NORMAL_GUY will then try to read the REDACT_ME table.

```
sqlplus overwatch/saw@pdb1

create table overwatch.redact_me
(col1 varchar2(200),
 col2 varchar2(200),
 col3 varchar2(200),
 col4 varchar2(200) );
```

```
insert into overwatch.redact_me (col1 , col2)
   values ('Is this ', 'safe to use 1');
insert into overwatch.redact_me (col1 , col2)
   values ('Is this ', 'safe to use 2');
COMMIT;

create user normal_guy identified by frederick
default tablespace users temporary tablespace temp;
grant connect, resource to normal_guy;
grant select on overwatch.redact_me to normal_guy;

select * from overwatch.redact_me;


COL1              COL2               COL3              COL4
---------------- ----------------- ----------------- ----------------------
Is this           safe to use 1
Is this           safe to use 2


BEGIN
DBMS_REDACT.ADD_POLICY(
object_schema => 'overwatch',
object_name   => 'redact_me',
column_name   => 'col2',
policy_name   => 'nullify_col2',
function_type => DBMS_REDACT.NULLIFY,
expression    => '1=1');
END;
/


PL/SQL procedure successfully completed.


sqlplus normal_guy/frederick@pdb1

select * from overwatch.redact_me;

COL1              COL2               COL3              COL4
---------------- ----------------- ----------------- ----------------------
Is this
Is this
```

Another new feature related to redaction in Oracle Database 12c Release 2 is adding *named* Oracle Data Redaction policies which enables you to redact data based on runtime conditions; in other words, you can redact based on session characteristics such as where the user is connecting from or even what time of day the query is run. For instance, the user NORMAL_GUY logs into the database. A named Data Redaction policy can use SYS_CONTEXT ('USERENV', 'SESSION_USER') to activate redaction on a column of a table. The policy can be reused with DBMS_REDACT.APPLY_POLICY_EXPR_TO_COL against other tables or columns. Let us look at a working example of how to use this feature with explanations at each step of the example that follows.

First, I create and load an example table:

```
create table overwatch.redact_me2
(col1 varchar2(200),
col2 varchar2(200),
col3 varchar2(200),
col4 varchar2(200) );

insert into  overwatch.redact_me2
(col3 , col4) values ('This is ', 'what I see 1');
insert into  overwatch.redact_me2
(col3 , col4) values ('This is ', 'what I see 2');
COMMIT;
grant select on overwatch.redact_me2 to normal_guy;
```

Confirm that NORMAL_GUY can read the table currently before the named policy is applied:

```
sqlplus normal_guy/fred@pdb1
select * from overwatch.redact_me2;
```

Build out the default redaction and give it a name:

```
sqlplus overwatch/seer@pdb1

BEGIN
   DBMS_REDACT.CREATE_POLICY_EXPRESSION(
      policy_expression_name        => 'NORMAL_GUY_REDACT_POL',
      expression                    =>
         'SYS_CONTEXT(''USERENV'',''SESSION_USER'') = ''NORMAL_GUY'''),
      policy_expression_description  => 'Enables policy for user NORMAL_GUY');
END;
/
```

To disable the overall redaction policy, you can use a conditional expression which will always evaluate to FALSE:

```
BEGIN
DBMS_REDACT.ADD_POLICY (
object_schema => 'OVERWATCH',
object_name   => 'REDACT_ME2',
policy_name   => 'OVERALL_POLICY',
expression    => '1=0');
END;
/
```

Next, I'll modify the policy to redact only the column COL4:

```
BEGIN
DBMS_REDACT.ALTER_POLICY (
object_schema => 'OVERWATCH',
object_name   => 'REDACT_ME2' ,
policy_name   => 'OVERALL_POLICY',
function_type => DBMS_REDACT.FULL,
action        => DBMS_REDACT.ADD_COLUMN,
column_name   => 'COL4' );
END;
/
```

Finally, I'll use the named policy NORMAL_GUY_REDACT_POL to apply to the column COL4:

```
BEGIN
DBMS_REDACT.APPLY_POLICY_EXPR_TO_COL (
object_schema             => 'OVERWATCH',
object_name               => 'REDACT_ME2',
column_name               => 'COL4',
policy_expression_name => 'NORMAL_GUY_REDACT_POL');
END;
/
```

Confirm that NORMAL_GUY can only read columns other than COL4:

```
sqlplus normal_guy/frederick@pdb1
select * from overwatch.redact_me2;
```

This enhancement to Oracle's redaction provides the database administrator with a more fine-grained approach to redaction. You may not want to redact a particular column for all users or even a single user all the time—you can now redact one or more columns based on the user's environment, whether it be the time of day or where they logged in from.

# Database Vault

In previous releases of Oracle Database, it was often difficult to use the Database Vault (DBV) options. When DBV was installed, it "locked down" the database and enforced separation of duties. From a security administrator's perspective, this was great, but from a development and day-to-day operation viewpoint, it meant "things just broke randomly." This "all or nothing" characteristic of DBV was seen as a drawback and a reason not to use it.

DBV in Oracle Database 12c Release 2 resolves this "all or nothing" characteristic with Simulation Mode Protection (hereafter "Simulation Mode" for simplicity's sake). In Simulation Mode, DBV records violations *without* enforcing DBV policies/realms.

| Code | Meaning |
|------|---------|
| 1000 | Realm violation |
| 1001 | Command rule violation |
| 1002 | Oracle Data Pump authorization violation |
| 1003 | Simulation violation |
| 1004 | Oracle Scheduler authorization violation |
| 1005 | DDL authorization violation |
| 1006 | PARSE_AS_USER violation |

**TABLE 5-1.**   *Database Vault Run-Time Error Messages*

Instead of an abrupt and disruptive halt to the operation being executed, a record is entered into the DVSYS.SIMULATION_LOG$ table. That record can then be viewed by DBAs in view DBA_DV_SIMULATION_LOG.

After reviewing DBA_DV_SIMULATION_LOG combined with the code information in Table 5-1, DBAs can take corrective actions before fully enforcing DBV policies/realms.

Let's see Database Vault in action and prove the value of DBV Simulation Mode. First, create the users involved in this example:

```
hattieh        Database Vault policy owner
bad_dba        who commits violations on the OVERWATCH.GPA table
bad_student    whose salary is the recipient of bad_dba's violations


GRANT CREATE SESSION TO hattieh      IDENTIFIED BY student123;
GRANT CREATE SESSION TO bad_dba      IDENTIFIED BY student123;
GRANT CREATE SESSION TO bad_student  IDENTIFIED BY student123;


GRANT DV_POLICY_OWNER TO hattieh;
```

Create the tables, load some data, and grant the SELECT privilege to the appropriate users:

```
sqlplus overwatch/seer@pdb1
create table OVERWATCH.GPA
( FNAME varchar2(20),
  LNAME varchar2(20),
  GPA number(3,2) );
insert into OVERWATCH.GPA  values ('Jane',   'Cheung', 4.25 );
```

```
insert into OVERWATCH.GPA  values ('Connie', 'Rose'   , 4.15 );
insert into OVERWATCH.GPA  values ('Carlie', 'Rose'   , 3.55 );
insert into OVERWATCH.GPA  values ('Emma',    'Rose'   , 3.50 );
insert into OVERWATCH.GPA  values ('Alex',    'Cheung', 3.85 );
insert into OVERWATCH.GPA  values ('bad_student',   'Cheung', 3.25 );
commit;
select * from OVERWATCH.GPA order by fname;
GRANT SELECT ON OVERWATCH.GPA TO bad_student;

BEGIN
   DBMS_MACADM.CREATE_REALM(
      realm_name    => 'OVERWATCH.GPA_REALM',
      description   => 'REALM TO PROTECT OVERWATCH.GPA',
      enabled       => DBMS_MACUTL.G_SIMULATION,
      audit_options => DBMS_MACUTL.G_REALM_AUDIT_FAIL,
      realm_type    => 0);
END;
/


BEGIN
   DBMS_MACADM.ADD_OBJECT_TO_REALM(
      realm_name   => 'OVERWATCH.GPA_REALM',
      object_owner => 'OVERWATCH',
      object_name  => 'GPA',
      object_type  => 'TABLE');
END;
/


BEGIN
DBMS_MACADM.CREATE_POLICY(
    policy_name => 'OVERWATCH.GPA_POL',
    description => 'POLICY TO PROTECT OVERWATCH.GPA',
    policy_state => DBMS_MACADM.G_SIMULATION);
END;
/


BEGIN
   DBMS_MACADM.ADD_REALM_TO_POLICY(
      policy_name => 'OVERWATCH.GPA_POL',
      realm_name  => 'OVERWATCH.GPA_REALM');
END;
/


BEGIN
   DBMS_MACADM.ADD_OWNER_TO_POLICY(
      policy_name => 'OVERWATCH.GPA_POL',
      owner_name => 'HATTIEH');
END;
/
```

As the BAD_DBA user, I update some rows:

```
UPDATE OVERWATCH.GPA
SET GPA = 3.95
WHERE FNAME = 'Carlie';

UPDATE OVERWATCH.GPA
SET GPA = 3.90
WHERE FNAME = 'Alex';

COMMIT;
select * from OVERWATCH.GPA order by fname;
```

View the violations that occurred (but were *not* prevented) when those UPDATE statements were run:

```
SELECT USERNAME, SQLTEXT, VIOLATION_TYPE, TIMESTAMP
FROM DBA_DV_SIMULATION_LOG
WHERE REALM_NAME = 'OVERWATCH.GPA_REALM';
```

Next, fix the data as SYSDBA and change it back to its original state:

```
UPDATE OVERWATCH.GPA
SET GPA = 3.55
WHERE FNAME = 'Carlie';

UPDATE OVERWATCH.GPA
SET GPA = 3.85
WHERE FNAME = 'Alex';

COMMIT;
select * from OVERWATCH.GPA order by fname;
```

Change the policy so that it's enforced going forward, preventing those UPDATEs from happening:

```
BEGIN
    DBMS_MACADM.UPDATE_POLICY_STATE(
        policy_name => 'OVERWATCH.GPA_POL',
        policy_state => 1);
END;
/
```

This simple case shows how to use the Simulation Mode of DBV. A more realistic use case would involve planning with the development team and implementing the DBV policies in Simulation Mode near the end of the Q&A process. Once there is enough data recorded, the DBA and security administrator can review the DBA_DV_SIMULATION_LOG and make adjustments accordingly.

## Auditing

Auditing in Oracle Database 12c Release 2 has improved in a number of ways. I'll focus here on the new feature that allows unified auditing to audit by *roles*. Auditing by role allows for an analysis of security violations by a role. For instance, auditing an APPLICATION or DBA role can identify unusual activity.

Our example of auditing by role involves auditing the DBA for using the system privileges CREATE ANY TABLE, ALTER ANY TABLE, and DROP ANY TABLE. But, before I get into creating the audit by role configuration, I need to enable unified auditing. Enabling unified auditing must be done at the CDB level:

```
SQL> sqlplus / as sysdba
SQL> select value from v$option where parameter = 'Unified Auditing';

VALUE
------
False

SQL> shutdown immediate

% cd $ORACLE_HOME/rdbms/lib
% make -f ins_rdbms.mk uniaud_on ioracle

SQL> startup

SQL> select value from v$option where parameter = 'Unified Auditing';

VALUE
------
True
```

Now that I have unified auditing configured, I can set up auditing by role. This example will use the pluggable database PDB1 and the OVERWATCH user. As the OVERWATCH user:

```
create user matt identified by intensity
    default tablespace users temporary tablespace temp;
grant dba to matt;

create audit policy table_privs
    privileges create any table, alter any table, drop any table
    container = current;

audit policy table_privs by users with granted roles dba;
```

I will purge the unified audit trail to make it easier to review from this point on:

```
select  count(*) from unified_audit_trail;

begin
   dbms_audit_mgmt.clean_audit_trail(
      audit_trail_type           =>  dbms_audit_mgmt.audit_trail_unified,
      use_last_arch_timestamp  =>  false);
end;
/

select  count(*) from unified_audit_trail;
```

Next, I use the MATT account (which has the DBA role) to run the following SQL:

```
create table overwatch.i_am_bad0 (col1 varchar2(200), col2 varchar2(200));
create table overwatch.i_am_bad1 (col1 varchar2(200), col2 varchar2(200));
create table overwatch.i_am_bad2 (col1 varchar2(200), col2 varchar2(200));

ALTER TABLE overwatch.i_am_bad0 ADD col3 varchar2(200);
ALTER TABLE overwatch.i_am_bad1 ADD col3 varchar2(200);
ALTER TABLE overwatch.i_am_bad2 ADD col3 varchar2(200);

DROP TABLE overwatch.i_am_bad0;
DROP TABLE overwatch.i_am_bad1;
DROP TABLE overwatch.i_am_bad2;
```

As the OVERWATCH user, I flush the memory and check results (not all records are shown due to space restrictions):

```
exec dbms_audit_mgmt.flush_unified_audit_trail;

select dbusername, ACTION_NAME ,
   dbms_lob.substr( SQL_TEXT, dbms_lob.getlength(SQL_TEXT), 1) SQL,
   EVENT_TIMESTAMP from unified_audit_trail
order by 4 desc;


DBUSERNAME            ACTION_NAME             SQL
EVENT_TIMESTAMP
------------------- ----------------------- -----------------------------------
--------------------------
MATT                  DROP TABLE              DROP TABLE overwatch.i_am_bad2
29-NOV-16 03.21.38.619379 PM
MATT                  ALTER TABLE             ALTER TABLE overwatch.i_am_bad1 ADD col3
29-NOV-16 03.21.28.832059 PM
                                              varchar2(200)
MATT                  CREATE TABLE            create table overwatch.i_am_bad2
29-NOV-16 03.21.21.287420 PM
                                              (col1 varchar2(200), col2 varchar2(200))
```

To remove the audit rule, I run the following commands:

```
noaudit policy table_privs by users with granted roles dba;
drop audit policy table_privs;
```

The improvements in auditing are not limited to the new audit by role functionality. Also included are improvements to the AUDSYS audit schema itself. The AUDSYS audit schema contains the unified audit data, and the schema is now accessible with the privilege of SELECT ANY DICTIONARY. Previously, the AUDSYS schema could be accessible with the SELECT ANY TABLE privilege. You can think of this as bringing in the AUDSYS schema into the data dictionary and protecting it in the same manner as other data dictionary tables.

Equally important as the protection of the unified audit trail is the capturing of the predicate clause when using Virtual Private Database (VPD). The predicate clause is essentially the WHERE clause that VPD appends to a user's SQL statement when VPD policies are enforced. Since the user's original SQL_TEXT is also included in the unified audit trail, with the predicate clause it is easier to know what SQL the user actually ran.

## Privilege Analysis

Understanding what privileges are being used, and not used, by users over time is the new feature we cover in this section. Privilege analysis (PA) now has an additional parameter called RUN_NAME. The RUN_NAME parameter can be used for multiple runs of the same PA policy. This functionality along with the use of the **diff** utility allows for monitoring of any changes in privileges.

To demonstrate privilege analysis below, I do the following:

- Create the users and grant the necessary privileges for the users PRIV_ADMIN and BAD_USER

- Run the DBMS_PRIVILEGE.CAPTURE.CREATE_CAPTURE to set up what will be captured for the analysis

- Run the DBMS_PRIVILEGE_CAPTURE.ENABLE_CAPTURE procedure with different values for the RUN_NAME parameter

- After some length of time where users are active, run the DBMS_PRIVILEGE_ CAPTURE.GENERATE_RESULT procedures with different values for the RUN_NAME parameter

Create the users with the necessary permissions:

```
sqlplus  sys/oracle@pdb1 as sysdba

CREATE USER  PRIV_ADMIN  IDENTIFIED BY password;
CREATE USER  BAD_USER    IDENTIFIED BY password;

GRANT CREATE SESSION, CAPTURE_ADMIN  TO PRIV_ADMIN;
GRANT CREATE SESSION, READ ANY TABLE TO BAD_USER;
```

Next, set up the privilege analysis to capture potential BAD_USER activity:

```
BEGIN
    DBMS_PRIVILEGE_CAPTURE.CREATE_CAPTURE(
        name        => 'READ_ANY_TABLE_PA',
        description => 'ANALYZES SYSTEM PRIVILEGE USE',
        type        =>  DBMS_PRIVILEGE_CAPTURE.G_CONTEXT,
        condition   => 'SYS_CONTEXT(''USERENV'', ''SESSION_USER'')=''BAD_USER''');
END;
/
```

Use ENABLE_CAPTURE to start the capture process:

```
BEGIN
DBMS_PRIVILEGE_CAPTURE.ENABLE_CAPTURE (
name       => 'READ_ANY_TABLE_PA',
run_name   => 'READ_ANY_TABLE_PA_POL_RUN_1');
END;
/
```

Here, the BAD_USER logs in and tries to view a table that they should not be viewing:

```
SQL> sqlplus bad_user/bad_password@pdb1
SQL> SELECT * FROM OVERWATCH.GPA ORDER BY FNAME;
```

After some time has passed, top the capture process with DISABLE_CAPTURE:

```
SQL> sqlplus  sys/oracle@pdb1 as sysdba

SQL> exec dbms_privilege_capture.disable_capture ('READ_ANY_TABLE_PA');
```

After some time passes, I can view any possible bad activity by BAD_USER by generating the report data:

```
BEGIN
    DBMS_PRIVILEGE_CAPTURE.GENERATE_RESULT (
        name     => 'READ_ANY_TABLE_PA',
        run_name => 'READ_ANY_TABLE_PA_POL_RUN_1');
END;
/
```

To see what privileges the user BAD_USER used, I query the data dictionary view DBA_USED_PRIVS:

```
SELECT USERNAME, SYS_PRIV, OBJECT_OWNER, OBJECT_NAME, RUN_NAME
FROM DBA_USED_PRIVS
WHERE USERNAME = 'BAD_USER' AND SYS_PRIV = 'READ ANY TABLE';

USERNAME SYS_PRIV        OBJECT_OWNER OBJECT_NAME RUN_NAME
-------- -------------- ------------ ----------- ---------------------------
BAD_USER READ ANY TABLE OVERWATCH    GPA         READ_ANY_TABLE_PA_POL_RUN_1
```

Having found out what I needed to know, I can now stop the capture process:

```
EXEC DBMS_PRIVILEGE_CAPTURE.DROP_CAPTURE ('READ_ANY_TABLE_PA');
```

The preceding example shows an iteration of the privilege analysis process. You can turn on the capture process on a schedule with different and meaningful values for RUN_NAME and perform additional analyses based on time of day or privilege usage over time.

## Separation of Duties

Oracle Database 12c Release 2 continues to implement the separation of duties best practices with the introduction of the SYSRAC role. The SYSRAC role is needed when using SRVCTL. The Grid Infrastructure clusterware agent also uses the SYSRAC role.

The following is a list of PL/SQL packages that a user with the SYSRAC role can execute:

- DBMS_DRS
- DBMS_SERVICE
- DBMS_SERVICE_PRVT
- DBMS_SESSION
- DBMS_HA_ALERTS_PRVT
- Dequeue messaging in SYS.SYS$SERVICE_METRICS

Additionally, Table 5-2 lists administrative actions and views that a user with the SYSRAC role can use.

| Administrative Actions | Access to Views |
|---|---|
| STARTUP | V$PARAMETER |
| SHUTDOWN | V$DATABASE |
| ALTER DATABASE MOUNT | V$PDBS |
| ALTER DATABASE OPEN | CDB_SERVICE$ |
| ALTER DATABASE OPEN READ ONLY | DBA_SERVICES |
| ALTER DATABASE CLOSE NORMAL | V$ACTIVE_SERVICES |
| ALTER DATABASE DISMOUNT | V$SERVICES |
| ALTER SESSION SET EVENTS | |
| ALTER SESSION SET _NOTIFY_CRS | |
| ALTER SESSION SET CONTAINER | |
| ALTER SYSTEM REGISTER | |
| ALTER SYSTEM SET | |
| local_listener \| remote_listener \| listener_networks | |

**TABLE 5-2.** *SYSRAC Role and Related Administrative Actions*

# User and Password Management

The management of user accounts is easier in Oracle Database 12c Release 2. User accounts can now be automatically locked after a period of inactivity. This period of inactivity can range from 15 to 24,855 days. Fractional days are not allowed when using this new functionality. A user is no longer considered inactive after logging into the database.

The implementation of automatically locking users is done with the use of profiles. The following example creates the profile INACTIVE_LIMIT with a 30-day inactivity limit. That profile is then assigned to the BAD_USER.

```
create profile inactive_limit limit
    inactive_account_time 30;

alter user bad_user profile inactive_limit;
```

In addition, the password verification functionality has changed in Oracle Database 12c Release 2; the default value for SQLNET.ALLOWED_LOGON_VERSION_SERVER in **sqlnet.ora** is now 12. This setting requires the use of stronger password verifiers. Do not set or use the database parameter SEC_CASE_SENSITIVE_LOGON in Oracle Database 12c Release 2. It has been deprecated since 12.1. Also, the combination of setting SEC_CASE_SENSITIVE_LOGON to FALSE and the default value of SQLNET.ALLOWED_LOGON_VERSION_SERVER causes all accounts to become inaccessible!

## STIG

For those of you working in a U.S. Government Sector (USGS), this section is for you. The Security Technical Implementation Guides (STIG) list requirements to gain the Authority to Operate (ATO) certification—in other words, the guides' requirements must be met before you can implement the application in production. In Oracle Database 12c Release 2, the new security features that help you pass the STIG are various password complexity functions and a specific user profile.

The three password complexity functions are ORA12C_VERIFY_FUNCTION, ORA12C_STIG_VERIFY_FUNCTION, and ORA12C_STRONG_VERIFY_FUNCTION. Each function provides varying levels of validation for password complexity. The STIG-related user profile is ORA_STIG_PROFILE and is listed in the following example.

One thing to notice about the profile ORA_STIG_PROFILE is the password verify function that is used. It is ORA12C_STRONG_VERIFY_FUNCTION by default.

```
create profile ora_stig_profile
    idle_time 15
    failed_login_attempts 3
    password_life_time 60
    password_reuse_time 365
    password_reuse_max 10
    password_lock_time unlimited
    password_grace_time 5
    password_verify_function ora12c_strong_verify_function;
```

## Summary

This chapter covered the most important new administrative, high availability (HA), and security features of Oracle Database 12c Release 2.

Administration of your Oracle database or even a widely distributed RAC database now has many more proactive and ease-of-use features, such as being able to perform even more types of database table partition operations with little or no downtime for the users.

The enhancements to ASM in conjunction with sharding can make your distributed databases even more heterogeneous and localized to meet the needs of each logical portion of the database application.

The covered security features include encryption and redaction, Database Vault, auditing, privilege analysis, separation of duties, user and password management, and STIG. You should try some or all of these features in your development and test environments. There is nothing like actually trying out a new feature to really appreciate it.

# CHAPTER
## 6

# RMAN New Features

Oracle Recovery Manager (RMAN) has been an integral part of Oracle Database since version 10*g*. Previous to Oracle Database 10*g*, you had to use manual backup methods such as OS file copies that didn't have the numerous recoverability and ease of maintenance options that RMAN does. Oracle Database 12*c* Release 2 offers several significant enhancements to RMAN, including a couple that directly support other new features such as multitenant pluggable database (PDB) archive files.

In this chapter, I'll explain all of these new features: more flexible table recovery options, duplicating Transparent Data Encryption (TDE) databases and tablespaces, cross-platform PDB transport, and enhanced backup and recovery options for sparse databases. In the case of the new table recovery feature and PDB archive file support, I'll provide a detailed real-world example that shows how to create a multitenant PDB archive to move a PDB from one CDB to another on the same or a different server.

# Table Recovery Enhancements

Before Oracle Database 12*c* Release 1, if you wanted to restore individual tables from a backup, the easiest way would be to have a recent Oracle Data Pump export dump file and import it from there. The downside to doing it that way was that the export was a logical point-in-time backup and your table may have changed quite a bit since that backup. If your database was in ARCHIVELOG mode and you had an RMAN backup, you could get the table from there, but you had to restore the entire database to get back one table.

In Oracle Database 12*c* Release 1, RMAN was enhanced to allow selective restoration of one or more tables without having to restore the entire database. If the table is critical but has a very small footprint in your database, using RMAN with the selective restore method saves a lot of I/O and disk space. However, the table has to be restored with the same name to the same schema.

Oracle Database 12*c* Release 2 makes your recovery operation easier and much more flexible: you can not only restore one or more tables to a different schema but also rename the files during the same restore operation. This is very useful, for example, if the current version of the table is incomplete but can't be renamed or moved because it's still in production and needed for ongoing DML operations. You can restore the table from the RMAN backup to a point in time before rows were erroneously dropped to a new schema and with a different name, and then reconcile the differences between the restored table and the table currently in production.

An example will show you how useful this feature is. The container database (CDB) REL2018 has two PDBs: DEV02 and DEV02A. In the PDB DEV02A, the two developer schemas are RJB and KLH. The schema RJB has a table called MY_OBJECTS. Figure 6-1 shows the location of this table when I browse the schemas in DEV02A within Oracle SQL Developer.

**FIGURE 6-1.** *Browsing the RJB schema in Oracle SQL Developer*

The REL2018 container database is in ARCHIVELOG mode, so my RMAN backups have archived redo logs to ensure that I can restore and recover the table MY_OBJECTS up to any point in time before the wrong table rows were dropped. I know that the table had all the rows earlier today, so I'll restore and recover the table using SYSDATE – 0.5 (12 hours earlier) in the UNTIL TIME clause of the RMAN RECOVER command. Here is what the output looks like:

```
[oracle@db122dev /home/oracle]$ rman target c##rjb/c##rjb@db122dev/rel2018
Recovery Manager: Release 12.2.0.1.0 - Production on Thu Apr 13 08:18:39 2017
Copyright (c) 1982, 2017, Oracle and/or its affiliates.  All rights reserved.
connected to target database: REL2018 (DBID=2572440253)
RMAN> recover table rjb.my_objects of pluggable database dev02a
2>      until time 'sysdate - 0.5'
3>      auxiliary destination '/u01/app/oracle/aux'
4>      remap table rjb.my_objects:klh.her_objects;
Starting recover at 13-APR-17
current log archived
using channel ORA_DISK_1
using channel ORA_DISK_2
using channel ORA_DISK_3
using channel ORA_DISK_4
Creating automatic instance, with SID='bije'
initialization parameters used for automatic instance:
db_name=REL2018
db_unique_name=bije_pitr_dev02a_REL2018
compatible=12.2.0
. . .
Performing export of tables...
EXPDP> Starting "SYS"."TSPITR_EXP_bije_vdtx":
. . .
EXPDP> . . exported "RJB"."MY_OBJECTS"          153.5 MB 1161968 rows
. . .
```

```
EXPDP> Job "SYS"."TSPITR_EXP_bije_vdtx"
      successfully completed at Thu Apr 13 08:41:34 2017 elapsed 0 00:00:18
Export completed
. . .
Performing import of tables...
IMPDP> Master table "SYS"."TSPITR_IMP_bije_zgzC" successfully loaded/unloaded
IMPDP> Starting "SYS"."TSPITR_IMP_bije_zgzC":
. . .
IMPDP> . . imported "KLH"."HER_OBJECTS"              153.5 MB 1161968 rows
. . .
IMPDP> Job "SYS"."TSPITR_IMP_bije_zgzC" successfully completed at Thu Apr 13
08:41:58 2017 elapsed 0 00:00:18
Import completed
auxiliary instance file
/u01/app/oracle/aux/REL2018/datafile/o1_mf_undotbs1_dgyzwshv_.dbf deleted
auxiliary instance file
/u01/app/oracle/aux/REL2018/4CC71C26D0B22EC7E0550A0027E39010/datafile
    /o1_mf_system_dgyzwbg1_.dbf deleted
. . .
Finished recover at 13-APR-17
RMAN>
```

**NOTE**
*You can also recover tables using RMAN and save them directly to an Oracle Data Pump dump file, bypassing the target database.*

There are several things to note here:

- The recovery operation is very similar to any point-in-time RMAN recovery operation where RMAN creates a temporary auxiliary instance to perform the recovery, dropping the auxiliary instance and any temporary files after the recovery operation is complete.

- Using RMAN to restore and recover one or more tables uses Oracle Data Pump under the covers to perform the export and import using the auxiliary instance.

- RMAN fully supports the multitenant architecture—you can back up and recover individual PDBs, but for this kind of recovery operation, you have to connect directly to the CDB when launching RMAN.

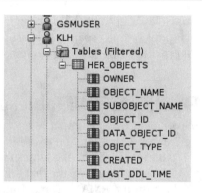

**FIGURE 6-2.** *Browsing the KLH schema in Oracle SQL Developer*

Looking at the KLH schema via SQL Developer in Figure 6-2, you can see that the MY_OBJECTS table has been successfully restored to a different schema with a different name, HER_OBJECTS.

# RMAN High Availability and Security Enhancements

Using RMAN should be at the top of your list for your backup and recovery strategy. It can perform any type of backup you'll need for any recovery scenario: full backups and two types of incremental backups supported by archived redo log files if your database is in ARCHIVELOG mode. You will often use other backup methods, such as Oracle Data Pump, for logical backups, but keep in mind that Oracle Enterprise Manager Cloud Control 13*c* Release 2 (Cloud Control) will use RMAN backups to recover individual tables with assistance from Data Pump. You might even make a cold backup of Oracle datafiles on occasion, but RMAN should be your primary backup and recovery tool whether you're managing a small departmental database in a virtual machine or a cluster of Exadata servers for an international e-commerce company.

In Oracle Database 12*c* Release 2, RMAN has been enhanced to increase your database availability and to make it easier to back up or migrate databases across different hardware and OS platforms or even sparse databases on engineered platforms such as Exadata. I'll provide a brief overview of these features in the following sections.

## Using RMAN to Duplicate TDE Tablespaces

If you have multiple platforms *and* you have tablespaces encrypted with TDE, Oracle Database 12*c* Release 2 eases your migration effort and minimizes downtime when copying or moving such tablespaces. Since the tablespace is encrypted, you must back up and restore the TDE key as well. So, the first thing you need to do is wrap the TDE key with a passphrase at the RMAN prompt, like this:

```
RMAN> set passphrase on identified by r45e0111;
```

To minimize downtime, you then perform an incremental RMAN level 0 backup with the ALLOW INCONSISTENT clause along with a series of incremental level 1 backups while the tablespace is still in READ WRITE mode. With one final incremental level 1 backup after the tablespace is put into READ ONLY mode, you will minimize the window during which the tablespace is not available for changes.

## Cross-Platform Transport Using RMAN

With the global nature of large organizations and their frequent acquisitions, it's rare for any larger organization to have the same version of Oracle Database on all of its servers, much less the same hardware and OS versions. For example, an organization may be using Intel-based servers in its data center, but its recently acquired former competitor may have all of its Oracle databases on Itanium servers, which have a different OS (but the same endian format). Because organizations in such scenarios want to maximize their return on investment from existing Oracle hardware, they demand support for cross-platform transport. Prior to Oracle Database 12*c* Release 1, they had to rely solely on tools such as Oracle Data Pump to migrate or copy databases.

Starting with Oracle Database 12*c* Release 1, you can use multitenant databases to make database migrations and cloning operations easier, but challenges with cross-platform movement of pluggable databases still exist in Release 1. To address these challenges, Oracle Database 12*c* Release 2 makes it much easier to use RMAN to migrate a PDB to a different platform (but with the same endian format). There are a few prerequisites for doing this kind of cross-platform migration:

- The COMPATIBLE parameter must be 12.2 or higher on both the source and target CDB.

- You must have both the XML metadata file and an RMAN backup of the source PDB.

- The source and target CDB must be on hardware with the same endian format.

The steps and commands you would use to do the actual clone operation are outlined as follows:

1. Close the PDB within RMAN.

2. Use the BACKUP PLUGGABLE DATABASE command with either the FOR TRANSPORT clause or TO PLATFORM clause to indicate that the backup will be used for a cross-platform operation.

3. Copy or move both the XML metadata and the backup file to a file system accessible to the target CDB.

4. At the target CDB, run the procedure DBMS_PDB.CHECK_PLUG_ COMPATIBILITY to ensure that the PDB you just backed up will successfully plug into the target CDB.

5. Run the RMAN RESTORE command with the FOREIGN PLUGGABLE DATABASE and FROM BACKUPSET clauses to plug in the PDB.

6. Open the PDB with the ALTER PLUGGABLE DATABASE . . . OPEN command as you would for any other PDB.

Note that the PDB is down while you're running the BACKUP command. If you want to minimize downtime, and your CDB is in ARCHIVELOG mode, use a series of inconsistent level 0 and 1 backups while the PDB is open, and then, when the activity in the PDB is somewhat low, shut down the PDB briefly to run one more incremental level 1 backup. This will almost certainly take less time than doing a full backup when the PDB is down.

# Backup and Recovery of Sparse Databases on Exadata

Sparse databases on Exadata (using disk groups specifically for storing snapshot copies of a database) have been available since Oracle Database 12c Release 1. Having sparse databases means that you can have several or even hundreds of different incarnations of a clone master that each have their own changes to the master.

What if you want to back up a sparse database on Exadata? You certainly don't want to back up the clone master along with your own local changes to the master. Therefore, in Oracle Database 12c Release 2, RMAN supports backups of only the deltas, and you can perform sparse backups at many different levels: datafile, tablespace, or the entire database. The only thing you have to do is add the SPARSE keyword like this:

```
RMAN> backup as sparse backupset tablespace users2;
```

Remember, you're not going to back up the entire USERS2 tablespace, just the changed table data in your sparse version of the database.

# Cloud Control, PDB Archives, and RMAN, Oh My!

This section presents a case study that combines a new feature of RMAN with Cloud Control to create a multitenant PDB archive to move a PDB from one CDB to another on the same or a different server. (Chapter 3 covers enhancements to Oracle Multitenant and Chapter 12 covers enhancements to Cloud Control 13*c*.)

In the following example, I demonstrate how to use RMAN within Cloud Control to move the pluggable database DEV02 in REL2018 to REL2017.

## Unplugging a PDB Using RMAN and Cloud Control

In Cloud Control, I navigate to the container database, which in this case is REL2018. From the Oracle Database drop-down list, I select Provision Pluggable Databases. This reveals several types of PDB operations, as shown in Figure 6-3.

I select the Unplug Pluggable Databases radio button and click Launch. In step 1 of the move (unplug) operation, I specify DEV02 as the PDB to be moved, as shown in Figure 6-4, and click Next.

Step 2 offers several ways to unplug, export, and move a PDB, as you can see in Figure 6-5. Oracle Database 12*c* Release 2 supports PDB archives (a single compressed file with all data and metadata), but not if the PDB is stored in Oracle Automatic Storage Management (ASM), so I'm selecting the next best option: a PDB metadata file and a full RMAN backup stored in an OS file system location. I'm using **/u01/app/oracle/pdbrman** to store both the backup DFB file and the XML metadata file. Any temporary files needed during the unplug operation will use **/tmp** for a working area. After selecting the PDB to be unplugged and migrated along with those OS file system locations, I click Next.

Step 3, shown in Figure 6-6, gives you the option to run the scheduler job either immediately or at a later date. To move this case study along to the final step, I selected Immediately and clicked Next. Figure 6-7 shows a summary of the job I'm about to submit, giving me one more chance to change things. Since everything looks good, I click Submit.

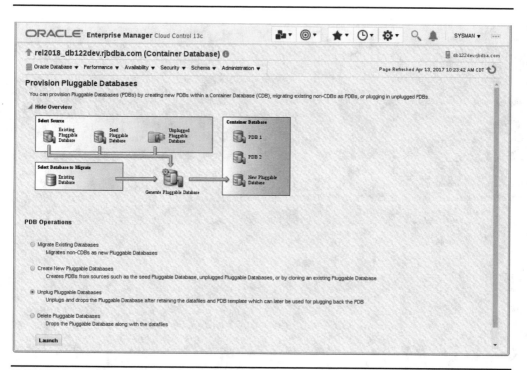

**FIGURE 6-3.** *Pluggable database provisioning options in Cloud Control*

I can monitor the progress of the job in real time as well. As shown in the Provisioning window in Figure 6-8, the unplug and drop of the PDB DEV02 has completed successfully with a detailed log. Looking in the location specified for the compressed RMAN backup and PDB metadata file, I can see that the two files are ready for plugging back into another container:

```
[oracle@db122dev /u01/app/oracle/pdbrman]$ ls -l
total 160968
-rw-r-----. 1 oracle dba 164823040 Apr 13 14:27 DEV02.dfb
-rw-r-----. 1 oracle dba      6523 Apr 13 14:27 DEV02.xml
[oracle@db122dev /u01/app/oracle/pdbrman]$
```

**FIGURE 6-4.** *Selecting the PDB to unplug*

In the next section, I'll show how to put PDB DEV02 back into a different CDB. The REL2017 CDB happens to reside on the same server, but it could easily be on another server in a different hemisphere since all I really need are those two files I created using Cloud Control and RMAN.

# Plugging In a PDB Using RMAN and Cloud Control

To plug the DEV02 PDB into REL2017, I navigate to the REL2017 database instance and select Oracle Database | Provisioning/Provision Pluggable Database. As shown in Figure 6-9, I select Create New Pluggable Databases and click Launch.

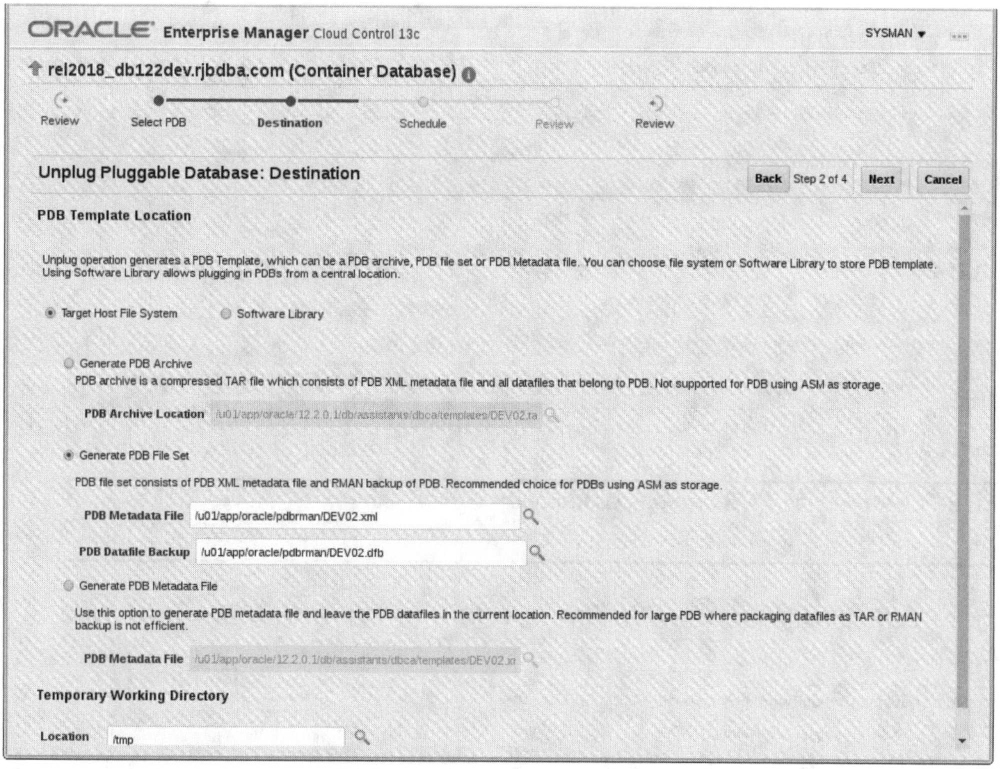

**FIGURE 6-5.** *Specifying PDB metadata and backup location for PDB file set*

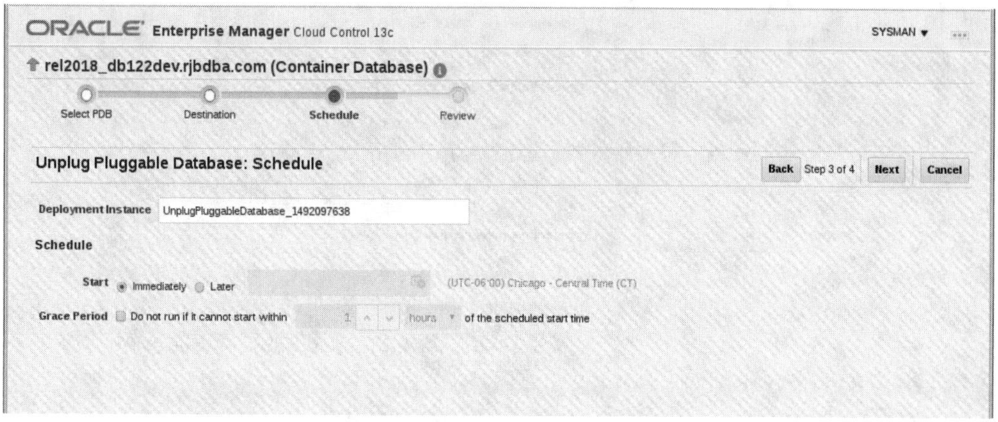

**FIGURE 6-6.** *Scheduling the PDB unplug job to start immediately*

**FIGURE 6-7.** *Reviewing PDB unplug parameters*

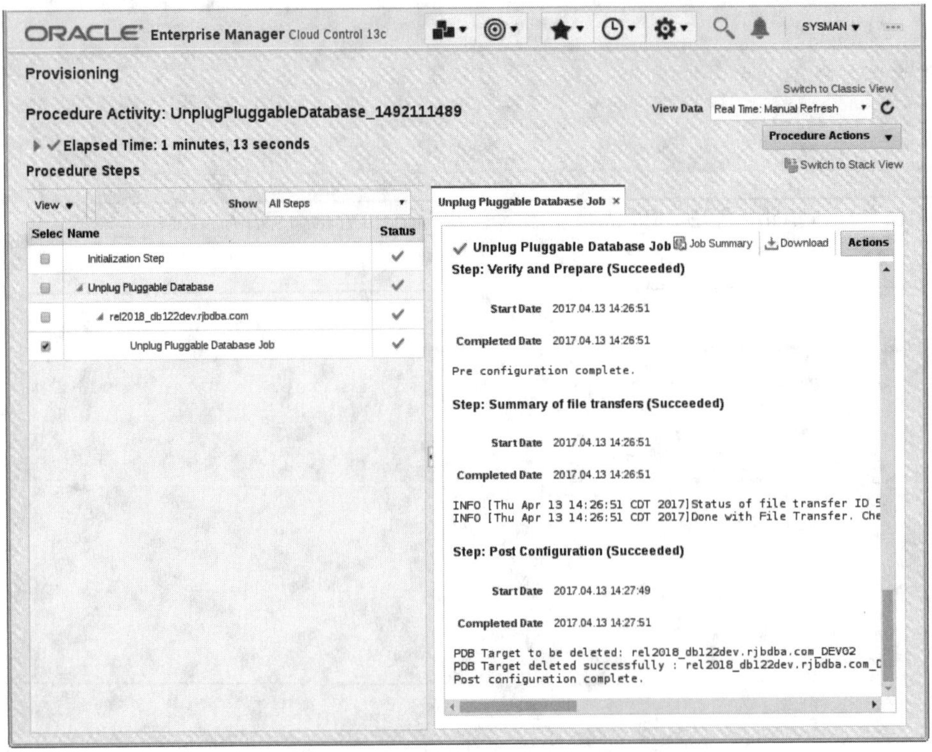

**FIGURE 6-8.** *Completion status of PDB unplug*

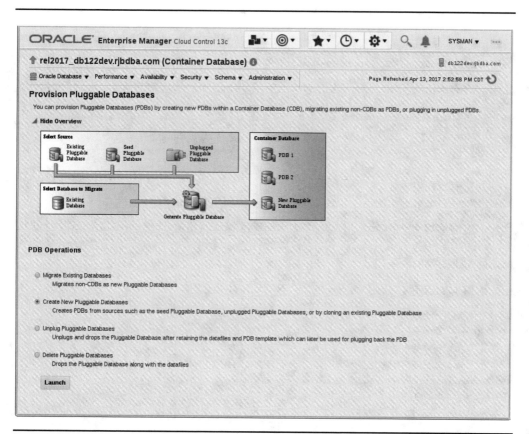

**FIGURE 6-9.**   *Launching the Create New Pluggable Database PDB operation*

Figure 6-10 shows the Create Pluggable Database window, where I have selected Plug an Unplugged PDB. The unplugged PDB is the XML metadata and the compressed RMAN backup created in the previous section.

In step 2, shown in Figure 6-11, I specify the new PDB name along with the PDB metadata and backup files, which are still at **/u01/app/oracle/pdbrman**.

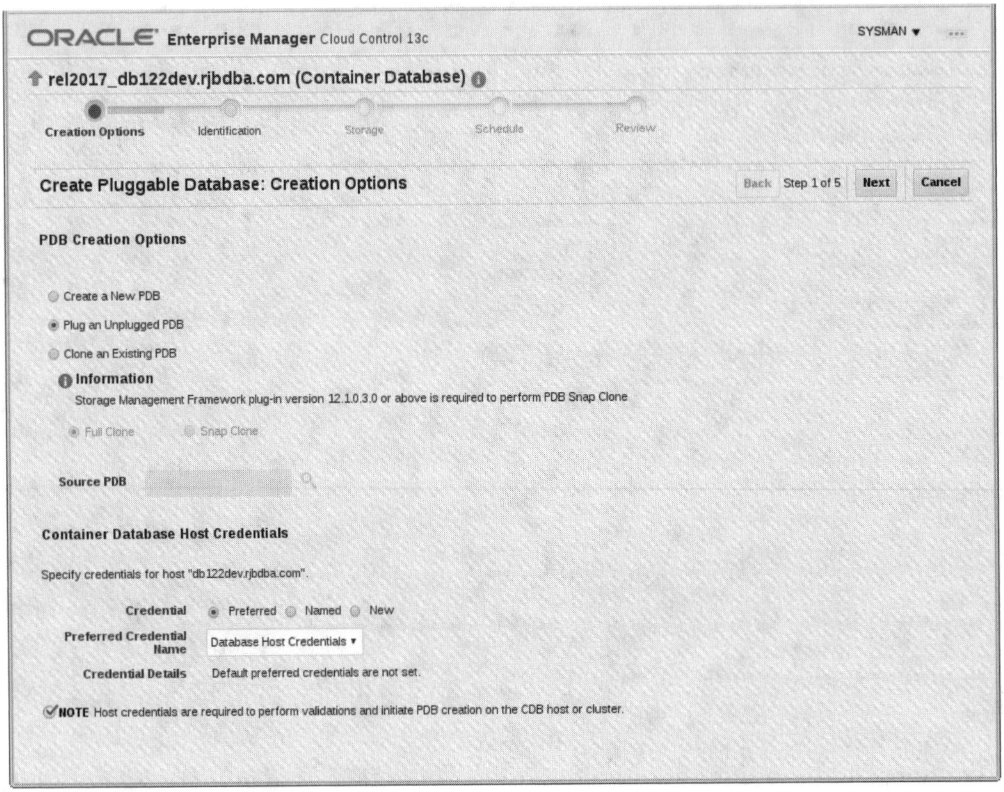

**FIGURE 6-10.** *Create Pluggable Database creation options*

After clicking Next, I add the additional details regarding where the plugged-in PDB will reside (in ASM in the +DATA disk group) and where to put the temporary files (**/tmp**), as shown in Figure 6-12. After providing these details, I click Next.

Step 4 shows a scheduling screen similar to that shown earlier in Figure 6-6, with the option to start the unplug PDB operation immediately or schedule it to run later. To complete this case study, I chose to run it immediately and clicked Next. Again, I have one more chance to change the job after confirming the details,

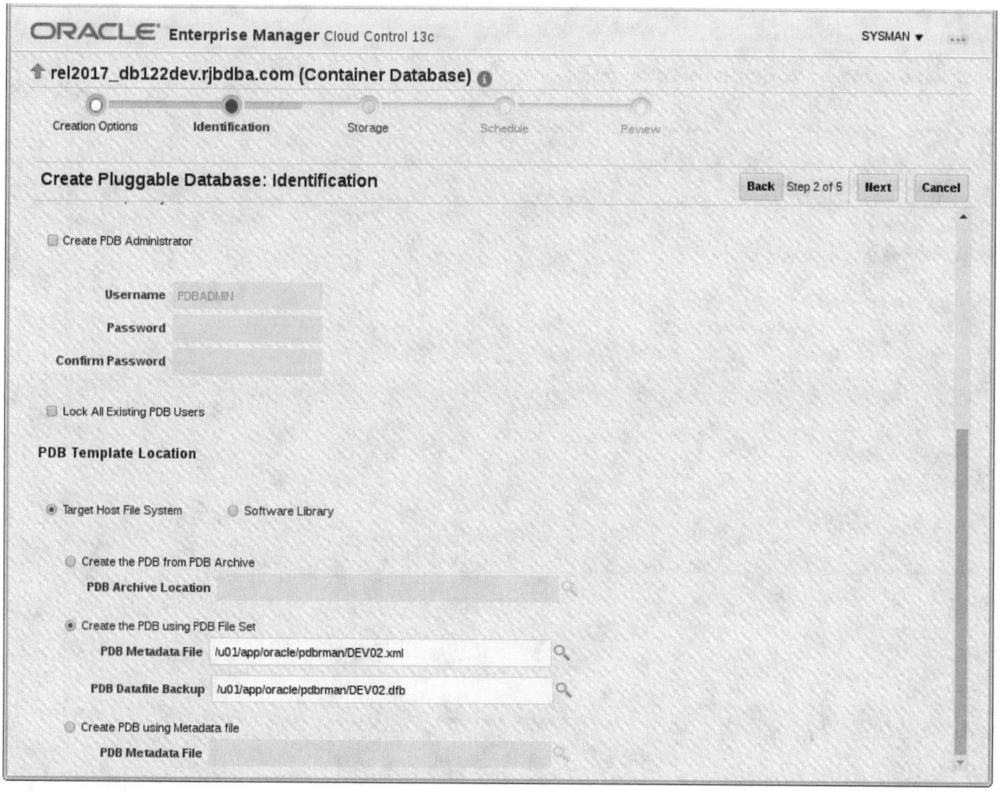

**FIGURE 6-11.** *Specifying PDB file set*

as shown in Figure 6-13. Note that the PDB Creation Options setting specifies an RMAN file set as input.

In Figure 6-13, I click Submit to start the import process. There are many more steps when you use Cloud Control to import a PDB created with RMAN—the status window in Figure 6-14 shows all the steps that Cloud Control performs under the covers for me (and which ones didn't need to be run!).

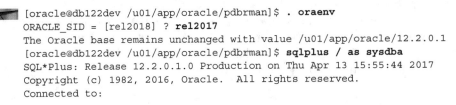

**FIGURE 6-12.** *Storage specification for PDB to be plugged in*

Looking inside the REL2017 CDB, I can see the newly plugged-in DEV02 PDB:

```
[oracle@db122dev /u01/app/oracle/pdbrman]$ . oraenv
ORACLE_SID = [rel2018] ? rel2017
The Oracle base remains unchanged with value /u01/app/oracle/12.2.0.1
[oracle@db122dev /u01/app/oracle/pdbrman]$ sqlplus / as sysdba
SQL*Plus: Release 12.2.0.1.0 Production on Thu Apr 13 15:55:44 2017
Copyright (c) 1982, 2016, Oracle.  All rights reserved.
Connected to:
```

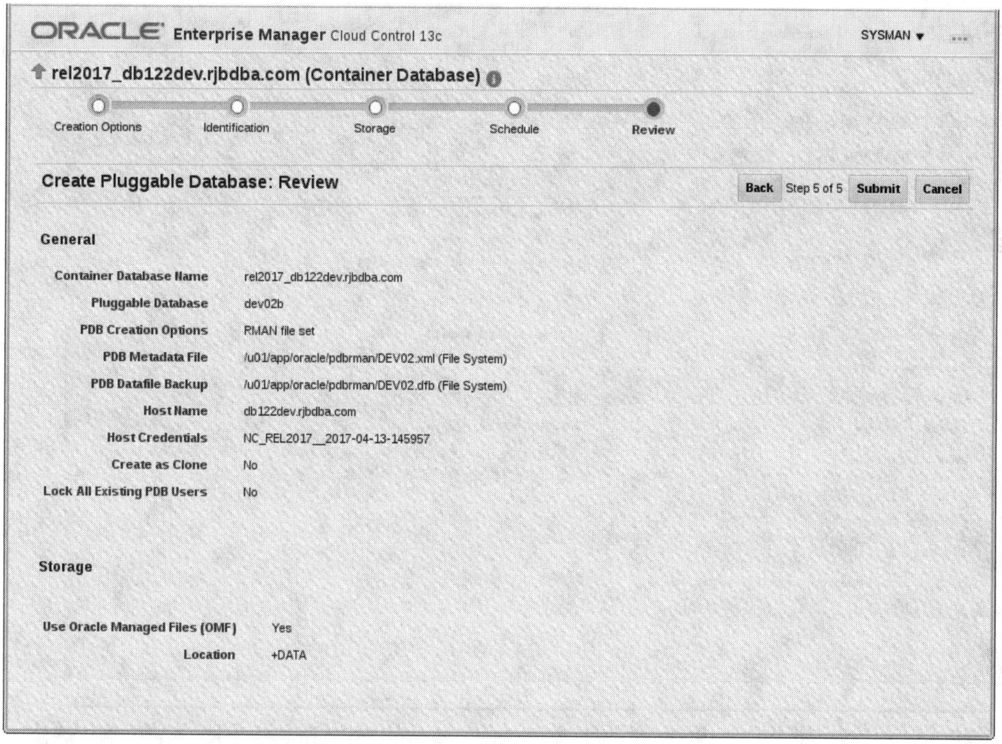

**FIGURE 6-13.**   *Reviewing parameters for PDB plug-in from RMAN datafile backup*

```
Oracle Database 12c Enterprise Edition Release 12.2.0.1.0 - 64bit Production
SQL> select name, open_mode, open_time, creation_time from v$pdbs;

NAME         OPEN_MODE  OPEN_TIME                            CREATION_TIME
-----------  ---------- ------------------------------------ -------------
PDB$SEED     READ ONLY  12-APR-17 10.15.06.853 PM -05:00     22-MAR-17
DEV01        READ WRITE 12-APR-17 10.15.17.676 PM -05:00     12-APR-17
DEV02        READ WRITE 13-APR-17 03.42.10.655 PM -05:00     13-APR-17
SQL>
```

ORACLE Enterprise Manager Cloud Control 13c    SYSMAN ▾

**Provisioning**

Switch to Classic View

Procedure Activity: CreatePluggableDatabase_1492116009    View Data  Real Time: Manual Refresh ▾ ↻

▶ ✓ Elapsed Time: 1 minutes, 59 seconds    **Procedure Actions** ▾

**Procedure Steps**    Switch to Stack View

View ▾    Show  All Steps ▾    | Pluggable Databases Creation × | Clone PDB - Post × | Prepare to configure ▶ ▾

| Selec | Name | Status |
|---|---|---|
| ☐ | Initialize | ✓ |
| ☐ | ▶ Create PDB Snapshot | |
| ☐ | ▶ Create PDB Profile | |
| ☐ | Create Snapshot - Prepare | |
| ☐ | PDB Metadata Violations | |
| ☐ | Clone Data Preparation | |
| ☐ | Update storage metadata | |
| ☐ | Clone PDB - Pre | |
| ☑ | ▶ Pluggable Databases Creation | ✓ |
| ☑ | Clone PDB - Post | ✓ |
| ☑ | Prepare to configure Data Encryption for new Pluggable Data | ✓ |
| ☐ | Import Wallet into new Pluggable Database | |

✓ **Pluggable Databases Creation**

Type  Parallel    Start Date  Apr 13, 2017 3:40:42
PM CDT

Elapsed Time  1 minutes, 47 seconds

Completed  Apr 13, 2017 3:42:29
Date  PM CDT

| S/N | Step Name | Status | Type |
|---|---|---|---|
| 1 | rel2017_db122dev.rjbdba.com | Succeeded | Database Instance |

**FIGURE 6-14.**  *PDB provisioning summary*

# Summary

New RMAN features in Oracle Database 12c Release 2 not only support the new features of multitenant databases but make it even easier to recover individual tables from an RMAN backup and give the recovered table a new name and schema location.

In a heterogeneous software and hardware environment, RMAN eases the transport of databases and individual tablespaces across platforms with minimal downtime. Even TDE tablespaces don't slow you down as long as you include the TDE key in the backup.

The case for using Enterprise Manager Cloud Control 13c Release 2 is strong even if you only need to manage a few databases and servers, given that Cloud Control automates PDB cloning and management within its user interface by leveraging both RMAN and Data Pump. You may never have to type another RMAN or Data Pump command again!

# CHAPTER
## 7

# Performance-Related
# New Features

When discussing "Oracle performance," it can mean one of a dozen different things. Regardless of how you describe Oracle performance, it usually boils down to optimizing your storage, ensuring that statistics are up to date, and leveraging your SGA and PGA as a first-tier storage device.

In this chapter, I'll first describe how index monitoring has been completely reinvented to provide a much higher level of granularity than previous incarnations of index monitoring. Next, I'll explain how the Optimizer Statistics Advisor can force you to stay "up to date" on Oracle statistics best practices by incorporating the best practices into maintenance window jobs. Finally, I'll discuss two memory-related enhancements: a new In-Memory feature that allows you to store more than just columns from a specific set of tables as well as controlling PGA memory usage on a per-session basis.

# Monitoring Index Usage

Inevitably, your database has too few indexes or too many. You want to have the best performance for your user queries by retrieving as few database blocks as possible to get the relatively small number of rows that would take much longer to retrieve if you used full table scans. Even if you err on the side of having more indexes, you need to keep in mind that indexes can take up a lot of disk space (sometimes they can be bigger than the table itself!) as well as require more CPU and I/O to maintain each index during DML statements (in particular during the nightly ETL window). For the sample table HR.EMPLOYEES, there are six indexes, shown in Figure 7-1. Depending on the types of reporting for the EMPLOYEES table, some of those indexes might be used very infrequently or not at all.

Since Oracle9*i* Database, up to and including Oracle Database 12*c* Release 1, Oracle has provided a somewhat rudimentary way to determine if an index is

| | INDEX_OWNER | INDEX_NAME | UNIQUENESS | COLUMNS |
|---|---|---|---|---|
| 1 | HR | EMP_JOB_IX | NONUNIQUE | JOB_ID |
| 2 | HR | EMP_NAME_IX | NONUNIQUE | LAST_NAME, FIRST_NAME |
| 3 | HR | EMP_EMAIL_UK | UNIQUE | EMAIL |
| 4 | HR | EMP_EMP_ID_PK | UNIQUE | EMPLOYEE_ID |
| 5 | HR | EMP_MANAGER_IX | NONUNIQUE | MANAGER_ID |
| 6 | HR | EMP_DEPARTMENT_IX | NONUNIQUE | DEPARTMENT_ID |

**FIGURE 7-1.**  *Default indexes for HR.EMPLOYEES*

being used or not with the MONITORING USAGE clause. You mark an index for
MONITORING like this:

```
alter index hr.emp_name_ix monitoring usage;
```

```
Index HR.EMP_NAME_IX altered.
```

Going forward, you query the V$OBJECT_USAGE dynamic performance view to
see if the index has been used or not:

```
select index_name,table_name,monitoring,used,start_monitoring
from v$object_usage
where index_name='EMP_NAME_IX';
```

```
INDEX_NAME       TABLE_NAME        MON USE START_MONITORING
---------------  ----------------  --- --- --------------------
EMP_NAME_IX      EMPLOYEES         YES NO  02/20/2017 09:27:22
```

There are a number of problems with this method. First, the indicator for the
index usage is only a binary indicator: either the index was used since 2/20/2017 or
it was not. That's not very granular. The index could have been used once by a report
writer who ran one ad hoc query and may never run that query again. That alone
would not be a justification for keeping that index. Worse yet, you don't even have
to run the query for the index monitoring flag to be set: if you run an EXPLAIN
PLAN on a query and the execution plan indicates that an index would be used to
run that query (and it might never be run!), the index monitoring flag will be set.

If you change index monitoring by running ALTER INDEX . . . NOMONITORING
USAGE, it will reset the flag, but that can be a labor-intensive and error-prone task.
The overhead for monitoring indexes can be significant using this method as well,
so it is not wise in Oracle Database 12c Release 1 to turn on index monitoring for
all indexes in the database at once!

**NOTE**
*The view V$OBJECT_USAGE still exists in Oracle
Database 12c Release 2 but is deprecated and is not
populated when an index is referenced.*

To address the index monitoring issue with a much more granular solution,
Oracle Database 12c Release 2 includes a new data dictionary view, DBA_INDEX_
USAGE, to monitor indexes over time, as well as a related dynamic performance
view, V$INDEX_USAGE_INFO.

# DBA_INDEX_USAGE

Oracle went from 0 to 60 in under 3 seconds on its index monitoring solution: DBA_INDEX_USAGE. This data dictionary view tracks every index, all the time. There is nothing to turn on or off, and it is very lightweight with negligible CPU overhead. Here is what the view looks like:

```
describe dba_index_usage
```

| Name | Null? | Type |
| --- | --- | --- |
| OBJECT_ID | NOT NULL | NUMBER |
| NAME | NOT NULL | VARCHAR2(128) |
| OWNER | NOT NULL | VARCHAR2(128) |
| TOTAL_ACCESS_COUNT | | NUMBER |
| TOTAL_EXEC_COUNT | | NUMBER |
| TOTAL_ROWS_RETURNED | | NUMBER |
| BUCKET_0_ACCESS_COUNT | | NUMBER |
| BUCKET_1_ACCESS_COUNT | | NUMBER |
| BUCKET_2_10_ACCESS_COUNT | | NUMBER |
| BUCKET_2_10_ROWS_RETURNED | | NUMBER |
| BUCKET_11_100_ACCESS_COUNT | | NUMBER |
| BUCKET_11_100_ROWS_RETURNED | | NUMBER |
| BUCKET_101_1000_ACCESS_COUNT | | NUMBER |
| BUCKET_101_1000_ROWS_RETURNED | | NUMBER |
| BUCKET_1000_PLUS_ACCESS_COUNT | | NUMBER |
| BUCKET_1000_PLUS_ROWS_RETURNED | | NUMBER |
| LAST_USED | | DATE |

Quite a few things to note here. This view tracks not only index usage but also the last time that the index was used. Therefore, even if the index has been accessed thousands of times, it might still be a candidate for retirement if the last time it was used was over a year ago (perhaps the application has been changed significantly in the last year, no longer requiring the index on a table).

It's even more granular than that: it's like a histogram for index usage. Each of the "buckets" in DBA_INDEX_USAGE accumulates a count for various levels of index access and rows returned. If an index has been accessed very infrequently but, when it is accessed, returns over 1000 rows, you may decide that some query tuning or application changes are required.

Last, but not least, note the distinction between TOTAL_ACCESS_COUNT and TOTAL_EXEC_COUNT. When running an EXPLAIN PLAN, an index will be marked as accessed but may not necessarily be used in the execution plan. Therefore, it's possible that TOTAL_ACCESS_COUNT could be very high but TOTAL_EXEC_COUNT could be close to zero. Conversely, an index could be used for every query running against a certain table, in which case the values of TOTAL_EXEC_COUNT and TOTAL_ACCESS_COUNT would be very similar.

In this example, the table called EMPLOYEES_HIST has over 1,000,000 rows and has a primary key index called PK_EMP_HIST on the column UPK:

```
describe employees_hist

Name            Null?    Type
------------    -------- ------------
UPK             NOT NULL NUMBER
EMPLOYEE_ID              NUMBER(6)
FIRST_NAME              VARCHAR2(20)
LAST_NAME       NOT NULL VARCHAR2(25)
EMAIL           NOT NULL VARCHAR2(25)
PHONE_NUMBER            VARCHAR2(20)
TERM_DATE       NOT NULL DATE
JOB_ID          NOT NULL VARCHAR2(10)
SALARY                  NUMBER(8,2)
```

The lookups in this table are almost always by the primary key UPK, as in this example:

```
select employee_id from employees_hist where upk in (500000,500010);
```

The execution plan shows that the index PK_EMP_HIST will be used to retrieve this row since we're retrieving only two rows out of over 1,000,000. That means we should see this index access in DBA_INDEX_USAGE:

```
select object_id,owner,name,total_access_count,
    total_exec_count,total_rows_returned,bucket_1_access_count,last_used
from dba_index_usage
where owner='HR';

OBJECT_ID  OWNER        NAME             TOTAL_ACCESS_COUNT TOTAL_EXEC_COUNT
---------- ----------   --------------- ------------------ ----------------
TOTAL_ROWS_RETURNED BUCKET_1_ACCESS_COUNT LAST_USED
------------------- --------------------- -------------------
    73682 HR           PK_EMP_HIST                       7                7
                27                         5 2017-02-23 08:14:29
```

A few things to note here. Since the index was created, it has been accessed five times and used in a query five times. Because it was a very selective index, retrieving only one or two rows at a time, the TOTAL_ROWS_RETURNED count is 27 across 7 executions that used the index. Finally, the index was last used on 2/23/2017. If you had been testing this index recently to determine how useful it is, then the LAST_USED column might not be very useful! If only there were a histogram for the LAST_USED dates too…maybe in Oracle Database 12.3!

**NOTE**
*To get the most accurate and complete index usage count, you must set the hidden parameter "_iut_ stat_collection_type" to ALL. Do not set hidden parameters without the advice of Oracle Support.*

## V$INDEX_USAGE_INFO

Remember that database views starting with V$ are called dynamic performance views. The *dynamic* part means that the views are not persistent—every time the database instance is restarted, the contents of the V$ views are cleared and are repopulated over time while the instance is open. The dynamic performance view V$INDEX_USAGE_INFO is no different, and it feeds into DBA_INDEX_USAGE, discussed in the previous section. It looks like this:

```
describe v$index_usage_info

Name                            Null? Type
------------------------------- ----- -------------
INDEX_STATS_ENABLED                   NUMBER
INDEX_STATS_COLLECTION_TYPE           NUMBER
ACTIVE_ELEM_COUNT                     NUMBER
ALLOC_ELEM_COUNT                      NUMBER
MAX_ELEM_COUNT                        NUMBER
FLUSH_COUNT                           NUMBER
TOTAL_FLUSH_DURATION                  NUMBER
LAST_FLUSH_TIME                       TIMESTAMP(3)
STATUS_MSG                            VARCHAR2(256)
CON_ID                                NUMBER
```

This view is updated when indexes are accessed, and is flushed to the Automatic Workload Repository (AWR) via the DBA_INDEX_USAGE view every 15 minutes. There isn't much granularity in this view, but a couple of columns are of interest:

```
select index_stats_enabled,index_stats_collection_type,
       active_elem_count,last_flush_time
from v$index_usage_info;

INDEX_STATS_ENABLED INDEX_STATS_COLLECTION_TYPE ACTIVE_ELEM_COUNT
    LAST_FLUSH_TIME
------------------- --------------------------- -----------------
                  1                           0                 1
-------------------------------
2017-02-23 10:59:40.599000000
```

The column INDEX_STATS_COLLECTION_TYPE with a value of 0 means that all index accesses are being recorded; a value of 1 means that index accesses are sampled. At this moment, there is one index access recorded in the column ACTIVE_ELEM_COUNT. That column will be set back to 0 after the next flush.

# Optimizer Statistics Advisor

Statistics on database tables and indexes, whether they be histograms, minimum and maximum values, row counts, or correlated, have been the key to optimal database performance for every version of Oracle Database that uses the cost-based optimizer (you shouldn't want or need to use the rule-based optimizer for any reason). Given the types of joins that Oracle can use even when you are joining only two tables, knowing the number of rows and the distribution of data for the join columns and predicates in the WHERE clause is key to a good execution plan. With bad cardinalities, a nested loop join on a 1-billion-row table when the optimizer only expected 10 rows means that you'll get a phone call at 3 A.M. when that critical report due tomorrow isn't finished yet.

Knowing that statistics are critical to a well-performing database, the next question is whether statistics are being kept up to date adequately using the default maintenance windows. Should statistics be collected on some tables more often than once a day—maybe several times during the day? Are statistics being collected too often? Oracle Database 12c Release 2 addresses this with the Optimizer Statistics Advisor (OSA). Figure 7-2 shows the components and inputs for the Optimizer Statistics Advisor.

Keep in mind that the Optimizer Statistics Advisor does not collect statistics itself—it only analyzes *how you are collecting statistics now* and suggests changes to your statistics collection strategy. In Figure 7-2, the DBA has set up manual statistics collection tasks that complement the automatic tasks that run in the default maintenance window. But the DBA might not be aware that the manual tasks or extra scheduled tasks may be redundant or that there are still tables that keep missing out on statistics collection. The busy DBA (which is *every* DBA) may not be aware of newer optimizer and statistics collection features. Newer Oracle recommendations for statistics collection include specifying AUTO_SAMPLE_SIZE for almost all statistics collection jobs. Many of the DBA's existing statistics collection jobs, having been set up in previous versions of Oracle Database, are likely specifying a sample size of 100 percent. This may be excessive and not beneficial for most tables.

Various other issues may plague the database and may be difficult or time consuming for the DBA to find. Table statistics may not be in sync with the table's indexes, causing more than expected fluctuations in elapsed time when an index is incorrectly chosen by the optimizer over a full table scan with the expectation that the index will drive fewer I/O requests.

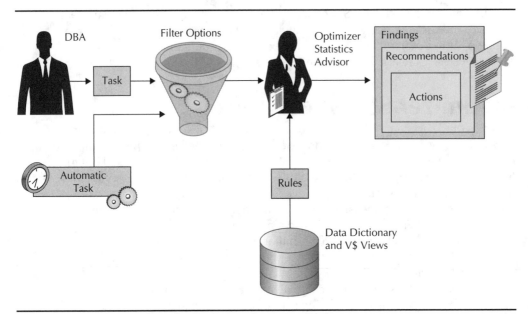

**FIGURE 7-2.** *Process flow for Optimizer Statistics Advisor*

The OSA automates many of the tasks that the DBA has been performing in previous releases of Oracle Database. Here are just a few of those tasks and features:

- When new statistics-related best practices are documented by Oracle with each release of Oracle Database, the OSA automatically incorporates those into its rule engine when analyzing the statistics collection in the database.

- The OSA generates findings, recommendations, and actions in HTML reports.

- The OSA provides scripts that can be run by the DBA to address findings and recommendations.

- By default, the OSA runs a task in the maintenance window called AUTO_STATS_ADVISOR_TASK once per day.

- The OSA is incorporated into the results of the SQL Tuning Advisor and the AWR reporting infrastructure.

- The OSA adds new procedures to DBMS_STATS to allow fine-tuning of the OSA analysis tasks.

- The OSA enables *filtering* of tasks or task results. For example, you may only want to see statistics staleness for a key subset of schemas.

**NOTE**
*The parameter STATISTICS_LEVEL must be set to
TYPICAL or ALL for the AUTO_STATS_ADVISOR_
TASK to run.*

The OSA framework is hierarchical in its deployment and use. Figure 7-3 shows the relationships between the OSA's components.

In the following sections, I'll go into more detail of each layer and how much interaction you'll have with each layer. Hint: It's a very automated process, as you've gathered by now, and if you're working too much in the rules layer, you're doing it wrong!

## Rules

The rules in the OSA often reflect new features in the current release, which further translates into recommended parameter settings. The OSA will tell you when you haven't followed the rules! Looking at the available rules is as easy as viewing the data dictionary view V$STATS_ADVISOR_RULES. This view doesn't have many columns, but it is a "parent" table from a data modeling perspective—the primary key of this table drives other tables and internal Oracle code to analyze the database for compliance with the rules. Here are the columns:

```
Name            Null?  Type
-----------     -----  -------------
RULE_ID                NUMBER
NAME                   VARCHAR2(64)
RULE_TYPE              VARCHAR2(9)
DESCRIPTION            VARCHAR2(150)
CON_ID                 NUMBER
```

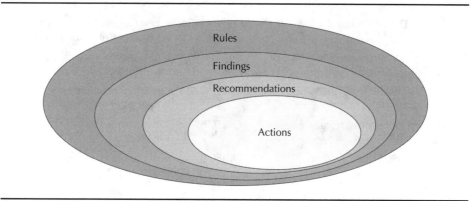

**FIGURE 7-3.** *Optimizer Statistics Advisor hierarchy*

In Oracle Database 12c Release 2 (12.2.0.1), there are only 24 rules, but they're big ones! The column RULE_TYPE can have one of three values:

- **SYSTEM** Preferences for statistics collection. Did you disable SQL Plan Baselines? Did all of your statistics jobs complete successfully?

- **OPERATION** Variations from defaults. Are you using the defaults for DBMS_STATS procedures?

- **OBJECT** Recommendations for specific types of objects or specific objects: volatile objects should have statistics locked, keeping table and index statistics updated together.

Here are the 24 rules. As you can see, most of the rule names are self-describing.

| RULE_ID | NAME | RULE_TYPE | DESCRIPTION |
|---------|------|-----------|-------------|
| 0 | | SYSTEM | |
| 1 | UseAutoJob | SYSTEM | Use Auto Job for Statistics Collection |
| 2 | CompleteAutoJob | SYSTEM | Auto Statistics Gather Job should complete successfully |
| 3 | MaintainStatsHistory | SYSTEM | Maintain Statistics History |
| 4 | UseConcurrent | SYSTEM | Use Concurrent preference for Statistics Collection |
| 5 | UseDefaultPreference | SYSTEM | Use Default Preference for Stats Collection |
| 6 | TurnOnSQLPlanDirective | SYSTEM | SQL Plan Directives should not be disabled |
| 7 | AvoidSetProcedures | OPERATION | Avoid Set Statistics Procedures |
| 8 | UseDefaultParams | OPERATION | Use Default Parameters in Statistics Collection Procedures |
| 9 | UseGatherSchemaStats | OPERATION | Use gather_schema_stats procedure |
| 10 | AvoidInefficientStatsOprSeq | OPERATION | Avoid inefficient statistics operation sequences |
| 11 | AvoidUnnecessaryStatsCollection | OBJECT | Avoid unnecessary statistics collection |
| 12 | AvoidStaleStats | OBJECT | Avoid objects with stale or no statistics |

| RULE_ID | NAME | RULE_TYPE | DESCRIPTION |
|---|---|---|---|
| 13 | GatherStatsAfterBulkDML | OBJECT | Do not gather statistics right before bulk DML |
| 14 | LockVolatileTable | OBJECT | Statistics for objects with volatile data should be locked |
| 15 | UnlockNonVolatileTable | OBJECT | Statistics for objects with non-volatile should not be locked |
| 16 | MaintainStatsConsistency | OBJECT | Statistics of dependent objects should be consistent |
| 17 | AvoidDropRecreate | OBJECT | Avoid drop and recreate object sequences |
| 18 | UseIncremental | OBJECT | Statistics should be maintained incrementally when it is beneficial |
| 19 | NotUseIncremental | OBJECT | Statistics should not be maintained incrementally when it is not beneficial |
| 20 | AvoidOutOfRange | OBJECT | Avoid Out of Range Histogram endpoints |
| 21 | UseAutoDegree | OBJECT | Use Auto Degree for statistics collection |
| 22 | UseDefaultObjectPreference | OBJECT | Use Default Object Preference for statistics collection |
| 23 | AvoidAnalyzeTable | OBJECT | Avoid using analyze table commands for statistics collection |

24 rows selected.

For example, rule 20, AvoidOutOfRange, will show you objects whose statistics may become stale quickly when key columns have timestamps and any low/high or histogram statistics could drive poor execution plans during the ETL to the data warehouse phase since the (stale) statistics may mislead the optimizer to think that there are no rows in the table with a given date or date range.

In summary, the rules fall into these three categories: how you should be gathering statistics, when to gather statistics, and how to optimize the efficiency of statistics gathering.

# Findings

The "findings" phase means that the OSA has examined the evidence, has sequestered the jury, and has decided if you have broken the rules or not. The sources for the findings include the statistics history in the data dictionary, the metrics gathered in the AWR, the log files from statistics gathering operations, and of course the existing state of statistics. You are very familiar with the location of statistics information: DBA_TAB_STATISTICS and DBA_TAB_COL_STATISTICS. Each finding references one of the 24 rules. However, as you might expect, especially with the object-level rules, a given rule may generate several or hundreds of findings.

# Recommendations

The OSA generates recommendations while running a scheduled task, which can be part of the auto-task framework or invoked manually at any time. These recommendations run the gamut from detecting obsolete settings to individual object recommendations. The data dictionary view you can use to view the recommendations is DBA_ADVISOR_RECOMMENDATIONS. Looking at one particular recommendation:

```
select owner, rec_id, task_name, finding_id, benefit_type
from dba_advisor_recommendations
where rec_id = 221;


OWNER          REC_ID TASK_NAME                      FINDING_ID BENEFIT_TYPE
----------- --------- ------------------------ ----------- -------------------
SYS              221 AUTO_STATS_ADVISOR_TASK            221 Use GATHER_SCHEMA_ST
                                                            ATS instead of GATHE
                                                            R_TABLE_STATS.
```

Apparently, some users are collecting statistics at the table level instead of the schema level, and the OSA is reminding them of that. Of course, these recommendations aren't always absolute—the developer may have had a very good reason to gather statistics on a specific table. If this is a legitimate frequent exception to the rule, you can filter out this particular recommendation going forward.

# Actions

In many cases, the recommendations generated by the OSA will be accompanied by SQL statements or a PL/SQL block to make it easier to implement the recommendation. The code to implement recommendations is stored in DBA_ADVISOR_ACTIONS. Not all recommendations have corresponding action code, however. Take the example in the previous section—the recommendation was to *not* do something. There is no code sample to prevent a developer from using a certain method for manual statistics gathering short of locking the developer out of the database! Other generated actions are more straightforward. If the current default statistics level is set to a fixed percentage instead of AUTO_SAMPLE_SIZE, the view DBA_ADVISOR_ACTIONS will have code to fix that. If one of the OSA actions is to set incremental statistics on a large partitioned table, the "fix code" will look something like this:

```
exec dbms_stats.set_table_prefs('HR', 'EMPLOYEE_HIST', 'INCREMENTAL', 'TRUE');
```

# In-Memory Enhancements

The Oracle In-Memory features introduced in Oracle Database 12c Release 1 were revolutionary, not evolutionary. In previous releases of Oracle Database, you could use memory-resident features such as pinning a table in the buffer cache or using the query result cache to take frequently referenced aggregate queries and keep them in a special memory area so that the aggregation process would not have to be repeated—assuming, of course, that the underlying table rows did not change.

In Oracle Database 12c Release 1, Oracle In-Memory takes one or more tables, or even specific columns of a table, and stores them in a special SGA area called, appropriately, the In-Memory cache. When these tables or columns are referenced in a query, the memory-resident versions of those tables or columns are used in the query, reducing the execution time by a factor of 10 or even 1,000 depending on the type of query and the number of rows needed from the In-Memory cache.

To ensure that In-Memory performs, Oracle Database 12c Release 1 leverages hardware features to process more than just one column at a time. To save space in memory (even with a terabyte of RAM, you still seem to run out of memory), Oracle In-Memory can use one of four levels of compression that trade CPU overhead for a smaller memory footprint.

There are some limitations to those features, however. First, In-Memory can only save actual table columns in memory, not virtual columns or expressions. In addition, if two memory-resident columns have different compression levels, they can't be used in a query join until they are uncompressed first. Finally, the contents of the In-Memory cache are lost when the database instance is shut down and restarted—but what if the table is truly read-only and it takes hours to repopulate?

Oracle Database 12c Release 2 addresses many of these limitations by adding two new types of columns that can reside in the In-Memory area and by giving you the option to persist an In-Memory area through an instance restart. The procedure DBMS_INMEMORY_ADMIN manages two of the new In-Memory features: In-Memory FastStart and In-Memory Expressions.

## Initialization Parameters

Oracle Database 12c Release 2 adds two new initialization parameters to support the new types of objects that can reside in the In-Memory cache: INMEMORY_EXPRESSIONS_USAGE and INMEMORY_VIRTUAL_COLUMNS.

The parameter INMEMORY_EXPRESSIONS_USAGE controls whether *any* types of expressions used in SELECT queries or JSON columns will be cached. The default is ENABLE. Numeric columns take up even less space when this parameter is set to ENABLE or STATIC_ONLY: other data types compress more effectively but now NUMBER columns can benefit from additional storage reductions as well.

The other new column, INMEMORY_VIRTUAL_COLUMNS, further refines what can be stored in the In-Memory area at the table level. It's likely that many of your tables have virtual columns that are used for a variety of purposes, such as for partitioning a table or hiding the business logic for a derived column used in a report. Allowing virtual columns to reside in the In-Memory cache avoids constant reevaluation and makes In-Memory joins on these columns possible too. The default for this column is MANUAL, meaning that you have to explicitly identify a virtual column as a candidate for In-Memory. Setting it to ENABLE means that all of a table's virtual columns are cached into the In-Memory area when the entire table or table partition is marked for In-Memory.

We'll talk more about these two parameters in the following sections when discussing specific new features.

## Dynamic Memory Area for In-Memory Objects

One of the limitations of the In-Memory feature in Oracle Database 12c Release 1 is that you can't change the memory allocated for In-Memory (either up or down) using the INMEMORY_SIZE parameter. You wouldn't want to allocate too little memory, knowing that you'd have a system downtime if newly added tables or columns needed to reside in the In-Memory area. Conversely, you wouldn't want to over-allocate memory for In-Memory objects since any unused memory in the In-Memory area could not be used for anything but table columns.

In Oracle Database 12c Release 2, you have much more flexibility and can change the value of the INMEMORY_SIZE parameter dynamically. You can now start out with INMEMORY_SIZE on the low end and keep as much memory available for the rest of the SGA objects (shared pool, buffer cache) until needed by In-Memory. Here, you add 2 GB to the In-Memory area:

```
SQL> show parameter sga_max_size

NAME                                 TYPE        VALUE
------------------------------------ ----------- --------------------------
sga_max_size                         big integer 40576M

SQL> show parameter inmemory_size

NAME                                 TYPE        VALUE
------------------------------------ ----------- --------------------------
inmemory_size                        big integer 10G

SQL> alter system set inmemory_size=12g;

System altered.
SQL>
```

There are a few restrictions when resizing In-Memory, but most of them make sense:

- In-Memory must be enabled (INMEMORY_QUERY=ENABLE).

- The COMPATIBLE parameter must be 12.2.0 or higher.

- You cannot decrease the value of INMEMORY_SIZE dynamically.

- You must be using an SPFILE to start the database.

- The increased size of the In-Memory area must be at least 128 MB.

If you are not using an SPFILE to start the database, you must edit your PFILE and restart the instance. Even if you are using an SPFILE, you must restart the instance if you want to decrease the value of INMEMORY_SIZE.

# New In-Memory Objects

Two new types of objects can reside in the In-Memory cache: query expressions and virtual columns. Your typical ad hoc or report query returns not only columns from one or more tables being joined but also the results of calculations against one or more columns. These calculations are generally arithmetic expressions (e.g., SALARY * 1.1) but can also be the result of single-row functions against one or more columns (e.g., COALESCE(LAST_NAME, FIRST_NAME, 'UNKNOWN'). The In-Memory cache now permits those types of expressions to be scanned and accessed just as quickly as any table column.

In addition, you may have one or more virtual columns defined on a table. These columns are now able to reside in the In-Memory cache. Virtual columns are very similar to query expressions in that some kind of transformation is occurring on another column in the same table, but there is a key distinction to query expressions: you don't want every expression for every query to be cached by In-Memory. Query expressions, therefore, must have a bit more infrastructure around them, including how Oracle tracks "hot" expressions and how you can make sure that Oracle thinks that one or more of your expressions should reside in the In-Memory cache regardless of how popular it is.

## Query Expressions

Query expressions, also known as In-Memory (IM) Expressions, add the full functionality of In-Memory columns to a wide range of expressions on table columns—and those table columns don't even have to be in the IM Expression itself. If the results of your frequently evaluated expressions are expensive to calculate, participate in a join condition for tables already using In-Memory, or are often a predicate in a WHERE clause, then those expressions are good candidates for IM Expressions.

An expression that's eligible for IM Expressions includes a combination of constants, single-row functions operating on table columns, arithmetic operators, and PL/SQL functions that return a value. Notice that columns are *not* eligible for IM Expressions— you can already put individual columns into the In-Memory cache using the existing ALTER TABLE syntax.

**NOTE**
*PL/SQL functions must be defined as DETERMINISTIC to be eligible for the In-Memory cache.*

Unlike tables whose columns are placed into the In-Memory cache by using the ALTER TABLE . . . INMEMORY MEMCOMPRESS statement, you use procedures in the DBMS_INMEMORY_ADMIN package to capture potential IM Expressions and populate the In-Memory cache. Here are the three procedures related to IM Expressions:

- **IME_CAPTURE_EXPRESSIONS**  Given a specific time range, identify the 20 most frequently accessed expressions across all queries recently executed in the database.

- **IME_POPULATE_EXPRESSIONS**  Take the expressions gathered by IME_CAPTURE_EXPRESSIONS and populate the IM Expression cache.

- **IME_DROP_ALL_EXPRESSIONS**  Remove all populated expressions from the IM Expression cache.

The workflow for using IM Expressions is very straightforward. IM Expressions are implemented as virtual columns in a table: we'll discuss explicitly defined virtual columns in the next section.

## Virtual Columns

Oracle virtual columns have been available for any of your tables since Oracle Database 10g. Virtual tables are somewhat like a row-level view: the virtual column occupies no space in the table itself (only the metadata in the data dictionary). The column is treated like any other column would in a join or report, except that the value of the column is calculated "on the fly" whenever the row is retrieved from the database. The obvious advantage to virtual columns is that no additional disk space is required, but on the flip side, the column's value must be recalculated every time it's accessed.

In Oracle Database 12c Release 1, virtual columns cannot be in the In-Memory cache even if you mark the entire table as INMEMORY. In Oracle Database 12c

Release 2, any expression including columns from the same table, SQL single-row functions, and user-defined functions declared as DETERMINISTIC can reside in the In-Memory cache right alongside the rest of the columns in the table. Once the virtual column is "materialized" in the In-Memory cache, it can participate in join operations and fast memory scans just like any column can.

However, what if you have a table with several virtual columns, but only want one or two to utilize the In-Memory cache? You can fine-tune the placement of virtual columns into the In-Memory cache by using the parameter INMEMORY_ VIRTUAL_COLUMNS. By default, this parameter is set to MANUAL, which means that when a table is marked as INMEMORY it leaves behind the virtual columns. However, you can still explicitly mark a virtual column for In-Memory use in the ALTER TABLE . . . INMEMORY MEMCOMPRESS statement. If you want virtual columns to automatically populate the In-Memory cache along with the rest of the table columns when the table itself is marked as INMEMORY, set INMEMORY_ VIRTUAL_COLUMNS to ENABLE.

**NOTE**
*In Oracle Database 12c Release 2, you can mark a regular or virtual column as INMEMORY without marking the table as INMEMORY.*

## In-Memory FastStart

You shouldn't have to restart your production database very often, but when you do, you lose all the information in the V$ views. Even worse, any tables or columns that occupied the In-Memory cache also have to be reloaded. Regardless of whether In-Memory tables are marked for high-priority population, on-demand, or just one column of that table, it could take minutes or even hours to get back the contents of the In-Memory tables given all the system activity that happens at startup. That results in yet another performance hit to queries that were relying on the contents of In-Memory.

If you have many tables residing in the In-Memory cache, and those tables rarely change, having the In-Memory cache repopulate more quickly is a huge advantage for the DBA who is already dealing with an unscheduled system restart. As a result, using the FastStart feature in Oracle Database 12c Release 2 you can designate a tablespace to hold the contents of the In-Memory cache that is continuously updated and available to repopulate the In-Memory cache when the instance is restarted.

Your initial thought may be that saving a copy of the In-Memory cache on disk is redundant or defeats the purpose of using In-Memory. However, the copy of the In-Memory cache on disk will occupy very little space—in fact, the amount of space occupied will be less than the size of your SGA. Once the FastStart area is updated after a new column or table is added to the In-Memory cache, there is virtually no activity against the tablespace until the database is restarted and the In-Memory cache can be reloaded from disk.

To manage the In-Memory FastStart functionality, you use several procedures in the DBMS_INMEMORY_ADMIN package:

- **FASTSTART_ENABLE**    Enable FastStart and assign a tablespace to hold the contents of the In-Memory cache.

- **FASTSTART_DISABLE**    Disable FastStart. The In-Memory cache will not be recoverable after an instance restart but the current state of the In-Memory cache is not changed.

- **GET_FASTSTART_TABLESPACE**    Identify which tablespace is being used for FastStart.

- **FASTSTART_MIGRATE_STORAGE**    Move the copy of the In-Memory cache and its associated metadata to another tablespace.

Note that for the FASTSTART_ENABLE procedure, you can specify whether the LOB used for FastStart is created with the LOGGING or NOLOGGING attribute, much like you would specify LOGGING or NOLOGGING for a table.

## Compress Join Groups

Much like the expression "no man is an island," it is often true that no table stands alone in a query: you'll more likely than not join that table to another. If all of those tables are marked as INMEMORY, you would assume that Oracle will perform the join completely from the In-Memory cache. However, if the compression types of the columns being joined are different, then a decompress operation must be performed before the join can occur. That's still faster than reading the rows from disk and joining them. In this example, a table has three different types of In-Memory compression defined:

```
select table_name, column_name, inmemory_compression
from v$im_column_level
where table_name='MY_OBJECTS';


TABLE_NAME       COLUMN_NAME            INMEMORY_COMPRESSION
---------------  ---------------------  --------------------------
MY_OBJECTS       OWNER                  FOR QUERY HIGH
MY_OBJECTS       OBJECT_NAME            FOR QUERY HIGH
MY_OBJECTS       SUBOBJECT_NAME         NO INMEMORY
MY_OBJECTS       OBJECT_ID              NO INMEMORY
MY_OBJECTS       DATA_OBJECT_ID         NO INMEMORY
MY_OBJECTS       OBJECT_TYPE            FOR QUERY LOW


select table_name, column_name, inmemory_compression
from v$im_column_level
where table_name='THEIR_OBJECTS';
```

| TABLE_NAME | COLUMN_NAME | INMEMORY_COMPRESSION |
|---|---|---|
| THEIR_OBJECTS | OWNER | FOR CAPACITY HIGH |
| **THEIR_OBJECTS** | **OBJECT_NAME** | **FOR CAPACITY HIGH** |
| THEIR_OBJECTS | SUBOBJECT_NAME | NO INMEMORY |
| THEIR_OBJECTS | OBJECT_ID | NO INMEMORY |
| THEIR_OBJECTS | DATA_OBJECT_ID | NO INMEMORY |
| THEIR_OBJECTS | OBJECT_TYPE | FOR QUERY HIGH |
| THEIR_OBJECTS | CREATED | DEFAULT |

If the OBJECT_NAME column is joined to another table that has an OBJECT_NAME column but defined with an In-Memory attribute of FOR ARCHIVE LOW, the join operation will be delayed because the column in both tables must be decompressed to perform the join operation.

Oracle Database 12c Release 2 solves this dilemma by using *join groups*. A new object called a common dictionary is created in the In-Memory cache to maintain the mapping between sets of columns that are frequently joined. The common dictionary is created the first time you create a mapping. Here is how you would create the mapping between the OBJECT_NAME table in MY_OBJECTS and THEIR_OBJECTS:

```
create inmemory join group obj_name
   (c##rjb.my_objects(object_name),c##rjb.their_objects(object_name));

Inmemory JOIN created.
```

Having the join group in place means that all operations occur directly on the compressed memory images. In addition, the join can use an array instead of building a hash table for the join. The data dictionary view DBA_JOINGROUPS shows that the join group has been instantiated:

```
select joingroup_name, table_name,
   column_name, gd_address
from dba_joingroups;
```

| JOINGROUP_NAME | TABLE_NAME | COLUMN_NAME | GD_ADDRESS |
|---|---|---|---|
| OBJ_NAME | MY_OBJECTS | OBJECT_NAME | |
| OBJ_NAME | THEIR_OBJECTS | OBJECT_NAME | |

# Per-Process PGA Limits

Sometimes the PGA does not get as much attention as it should and is treated by Oracle as a bit player in an off-Broadway musical. Even though the PGA per client session might never reach the theoretical limit of 2 GB, in aggregate the PGA is using up memory on the database server, sometimes at a rate that can exceed that of the entire SGA. I've seen occasions where the simultaneous allocation of PGA for dozens of query sessions has taken down the database server because the DBA thought he had set PGA_AGGREGATE_TARGET and PGA_AGGREGATE_LIMIT high enough. Even PGA_AGGREGATE_LIMIT can be exceeded on a rare occasion.

Oracle Database Resource Manager is now capable of managing the use of the PGA at the session level. When creating the plan directive, you can set the SESSION_PGA_LIMIT parameter to control how much PGA memory a given session assigned to a consumer group is allowed to use. So, depending on the consumer group, a given session's limit may well vary. This limit won't apply to background or system processes, though it can have impacts on parallel queries and any jobs running via the Oracle Scheduler.

# Summary

Many of the new performance features in Oracle 12c Release 2 appear at first glance to be extensions to existing features. But when you look more closely, many of these features don't even resemble the features they extend!

The Optimizer Statistics Advisor keeps you honest and up to date with all current Oracle best practices. When you wander from a solid statistics collection configuration, Optimizer Statistics Advisor will even give you scripts to get your objects and statistics collection tasks back on track.

Index monitoring in Oracle Database 12c Release 2 is no longer a "yes/no" flag for each index. Each index now has a multitude of statistical information available on a continuous basis: how often it is accessed, how many rows were retrieved for each execution plan using the index, and when the index was used last. Having this metadata makes it much easier to decide if the index is worthy of the space it's using on disk.

The In-Memory enhancements let you add new types of objects in addition to table columns. Virtual columns defined on a table can be added to the In-Memory cache one at a time or all at once. Frequently accessed expressions, called IM Expressions, are tracked on a continuous basis and can be populated into the In-Memory cache on demand. IM Expressions are much like virtual columns except that IM Expressions are not explicitly tied to a table and populate the In-Memory cache based on a popularity contest! The more often a query expression is referenced in a given timeframe, the more likely it is to end up as an IM Expression when you run the IME_POPULATE_EXPRESSIONS procedure.

Last, but not least, you can use the Resource Manager to more tightly control how much PGA a given session can use. PGA_AGGREGATE_LIMIT is just not granular enough to effectively allocate and manage one of the most critical memory areas in your database.

# CHAPTER
## 8

# Compression
# and Archiving

I n this chapter, we focus on three new features that mainly relate to expanded database capability, compression, and archiving of data:

- NFS server in the database

- New Oracle Advanced Index Compression type

- Improvements to Hybrid Columnar Compression (HCC) on Exadata

The use of these new features provides greater flexibility in implementation, eases administration, and reduces storage costs. With the NFS server feature, you add a high-availability component to NFS that you might not have in a traditional NFS server environment.

# NFS Server in the Database

Oracle Database 12c Release 2 can now be used as an NFS server. Files and their related metadata can be stored in the database. This opens the opportunity to store files, such as Bash and SQL scripts, in the database. Those files can then be replicated and manipulated using database technologies such as PL/SQL and Java stored procedures.

Clients on other servers and desktops use a standard NFS **mount** command to access the exported file system. At the OS level, the Oracle database responds directly to requests from the NFS daemon in the OS kernel.

Notice that the Oracle documentation uses OFS and NFS somewhat interchangeably. NFS is the industry standard for network file system sharing (thus the acronym). Oracle provides a combination of OS features in Oracle File System (OFS): creating file systems, mounting file systems, dropping file systems, and making those file systems available via the NFS functionality native to the OS.

To create the file system to export, you need something for OFS to export via the DBMS_FS package, such as an Oracle Database File System (DBFS), so first we'll review how DBFS works before setting up NFS. DBFS has been available since Oracle Database 11g, but it has its own set of enhancements in Oracle Database 12c Releases 1 and 2.

## Prerequisites for Setting Up an NFS Server in the Database

These are the prerequisites to installing an in-database NFS server:

- To provide NFS access, you must have a DBFS file system already created.

- The client(s) must be able to mount the file systems you'll be exporting with NFS server.

- For Oracle Database 12c Release 2, OFS is only available for Solaris and Linux:

  - For Linux, the kernel module found in the **fuse** package must be installed.

  - For Solaris, the kernel module is found in **libuvfs.so**.

Keep in mind that DBFS already had many of the features of NFS but required Oracle-specific tools and drivers to access the files in DBFS. With an in-database NFS server, no additional tools are required for any remote server or PC that has a generic, industry-standard NFS client installed.

# Creating a DBFS File System

Creating a DBFS file system using Oracle Database 12c Release 2 is even easier than in previous releases. Remember that DBFS creates a file system within an Automatic Storage Management (ASM) disk group and exposes it at the OS level to look like another mount point. Once the DBFS file system is ready, you can set up the NFS server next. Before all else, however, you need to install the **fuse** package, as described next, to allow mounting the DBFS file system on Linux.

### Installing Kernel Modules for fuse

To install the **fuse** RPM package to use DBFS, install it with **yum**:

```
[root@db122dev ~]# yum install fuse fuse-libs kernel-devel
. . .
Installed:
  kernel-devel.x86_64 0:3.10.0-514.10.2.el7
Complete!
```

Verify that the **fuse** group exists and add the **oracle** user to that group:

```
[root@db122dev ~]# grep fuse /etc/group
fuse:x:981:
[root@db122dev ~]# usermod -a -G fuse oracle
[root@db122dev ~]# grep fuse /etc/group
fuse:x:981:oracle
[root@db122dev ~]#
```

Finally, make sure your Linux library directory can find the module **libfuse.so**:

```
[root@db122dev ~]# cd /usr/local/lib
[root@db122dev lib]# locate libfuse.so
/usr/lib64/libfuse.so.2
/usr/lib64/libfuse.so.2.9.4
[root@db122dev lib]# pwd
/usr/local/lib
[root@db122dev lib]# ln -s /usr/lib64/libfuse.so.2 libfuse.so
[root@db122dev lib]#
```

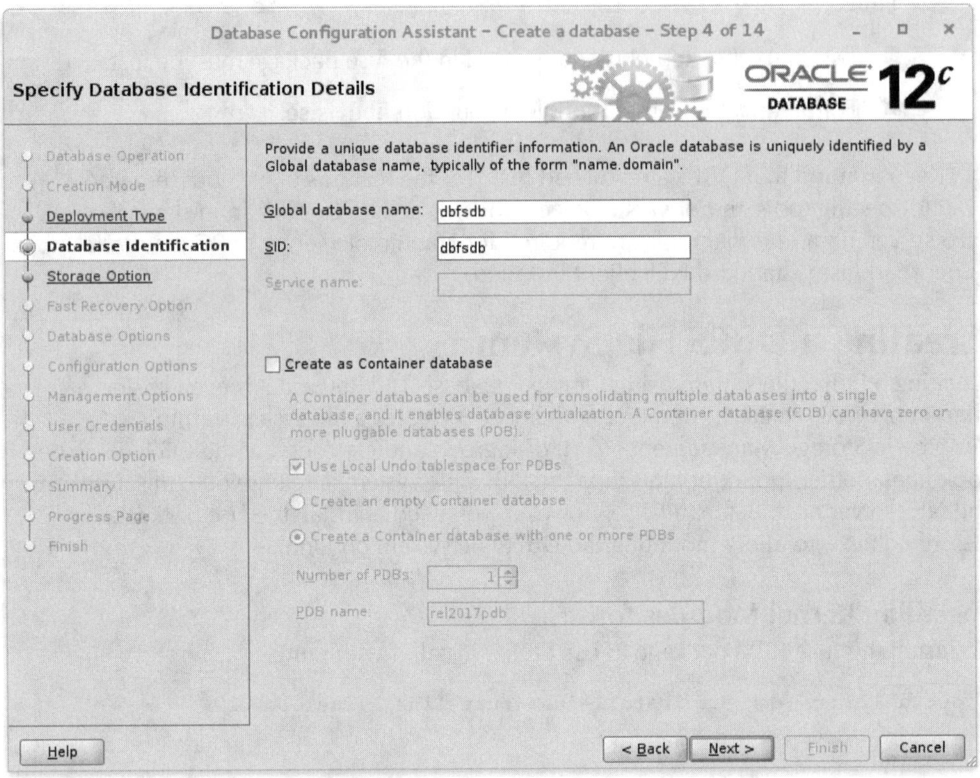

**FIGURE 8-1.** *Creating a database for DBFS*

## Create a Database for DBFS

A standalone, non-CDB database is required to host DBFS. Use the Database Configuration Assistant (**dbca**) to create the database. Figure 8-1 shows the creation of a non-CDB named DBFSDB.

## Creating the DBFS Tablespace and File System

Setting up a user to manage DBFS is straightforward and needs to be done only once. You can create a DBFS file system in an existing ASM disk group, but in this case I've dedicated a disk group called DBFS_FS to host DBFS. Here are the commands:

```
create tablespace dbfs_ts
    datafile '+dbfs_fs' size 500m autoextend on next 500m maxsize 10g;
create user dbfs_owner identified by dbfs_owner
```

```
default tablespace dbfs_ts quota unlimited on dbfs_ts;
grant create session, resource,
    create table, create view, create procedure, dbfs_role to dbfs_owner;
```

The next step happens at the OS level by running the SQL script **dbfs_create_ filesystem.sql**. You connect as the user DBFS_OWNER and specify the tablespace you created to hold the DBFS files as well as the external name of the file system— in this case it is FS122:

SQL> **@$ORACLE_HOME/rdbms/admin/dbfs_create_filesystem.sql dbfs_ts FS122**
No errors.
SQL>

The script **dbms_create_filesystem.sql** simplifies your work by calling these procedures and steps:

- **DBMS_DBFS_SFS.CREATEFILESYSTEM**   Create the file system

- **DBMS_DBFS_CONTENT.REGISTERSTORE**   Register the content store

- **DBMS_DBFS_CONTENT.MOUNT**   Mount the file system

- **DBMS_FUSE.FS_CHMOD**   Permissions on file system

Now that the DBFS file system is in place, present it to the OS file system using the **root** account:

```
[root@db122dev ~]# mkdir /u02dbfs
[root@db122dev ~]# chown oracle:dba /u02dbfs
[root@db122dev ~]#
```

Next, as the **oracle** user, mount the DBFS file system using the **dbfs_client** command with the DBFS database owner DBFS_OWNER:

```
[oracle@db122dev]$ dbfs_client dbfs_owner/dbfs_owner@db122dev/dbfsdb /u02dbfs
Password:
```

Enter the password for the DBFS_OWNER account (again). The session appears to hang—but remember that the DBFS client is running in this session. You can set this up as a background process on server startup using an Oracle Wallet, but that is beyond the scope of this chapter; you can use a spawned process with a password file as well:

```
[oracle@db122dev]$ nohup dbfs_client
    dbfs_owner/dbfs_owner@db122dev/dbfsdb /u02dbfs < dbfs_pass.txt &
```

Moving on to NFS, you can see from the following session that the file system is in place and you can create files there. The files are actually stored in ASM.

```
[oracle@db122dev /home/oracle]$ df
Filesystem                             1K-blocks     Used  Available Use% Mounted on
/dev/mapper/ol-root                    43273580  28249284  15024296  66% /
. . .
dbfs-dbfs_owner@db122dev/dbfsdb:/      10484736       128  10484608   1% /u02dbfs
[oracle@db122dev /home/oracle]$ ls -la /u02dbfs
total 4
drwxr-xr-x.  3 root root     0 Mar 23 11:40 .
dr-xr-xr-x. 20 root root  4096 Mar 23 10:07 ..
drwxrwxrwx.  3 root root     0 Mar 23 09:46 FS122
[oracle@db122dev /home/oracle]$ cp /etc/oratab /u02dbfs/FS122/temp.tab
[oracle@db122dev /home/oracle]$ ls -l /u02dbfs/FS122
total 1
-rw-r--r--. 1 oracle oinstall 889 Mar 23 11:41 temp.tab
[oracle@db122dev /home/oracle]$
```

Notice that the subdirectory **FS122** under **/u02dbfs** is the name we gave to the DBFS file system when we ran **dbfs_create_filesystem.sql**.

## Installing NFS Server in the Database

To use an in-database NFS server, you need to enable OFS at the OS level first. To enable OFS, you simply need to "make" the corresponding file:

```
cd $ORACLE_HOME/rdbms
make ofs_on
```

To disable OFS:

```
cd $ORACLE_HOME/rdbms
make ofs_off
```

At the database level, you use the DBMS_FS PL/SQL package to manage the OFS and DBFS mount points.

## Using the NFS Client Interface

The DBMS_FS package contains four procedures that create, mount, unmount, and destroy an Oracle File System. To use this package, the user needs to have SYSDBA administrative privilege in the database and root permissions on the operating system. The following are some examples of using the procedure in the DBMS_FS package and their related parameters.

The first step is to create an Oracle File System (OFS) using the MAKE_ORACLE_FS procedure. Here, I'm creating a file system of type **ofs** and a name of **fs122dev** and storing it in the tablespace DBFS_TS:

```
begin
    dbms_fs.make_oracle_fs (
        fstype => 'ofs',
        fsname => 'fs122dev',
        mount_options => 'tablespace=dbfs_ts');
end;
/
```

Table 8-1 gives a more detailed description of each parameter to MAKE_ORACLE_FS. To mount the file system, I'll use the mount point **/u01/app/oracle/u03dbfs2**, which already exists:

```
[oracle@db122dev /home/oracle]$ ls -l /u01/app/oracle
drwxr-xr-x. 13 oracle oinstall 4096 Mar 22 20:32 12.2.0.1
drwxrwx---.  6 oracle oinstall   97 Mar 22 17:37 oraInventory
drwxr-xr-x.  2 oracle oinstall    6 Mar 25 09:46 u03dbfs2
[oracle@db122dev /home/oracle]$
```

Run the procedure DBMS_FS.MOUNT_ORACLE_FS to mount the new OFS file system:

```
begin
    dbms_fs.mount_oracle_fs (
    fstype => 'ofs',
    fsname => 'fs122dev',
    mount_point => ' /u01/app/oracle/u03dbfs2',
    mount_options => 'default_permissions, allow_other, persist');
end;
/
```

| Parameter | Description |
|---|---|
| FSTYPE | File system type. Enter **ofs** to create an OFS file system, **dbfs** for a DBFS file system. |
| FSNAME | Name of the file system. Enter a string no longer than 256 characters, using alphanumeric characters. |
| FSOPTIONS | Specify an existing tablespace to use for the OFS file system, using the following format:<br>"tablespace=tablespace_name"<br>The tablespace that you specify must exist prior to use. |

**TABLE 8-1.** *MAKE_ORACLE_FS Parameters*

| Parameter | Description |
|---|---|
| FSTYPE | File system type. Valid options are<br>    DBFS<br>    OFS |
| FSNAME | Name of the file system. Enter a string no longer than 256 characters, using alphanumeric characters. |
| MOUNT_POINT | Local directory where the file system should be mounted. This directory must already exist. Enter an absolute path. The maximum number of mount points that you can create is 64. |
| MOUNT_OPTIONS | Comma-separated mount options, listed in Table 8-3. |

**TABLE 8-2.**   *MOUNT_ORACLE_FS Parameters*

Table 8-2 shows the rest of the options available; Table 8-3 has the various mount options for the file system.

| Parameter | Description |
|---|---|
| DEFAULT_ PERMISSIONS | Enables permission check and restricts access based on file mode. This option is useful with the **allow_other** mount option. |
| ALLOW_ OTHER | Allows other users apart from the operating system user that did the mount to access the files. This is used in conjunction with permission checks to determine the file access. This option requires setting the **user_ allow_other** parameter in the **/etc/fuse.conf** configuration file on Linux. |
| MAX_READ | Maximum size of the read operation. No maximum size is set by default. |
| MAX_WRITE | Maximum write size in a single request. The default is 128K. |
| DIRECT_IO | Indicates to the operating system kernel to not use file system cache. |
| NOPERSIST | Does not store the mount options for use in the next instance startup. |
| PERSIST | Stores the mount entry persistently so that on subsequent instance startup it is automatically mounted again. |
| RO | Mounts the file system in READ-ONLY mode. Files cannot be modified. |
| RW | Mounts the file system as READ-WRITE. This is the default. |
| NOSUID | Specifies that the file system cannot contain set userid files. |
| SUID | Specifies that the file system can contain set userid files. This is the default. |

**TABLE 8-3.**   *Mount Options for MOUNT_ORACLE_FS Procedure*

| Parameter | Description |
|---|---|
| FSNAME | Name of the file system. Enter a string no longer than 256 characters, using alphanumeric characters. |
| MOUNT_ POINT | Local directory where the file system has been mounted. Enter an absolute path. |
| UNMOUNT_ OPTIONS | Optionally, enter **force** to unmount the file system forcibly. This setting prevents new requests from being sent to the file system. All pending requests on the file system are either completed or cancelled. If you omit this setting, then attempts to unmount a busy file system cause an EBUSY error. |

**TABLE 8-4.** *UNMOUNT_ORACLE_FS Parameters*

Unmounting the file system at some point is inevitable, so use the procedure DBMS_FS.UNMOUNT for that, as shown next. Table 8-4 has the full parameter list.

```
begin
dbms_fs.unmount_oracle_fs (
    fsname => 'fs122dev',
    mount_point => '/u01/app/oracle/u03dbfs2',
    unmount_options => 'force');
end;
/
```

Once unmounted, you can drop the file system as easily as you created it:

```
begin
    dbms_fs.destroy_oracle_fs (
    fstype => 'ofs',
    fsname => 'fs122dev');
end;
/
```

Table 8-5 shows the parameters available for DESTROY_ORACLE_FS. Overall, this is much easier to manage than DBFS.

Having an in-database NFS server allows for greater design flexibility by storing files and their related metadata in the database. This new feature combined with either Oracle Data Guard or Oracle GoldenGate opens up new opportunities for replicating files and ensuring high availability.

| Parameter | Description |
|-----------|-------------|
| FSTYPE | File system type. Valid options are |
| | DBFS |
| | OFS |
| FSNAME | Name of the file system. |

**TABLE 8-5.** *DESTROY_ORACLE_FS Parameters*

## Tuning NFS Server in the Database

There is one parameter related to an in-database NFS server, OFS_THREADS, which controls the initial number of worker threads that are started (the default is 4). As server load increases, additional threads are automatically started. You can adjust the OFS_THREADS parameter with the ALTER SYSTEM command, as shown in this example:

```
SQL> alter system set ofs_threads=12 scope=both;
```

The value for OFS_THREADS in a RAC environment should be the same across all instances; you can set this parameter only in a Linux environment.

## OFS Dynamic Performance and Data Dictionary Views

The primary dynamic performance view you use with OFS is V$OFSMOUNT. The data dictionary view USER_DBFS_HS_FILES shows the files in the mounted OFS file system owned by the current user. These files are also visible from the OS.

# Using Advanced Index Compression

In Oracle Database 12c Release 2, Advanced Index Compression has another option in addition to COMPRESS ADVANCED LOW; you can now also specify COMPRESS ADVANCED HIGH. This new option for index compression compresses at a higher compression ratio than in Oracle Database 12c Release 1. Of course, this greater compression ratio comes at a cost of CPU overhead. It is also necessary to set the database parameter COMPATIBLE to 12.2.0 or higher to use this new feature.

This section quickly reviews the index compression types available in previous releases before diving into the latest compression enhancements. Index compression has been available since Oracle8i Database as a deduplication mechanism, but it wasn't until Oracle Database 12c Release 1 that Oracle completely reinvented index compression. Of course, you can still use the previous index compression methods—in fact, that is your only option if you don't have the license for Advanced Index Compression.

## Using COMPRESS in Oracle Database 11*g*

The COMPRESS option for most index types has been available since Oracle8*i* Database and operates much like Advanced Index Compression works on heap tables: it coalesces duplicate index values in leaf blocks. It's a *logical* deduplication of index entries, not a binary compression of the index block. The COMPRESS clause in a CREATE INDEX statement defaults to all columns in the index for a nonunique index, and defaults to all columns except the last one for a multikey unique index. An example of two indexes compressed with the COMPRESS clause on a copy of the DBA_OBJECTS table shows how well (or how poorly) the legacy compression algorithm works. As a prerequisite to the discussion on Advanced Index Compression, let's create a few indexes on that table, one multicolumn unique index and one nonunique index on a couple of columns with many duplicate values:

```
create table my_objects_no_ci as select * from dba_objects;
create unique index ak1_my_objects_no_ci
   on my_objects_no_ci(owner,object_name,subobject_name,object_id);
create index ie1_my_objects_no_ci
   on my_objects_no_ci(object_type,status);

create table my_objects_with_ci as select * from dba_objects;
create unique index ak1_my_objects_with_ci
on my_objects_with_ci(owner,object_name,subobject_name,object_id) compress;
create index ie1_my_objects_with_ci
   on my_objects_with_ci(object_type,status) compress;

select index_name,leaf_blocks
from dba_indexes
where index_name like '%MY_OBJECTS%'
order by index_name;

INDEX_NAME                  LEAF_BLOCKS
------------------------- -----------
AK1_MY_OBJECTS_NO_CI               566
AK1_MY_OBJECTS_WITH_CI             622
IE1_MY_OBJECTS_NO_CI               267
IE1_MY_OBJECTS_WITH_CI             112
```

The results are not too surprising—unique or primary keys won't compress well or will even get larger! Indexes with many duplicates will compress very well, especially with duplicates on the trailing column of the index.

Although the CPU overhead is somewhat low for using the COMPRESS clause and can significantly reduce index storage space requirements, it has a couple of downsides.

As you can see in the previous examples, it doesn't help at all with unique or primary key indexes. You might have a multicolumn index that has lots of duplicates on the leading edge of the index or only occasional groups of rows whose trailing index column is duplicated. Daily changes to the indexed table may favor a COMPRESS level of 3 one day, but COMPRESS level 2 another day. As in the previous example, your index may even be *larger* with compression! In those cases, you get limited compression benefits. Oracle Advanced Index Compression addresses all of these issues.

## Using COMPRESS ADVANCED LOW in Oracle Database 12c Release 1

Oracle Database 12c Release 1 introduced a new type of index compression called Advanced Index Compression. It made index compression more automated because you no longer had to guess how many prefix columns you needed for any given index: Oracle figures out the optimal number of prefix columns on a *block by block basis*. Some index blocks may not compress at all. Thus, it's rare that an index compressed in Oracle Database 12c Release 1 will grow larger. Following our previous example, let's re-create those indexes with COMPRESS ADVANCED LOW:

```
create unique index ak1_my_objects_with_rca1_low
    on my_objects_with_rca1_low(owner,object_name,subobject_name,object_id)
    compress advanced low;

create index ie1_my_objects_with_rca1_low
    on my_objects_with_rca1_low(object_type,status)
    compress advanced low;
```

```
INDEX_NAME                      LEAF_BLOCKS
------------------------------- -----------
AK1_MY_OBJECTS_NO_CI                    566
AK1_MY_OBJECTS_WITH_CI                  622
AK1_MY_OBJECTS_WITH_RCA1_LOW            517
IE1_MY_OBJECTS_NO_CI                    267
IE1_MY_OBJECTS_WITH_CI                  112
IE1_MY_OBJECTS_WITH_RCA1_LOW            112
```

The unique index with Advanced Index Compression dropped in size significantly, and the nonunique index compressed to the same level.

## Using COMPRESS ADVANCED HIGH

In Oracle Database 12c Release 2, you can use COMPRESS ADVANCED HIGH in addition to the two compression methods previously discussed. The differences between COMPRESS ADVANCED HIGH and COMPRESS ADVANCED LOW are almost as significant as those between COMPRESS ADVANCED LOW and COMPRESS!

To finish our index compression face-off, let's compress those two indexes with COMPRESS ADVANCED HIGH instead:

```
create unique index ak1_my_objects_with_rca2_high
    on my_objects_with_rca2_high(owner,object_name,subobject_name,object_id)
    compress advanced high;
create index ie1_my_objects_with_rca2_high
    on my_objects_with_rca2_high(object_type,status)
    compress advanced high;
```

```
INDEX_NAME                        LEAF_BLOCKS
-----------------------------     -----------
AK1_MY_OBJECTS_NO_CI                      566
AK1_MY_OBJECTS_WITH_CI                    622
AK1_MY_OBJECTS_WITH_RCA1_LOW              517
AK1_MY_OBJECTS_WITH_RCA2_HIGH             231
IE1_MY_OBJECTS_NO_CI                      267
IE1_MY_OBJECTS_WITH_CI                    112
IE1_MY_OBJECTS_WITH_RCA1_LOW              112
IE1_MY_OBJECTS_WITH_RCA2_HIGH              21
```

Those aren't typos or Oracle bugs—the unique index is now less than *half* the size of the uncompressed index, and for the nonunique index, the size is *one-tenth* of the original.

Here are several reasons why COMPRESS ADVANCED HIGH is an even better method for generating a smaller index footprint:

- Additional binary compression methods are available, with different methods available for each index block.

- HCC methods from Exadata use a column-based index structure instead of row-based index structure.

- Any index block can have a compressed section and a noncompressed section.

- New INSERTs into an index block can trigger recompression (as with table compression) and avoid the allocation of new leaf blocks.

- ROWID list compression reduces the ROWID footprint even with single-column unique indexes.

Still, the better compression level doesn't come for free; the CPU requirements for compress and decompress operations with COMPRESS ADVANCED HIGH are measurably higher—but if you have extra CPU cycles available, your increased CPU wait time may be offset by reduced I/O because you'll be reading fewer index blocks for almost every type of index access method.

**NOTE**
*To use COMPRESS ADVANCED LOW, the COMPATIBLE parameter must be set at 12.1.0 or higher; COMPRESS ADVANCED HIGH requires COMPATIBLE to be set to at least 12.2.0.*

You can't use either level of Advanced Index Compression with these index types:

- Bitmap indexes
- Index-organized tables (IOTs), but you *can* use basic index compression
- Function-based indexes

# Improvements to Hybrid Columnar Compression (HCC)

There are two new features in Oracle Database 12c Release 2 related to HCC (available on Oracle ZFS or Exadata storage). The first feature is the use of *array inserts* with HCC. The second feature relates to HCC use with Automatic Data Optimization (ADO) row-level policies. Let's take a look at how to use each of these new features along with some possible scenarios in which they can be used.

## HCC Array Inserts

Prior to Oracle Database 12c Release 2, if you were using HCC during loading or inserting of data, you needed to be aware of certain limitation or optimization methods. The use of direct path technique such as the INSERT . . . APPEND hint, Parallel DML, Direct Path SQL*Loader, and Create Table as Select (CTAS) was recommended to maximize storage savings. With Oracle Database 12c Release 2, that restriction has been loosened. HCC can now use array inserts for loading or inserting data. This new feature can be used to load tables with HCC using an INSERT . . . SELECT statement without the APPEND hint. Array inserts used in PL/SQL and Oracle Call Interface (OCI) code can also take advantage of this new feature. This new flexibility makes loading tables with HCC easier.

## HCC with Automatic Data Optimization (ADO)

Information Lifecycle Management (ILM) continues to evolve in Oracle Database 12c Release 2. DBAs now can use row-level policies with HCC. This new feature should be of interest to those running Exadata, and other supported Oracle Storage, in a data warehouse environment.

Here is an example of a partitioned table with a row-level policy defined:

```
CREATE TABLE orders_ilm_ado
(
  ORDER_ID       NUMBER        NOT NULL,
  PROD_ID        NUMBER        NOT NULL,
  CUST_ID        NUMBER        NOT NULL,
  ORDER_DATE     DATE          NOT NULL,
  CHANNEL_ID     NUMBER        NOT NULL,
  PROMO_ID       NUMBER        NOT NULL,
  QUANTITY_SOLD  NUMBER(10,2)  NOT NULL,
  PRICE          NUMBER(10,2)  NOT NULL,
  DISCOUNT_PCT   NUMBER(10,2)  NOT NULL
)
PARTITION BY RANGE (ORDER_DATE)
( PARTITION sales_q1_2015 VALUES LESS THAN (TO_DATE('01-APR-2017','dd-MON-yyyy')),
  PARTITION sales_q2_2015 VALUES LESS THAN (TO_DATE('01-JUL-2017','dd-MON-yyyy')),
  PARTITION sales_q3_2015 VALUES LESS THAN (TO_DATE('01-OCT-2017','dd-MON-yyyy')),
  PARTITION sales_q4_2015 VALUES LESS THAN (TO_DATE('01-JAN-2018','dd-MON-yyyy'))
)
ILM ADD POLICY ROW STORE COMPRESS ADVANCED
ROW AFTER 30 DAYS OF NO MODIFICATION;
```

When upgrading to Oracle Database 12c Release 2, the choice of simply altering tables to use row-level policy with HCC might be easier than rewriting all of your table creation DDL. During the upgrade process, consider using use Advanced Index Compression for the rows, where appropriate, for even greater storage savings. The following examples demonstrate altering a table to use an ADO row-level policy with different compression levels.

The first example alters a table on HCC storage to use ADO row-level policy with COMPRESS FOR QUERY HIGH:

```
ALTER TABLE products_ilm_ado
    ILM ADD POLICY COLUMN STORE COMPRESS FOR QUERY HIGH
    ROW AFTER 180 DAYS OF NO MODIFICATION;
```

This example alters a table on HCC storage to use ADO row-level policy with Advanced Index Compression:

```
ALTER TABLE sales_ado
    ILM ADD POLICY ROW STORE COMPRESS ADVANCED
    ROW AFTER 60 DAYS OF NO MODIFICATION;
```

# Summary

This chapter covered some new features that can help make your life as a DBA easier. Having the in-database NFS server feature opens up new possibilities for how data is shared when used in combination with Oracle Data Guard or Oracle GoldenGate. Improvements in loading HCC tables removes a prior limitation that was once corrected using SQL hints. Indexes can now use the option of COMPRESS ADVANCED HIGH, which can save even more storage than in Oracle Database 12c Release 1. The development and testing of Oracle Database 12c Release 2 took some time but is well worth the wait. In the next chapter, we'll take a look at the new features for big data, business intelligence, and data warehousing.

# CHAPTER
## 9

# Big Data, Business Intelligence, and Data Warehousing New Features

Oracle Database has always had features to help you scale your database size for almost any application, whether it be for OLTP or data warehouse applications. The key database feature for scaling both of those application types is table and index partitioning: the less data you have to sift through to get the results you want, the better your response time will be when you run queries or run your nightly ETL. In the first part of this chapter, I'll cover a few of the new partitioning features in Oracle Database 12*c* Release 2, including enhancements to list partitioning and partitioning external tables.

In the last part of the chapter, I'll describe a key enhancement to materialized views: real-time materialized view refresh. I'll demonstrate how that feature can minimize the frequency of full materialized refreshes as well as meet the SLA with your user community to ensure consistent (and fast) query execution times when leveraging materialized views.

# Leveraging New Partitioning Methods

Leveraging Oracle partitioning is the key to scaling any "big data" or data warehouse application that approaches the terabyte size. Partitioning is even beneficial for large OLTP applications that need to retrieve more a than few rows for a specific date range while e-commerce applications are servicing customer-facing web page and shopping cart checkout requests.

To recap the architecture and types of Oracle partitioning available for tables and indexes, here are the five you'll have available to you in your partitioning toolbox:

- **Range** Each partition contains rows for a specific numeric or date range, most often a date range (year, month, week, day, even minutes if you want!).

- **Hash** Rows are spread out based on a hashing algorithm of the partitioning key to *N* different partitions, with each partition containing about the same number of rows.

- **List** Values of the partitioning key are explicitly mapped to a specific partition.

- **System** Partition mapping is determined within the application.

- **External** Partitions are stored as files on an OS file system, in Apache Hive storage, or on a Hadoop Distributed File System (HDFS).

Figure 9-1 shows typical examples of how you'd use list, range, and hash partitioning. In this chapter, I'll describe the features and benefits of external table partitioning, new to Oracle Database 12*c* Release 2.

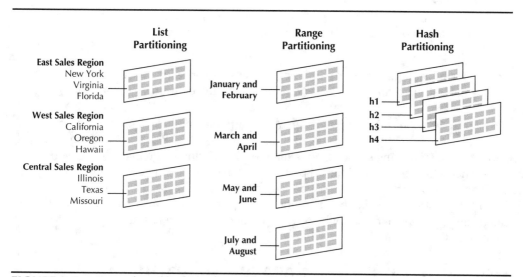

**FIGURE 9-1.**   *Examples of list, range, and hash partitioning*

Furthermore, you can extend partitioning to a second level. In other words, you can use one primary partitioning method and, within each of those partitions, use another partitioning method to logically divide each primary partition. Secondary partitioning is also known as *composite* partitioning. All nine combinations of range, hash, and list partitioning are supported for composite partitioning: for example, range-hash, hash-range, list-list, and so forth.

There are many extensions to partitioning:

- **Interval partitioning**   Creates a new range-based partition automatically when a new row doesn't currently have an existing partition

- **Interval subpartitioning**   Uses interval partitioning at the first level of a composite-partitioned table

- **Reference partitioning**   Partitions a child table based on the foreign key column referencing the parent table with a foreign key constraint

- **Multicolumn list partitioning**   An extension to list partitioning that uses more than one column to map a row to a partition based on each combination of values in those columns

- **Automatic list partitioning**   Creates new partitions for a list partition when all values for the partition key are not known or new values will appear in the future

- **Virtual column-based partitioning**   Uses an expression based on table columns instead of a physical column to calculate destination partition

Of the extensions listed above, interval subpartitions, multicolumn list partitions, and automatic list partitions are new to Oracle Database 12*c* Release 2 and are covered in the following sections. For example, when using range partitioning, you can further refine it by using interval partitioning to automatically create new partitions (which keeps rows out of your "catch-all" partition often called PMAX!). The biggest restriction on interval partitioning in general is that the column used for calculating the interval must not be NULL—otherwise, Oracle has no way to know which partition to put the new row into.

# Using Interval Partitioning with Subpartitions

Interval partitioning was one of the most useful new features introduced in Oracle Database 11*g* Release 1 to enhance scalability and ease of maintenance for range-partitioned tables. If you have a partitioned table whose partition key is a date column (or a numeric column with values generated by a sequence), you have to stay ahead of the current possible values for the partitioning key—for example, your ORDERS table is likely partitioned by ORDER_DATE. If you want to make sure all new orders don't end up in the partition defined by MAXVALUE, you have to stay at least one interval ahead of today's date. In other words, if today is April 30, 2017, you want to make sure that a new partition is available for May 1, 2017, before the first order is placed after midnight on May 1.

Oracle Database 11*g* Release 1 solved this issue by allowing you to create range-partitioned tables with the INTERVAL clause, as in this example:

```
create table orders
(order_date      date,
 cust_id         number,
 . . .)
partition by range (order_date)
interval (numtoyminterval(1,'MONTH'))
. . .
(partition p0 values less than (to_date('2001/01/01','YYYY/MM/DD')));
```

Your interval can be any unit of time or numeric value as long as you don't exceed the 1 million partition limit for a partitioned table.

In Oracle Database 12*c* Release 2, you can use interval partitioning as the *first* level of a composite-partitioned table, with the *second* level being range, hash, or list partitioned. Here's an example I created with composite range-list partitioning and the range partition using interval partitioning:

```
create table orders
(
 order_id        number generated always as identity,
 customer_id     number,
 order_dt        date,
 order_st_cd     varchar2(2)
)
partition by range (order_dt)
    interval (numtodsinterval(1,'DAY'))
        subpartition by list(order_st_cd)
            subpartition template
            (subpartition eastcoast values('NY','RI','ME'),
             subpartition westcoast values('CA','OR','NV'),
             subpartition midwestcoast values('WI','MN','IA','IL'),
             subpartition othercoast values(default))
    (partition p0 values less than (to_date('2001/01/01','YYYY/MM/DD')));
```

There are a few things to note in this example. This ORDERS table is range partitioned by day—every day's set of orders has its own partition, but if there were any orders before January 1, 2001, they will end up in partition P0 with system-generated partitions for every day starting on January 1, 2001 if there is a row inserted for a given day.

Within each daily partition, there can be up to four subpartitions called EASTCOAST, WESTCOAST, MIDWESTCOAST, and OTHERCOAST. Rows that have a state code of WI will end up in the MIDWESTCOAST subpartition, rows with a state code of CA will end up in the WESTCOAST subpartition, and so forth. Any state codes not explicitly declared in the subpartition template will end up in the OTHERCOAST subpartition.

To find out what the partition structure looks like for the ORDERS table after a few days of orders from around the country, I ran a couple of queries like this:

```
select table_owner,table_name,composite,partition_name,high_value
from dba_tab_partitions
where table_owner='RJB' and table_name='ORDERS'
order by partition_position;
```

| TABLE_OWNER | TABLE_NAME | COMPOSITE | PARTITION_NAME | HIGH_VALUE |
|---|---|---|---|---|
| RJB | ORDERS | YES | P0 | TO_DATE(' 2001-01-01 ... |
| RJB | ORDERS | YES | SYS_P332 | TO_DATE(' 2017-04-16 ... |
| RJB | ORDERS | YES | SYS_P327 | TO_DATE(' 2017-04-17 ... |
| RJB | ORDERS | YES | SYS_P322 | TO_DATE(' 2017-04-18 ... |

New orders over the last few days have created three new range partitions on
ORDER_DT. Digging deeper into the subpartitions, I ran this query:

```
select partition_name,subpartition_name,high_value
from dba_tab_subpartitions
where table_owner='RJB'
  and table_name='ORDERS'
order by partition_position,subpartition_position;

PARTITION_NAME SUBPARTITION_NAME HIGH_VALUE
-------------- ----------------- ------------------
P0             P0_EASTCOAST      'NY', 'RI', 'ME'
P0             P0_WESTCOAST      'CA', 'OR', 'NV'
P0             P0_MIDWESTCOAST   'WI', 'MN', 'IA', 'IL'
P0             P0_OTHERCOAST     default
SYS_P332       SYS_SUBP328       'NY', 'RI', 'ME'
SYS_P332       SYS_SUBP329       'CA', 'OR', 'NV'
SYS_P332       SYS_SUBP330       'WI', 'MN', 'IA', 'IL'
SYS_P332       SYS_SUBP331       default
SYS_P327       SYS_SUBP323       'NY', 'RI', 'ME'
SYS_P327       SYS_SUBP324       'CA', 'OR', 'NV'
SYS_P327       SYS_SUBP325       'WI', 'MN', 'IA', 'IL'
SYS_P327       SYS_SUBP326       default
SYS_P322       SYS_SUBP318       'NY', 'RI', 'ME'
SYS_P322       SYS_SUBP319       'CA', 'OR', 'NV'
SYS_P322       SYS_SUBP320       'WI', 'MN', 'IA', 'IL'
SYS_P322       SYS_SUBP321       default
```

Each of the partitions in the previous query has four subpartitions whether they
have rows inserted or not; if you create those partitions with the clause SEGMENT
CREATION DEFERRED, they won't occupy any space other than as a row in the
data dictionary.

## List Partitioning Enhancements

Distinct values for a partitioned table help your performance and scalability in this
way: referencing a partitioning column in a WHERE clause will perform partition
pruning much like any other partitioning method—fewer partitions need to be
considered for returning results to the query, which means less I/O and less elapsed
time. However, with list partitioning in Oracle Database 12c Release 1 and earlier,
you have to declare a DEFAULT partition for list-partitioned tables so that any
partition key that is not part of any partition's VALUE clause maps to the DEFAULT
partition instead of generating an error. However, the DEFAULT partition may end
up having quite a few values that might make that partition much larger than the
other partitions—as a result, performance for queries referencing rows in the
DEFAULT partition will likely suffer.

In the next two sections, I'll describe two enhancements to list partitioning to enhance both scalability and manageability: automatic list partitioning and multicolumn list partitioning.

## Automatic List Partitioning

List partitioning has been available for several previous versions of Oracle Database, and its first incarnation let you specify one or more partition key values that map to one or more partitions, as in this example:

```
create table customers
(
  customer_id    number generated always as identity,
  join_dt        date,
  cust_st_cd     varchar2(2)
)
partition by list (cust_st_cd)
    (
      partition eastcoast values('NY','RI','ME'),
      partition westcoast values('CA','OR','NV'),
      partition midwestcoast values('WI','MN','IA','IL')
    )
;
```

That worked fine when you did an INSERT like this:

```
insert into customers(join_dt,cust_st_cd) values('2016/05/20','WI');
1 row inserted.
```

But this was a problem:

```
insert into customers(join_dt,cust_st_cd) values('2016/05/22','AZ');
Error starting at line : 75 in command -
insert into customers(join_dt,cust_st_cd) values('2016/05/22','AZ')
Error report -
ORA-14400: inserted partition key does not map to any partition
```

To solve this issue in Oracle Database 12c Release 1 and earlier, you had to create the table like this instead:

```
create table customers
(
  customer_id    number generated always as identity,
  join_dt        date,
  cust_st_cd     varchar2(2)
)
partition by list (cust_st_cd)
    (
```

```
    partition eastcoast values('NY','RI','ME'),
    partition westcoast values('CA','OR','NV'),
    partition midwestcoast values('WI','MN','IA','IL'),
    partition othercoast values(default)
    )
;
```

The second INSERT would then work fine:

```
insert into customers(join_dt,cust_st_cd) values('2016/05/22','AZ');
1 row inserted.
```

There was still a problem: unless you constantly monitored for customers in states that never ordered before, all other customer rows outside of the states defined in EASTCOAST, WESTCOAST, and MIDWESTCOAST ended up in OTHERCOAST, potentially making the OTHERCOAST partition so big that the benefits of partitioning were diminished when looking for a row in OTHERCOAST. Oracle Database 12*c* Release 2 addresses this issue by allowing *automatic* list partitioning.

Automatic list partitioning is much like interval partitioning (reviewed extensively at the beginning of the chapter) except that you can use new discrete column values (numeric or character strings) to automatically create a new partition or subpartition to hold the new row. Modifying the structure of the CUSTOMERS table one more time, I use the AUTOMATIC keyword so that I don't have to worry about creating new partitions manually when new values suddenly show up in the daily INSERT statements:

```
create table customers
 (
  customer_id    number generated always as identity,
  join_dt        date,
  cust_st_cd     varchar2(2)
 )
partition by list (cust_st_cd) automatic
    (
     partition eastcoast values('NY','RI','ME'),
     partition westcoast values('CA','OR','NV'),
     partition midwestcoast values('WI','MN','IA','IL')
    )
;
```

Using the AUTOMATIC keyword is not compatible with the DEFAULT list partitioning method, and that makes sense because you no longer need a DEFAULT partition if new partitions are automatically created every time a row with a new value for the partition key is inserted into the table. When I perform a number of inserts like this:

```
insert into customers(join_dt,cust_st_cd) values('2016/06/15','WI');
insert into customers(join_dt,cust_st_cd) values('2016/06/16','AZ');
insert into customers(join_dt,cust_st_cd) values('2016/07/01','MN');
insert into customers(join_dt,cust_st_cd) values('2016/07/22','IL');
```

I can query DBA_TAB_PARTITIONS and see that a new partition was automatically created for the INSERT statement with ST_CD='AZ' since there was no existing partition that had AZ in its value list:

```
select table_owner,table_name,composite,partition_name,high_value
from dba_tab_partitions
where table_owner='RJB' and table_name='CUSTOMERS'
order by partition_position;
```

| TABLE_OWNER | TABLE_NAME | COMPOSITE | PARTITION_NAME | HIGH_VALUE |
| --- | --- | --- | --- | --- |
| RJB | CUSTOMERS | NO | EASTCOAST | 'NY', 'RI', 'ME' |
| RJB | CUSTOMERS | NO | WESTCOAST | 'CA', 'OR', 'NV' |
| RJB | CUSTOMERS | NO | MIDWESTCOAST | 'WI', 'MN', 'IA', 'IL' |
| RJB | CUSTOMERS | NO | **SYS_P333** | **'AZ'** |

No new partitions were created for rows containing a state code of WI, MN, and IL since those partitions already existed right after the table was created.

## Multicolumn List Partitioning

In Oracle Database 12c Release 1, you can create multicolumn range-partitioned tables with up to 16 columns in the PARTITION BY RANGE clause. For example, if you have separate numeric columns in your table for year and month instead of a single column with a DATE datatype, you can create a range-partitioned table using the YEAR and MONTH columns like this:

```
. . .
partition by range (year,month)
   ( partition old_data    values less than (2000,1),
     partition q1_2000     values less than (2000,4),
     partition q2_2000     values less than (2000,7),
   . . .
```

What if you want to have a *multicolumn* list-partitioned table? That's not possible in Oracle Database 12c Release 1, but it is in Oracle Database 12c Release 2! For example, I just added the column CUST_TYP_CD to my CUSTOMERS table, and I want to further subdivide a given state's customers by CUST_TYP_CD. However, because of how small the Wisconsin customer base is overall, I want all customer types in the same partition. I'm in luck, because in Oracle Database 12*c* Release 2, I can create a table with multicolumn list partitioning. Here's the latest version of the CUSTOMERS table:

```
create table customers
(
 customer_id    number generated always as identity,
 join_dt        date,
 cust_st_cd     varchar2(2),
 cust_typ_cd    varchar2(1) -- B=Business, C=Consumer
)
partition by list (cust_st_cd,cust_typ_cd)
   (
    partition eastcoast_bus values(('NY','B'),('RI','B'),('ME','B')),
    partition eastcoast_con values(('NY','C'),('RI','C'),('ME','C')),
    partition westcoast_bus values(('CA','B'),('OR','B'),('NV','B')),
    partition westcoast_con values(('CA','C'),('OR','C'),('NV','C')),
    partition midwestcoast_bus values(('MN','B'),('IA','B'),('IL','B')),
    partition midwestcoast_con values(('MN','C'),('IA','C'),('IL','C')),
    partition midwestcoast values(('WI','B'),('WI','C')),
    partition other_coasts values(default)
   )
;
```

All business customers from New York will be stored in the EASTCOAST_BUS partition and all retail consumers from California will end up in the WESTCOAST_CON partition. All customers from Wisconsin, regardless of their customer type, will be stored in the MIDWESTCOAST partition. Any other combinations of state code and customer type will end up in the OTHER_COASTS partition—I specify that mapping by using the familiar VALUES(DEFAULT) clause.

You can have up to 16 columns in a multicolumn list-partitioned table. In this example, I have four identifiers in each table row and I want certain combinations to end up in specific partitions:

```
create table bigdim
(
  id1      number,
  id2      number,
  id3      number,
  id4      number,
  rec_date date
)
partition by list (id1,id2,id3,id4)
(
   partition grp1 values ( (5,10,7,3),  (88,10,7,1),  (17,1,1,8) ),
   partition grp2 values ( (50,0,17,4),  (101,2,80,8) ),
   partition grpx values (default)
);
```

This can get quite complicated very quickly—not necessarily from a performance perspective but from a partition management perspective. However, it could be useful in cases where you want to more precisely control partition placement and therefore have more control over query performance.

# Partitioning External Tables

The capability to partition external tables in Oracle Database 12*c* Release 2 is a natural extension to partitioning internal tables and has many of the advantages such as partition pruning and partition-wise joins. Partitioned external tables have similar restrictions to nonpartitioned external tables that you are already familiar with, such as being read-only and not supporting indexes. In the following sections, I'll show you how to create and use partitioned external tables and also tell you what to watch out for.

### New Access Drivers for Partitioned External Tables

As of Oracle Database 12*c* Release 1, the only two access drivers for external tables were ORACLE_LOADER and ORACLE_DATAPUMP. The ORACLE_LOADER driver looks much like a control file for the SQL*Loader utility, and that's no accident—the ORACLE_LOADER driver enables you to create an external table that lets you access an OS flat file as if it were a native database table using syntax from a SQL*Loader control file. The other driver, ORACLE_DATAPUMP, enables you to write table data to an OS file and load it back into another Oracle database using the same driver.

In Oracle Database 12*c* Release 2, the ORACLE_HIVE driver enables you to access Apache Hive data as if it were a native database table; similarly, the ORACLE_HDFS access driver can map data in a Hadoop Distributed File System (HDFS) to database tables. To demonstrate how partitioned external tables work, I'll use the ORACLE_ LOADER driver because an in-depth discussion of Apache Hive and HDFS is beyond the scope of this book.

### Creating Partitioned External Tables

Creating a partitioned external table is not much different from creating an external table in previous releases of Oracle Database, and most of the partitioning options available for native Oracle tables are available for external tables. Before you can access the data in an external table, you need to perform these four steps:

1. Establish one or more directories on the OS file system that are accessible to the **oracle** OS user.

2. Create flat files in the OS file system directories containing the data to be mapped to external table partitions.

3. Create one or more Oracle directory objects that point to the OS directories containing the external table data.

4. Create the external table referencing the structure of the flat file and the Oracle directory objects that point to the OS file system.

**Create OS File System Directory Locations** There is nothing special about the OS file location where your external table data is located other than that it needs to be accessible by the **oracle** OS user. In this example, I'm creating the subdirectory **exttab** under **/u01/app/oracle** to hold my external table partitions:

```
[oracle@db122dev /u01/app/oracle]$ ls
12.2.0.1  aux  cc  oraInventory  pdbarch  pdbrman  u03dbfs2
[oracle@db122dev /u01/app/oracle]$ mkdir exttab
[oracle@db122dev /u01/app/oracle]$ ls -l
total 8
drwxr-xr-x. 13 oracle oinstall 4096 Mar 22 20:32 12.2.0.1
drwxr-xr-x.  4 oracle oinstall   51 Apr 13 08:41 aux
drwxr-xr-x.  6 oracle oinstall   63 Apr  9 08:42 cc
drwxr-xr-x.  2 oracle oinstall    6 Apr 18 21:03 exttab
drwxrwx---.  7 oracle oinstall 4096 Apr 18 08:46 oraInventory
drwxr-xr-x.  3 oracle oinstall   32 Mar 31 10:13 pdbarch
drwxr-xr-x.  2 oracle oinstall   76 Apr 14 08:03 pdbrman
drwxr-xr-x.  2 oracle oinstall    6 Mar 25 09:46 u03dbfs2
[oracle@db122dev /u01/app/oracle]$ cd exttab
[oracle@db122dev /u01/app/oracle/exttab]$
```

Since I'm creating an external partitioned table, I might have several or hundreds of flat files and they don't all need to be in the same directory. In fact, even if your external table is *not* partitioned, you can logically coalesce any number of flat files in several different directories and access them all through a single external table.

**Populate the OS File System** Here is the test data I'll use to demonstrate partitioned external tables. It consists of three **csv** files: one for Wisconsin, one for California, and a third for all other states.

**cust_wi.csv:**

```
101,'WI','C'
102,'WI','C'
103,'WI','B'
```

**cust_ca.csv:**

```
110,'CA','C'
120,'CA','B'
```

**cust_other.csv:**

```
151,'NY','C'
152,'ME','C'
```

The traditional partitioned table that would hold this data would look like this:

```
create table customers_nonext
(
  customer_id      number,
  cust_st_cd       varchar2(2),
  cust_typ_cd      varchar2(1)
)
partition by list (cust_st_cd)
    (
      partition eastcoast values('WI'),
      partition westcoast values('CA'),
      partition other_coasts values(default)
    )
;
```

All three of these files are stored in **/u01/app/oracle/exttab** on my server:

```
[oracle@db122dev /u01/app/oracle/exttab]$ ls -l
total 12
-rw-r--r--. 1 oracle oinstall 26 Apr 19 06:56 cust_ca.csv
-rw-r--r--. 1 oracle oinstall 26 Apr 19 06:57 cust_other.csv
-rw-r--r--. 1 oracle oinstall 39 Apr 19 06:56 cust_wi.csv
[oracle@db122dev /u01/app/oracle/exttab]$
```

**Create Oracle Directory Objects**   Creating the directory object to reference the external table partitions is the same as in previous releases:

```
create directory cust_ext as '/u01/app/oracle/exttab';
```

**Create the Partitioned External Table**   Finally, I get to the good part: creating the table itself. It looks much like creating an external table in previous releases but with the addition of the PARTITION BY clause:

```
create table customers_ext
(
  customer_id      number,
  cust_st_cd       varchar2(2),
  cust_typ_cd      varchar2(1)
)
organization external
(
  type oracle_loader
```

```
default directory cust_ext
access parameters
(
 records delimited by newline
 badfile 'bad_cust%a_%p.bad'
 logfile 'log_cust%a_%p.log'
 fields terminated by ","  optionally enclosed by "'"
)
)
partition by list (cust_st_cd)
   (
    partition eastcoast values('WI') location('cust_wi.csv'),
    partition westcoast values('CA') location('cust_ca.csv'),
    partition other_coasts values(default) location('cust_other.csv')
   )
;
```

The new part of this CREATE TABLE statement is the PARTITION BY LIST clause where I specify not only the partition values but also the flat file location in the directory where those rows are stored.

**Querying the Partitioned External Table**   Running a couple of queries on the CUSTOMERS_EXT table looks like running queries on a table stored natively in the database, and you wouldn't suspect otherwise if the name of the table didn't have EXT in it!

```
select * from customers_ext;

CUSTOMER_ID CU C
----------- -- -
        101 WI C
        102 WI C
        103 WI B
        110 CA C
        120 CA B
        151 NY C
        152 ME C
7 rows selected.

select * from customers_ext where cust_st_cd = 'CA';

CUSTOMER_ID CU C
----------- -- -
        110 CA C
        120 CA B
```

| OPERATION | OBJECT_NAME | OPTIONS | PARTITION_START | PARTITION_STOP |
|---|---|---|---|---|
| ⊟─● SELECT STATEMENT | | | | |
|    ⊟─● PARTITION LIST | | SINGLE | KEY | KEY |
|         ⊞ EXTERNAL TABLE ACCESS | CUSTOMERS_EXT | FULL | 2 | 2 |
|   ⊞─ Other XML | | | | |

**FIGURE 9-2.**  *EXPLAIN PLAN on the CUSTOMERS_EXT query*

One of the best reasons to use partitioned external tables is to leverage partition pruning and as a result reduce the number of external files you need to scan every time you access the CUSTOMERS_EXT table. But how do you know that partition pruning is happening in the second SELECT statement? Check the execution plan! Figure 9-2 shows the output from an EXPLAIN PLAN in Oracle SQL Developer.

The columns PARTITION_START and PARTITION_STOP in Figure 9-2 confirm that the query will only be accessing one partition (and therefore only one external table), which in this case is the external table with the rows from California.

### Restrictions on Partitioned External Tables

There are a few restrictions on partitioned external tables besides the restrictions you would expect on nonpartitioned external tables, such as not being able to create indexes on external tables. Here are the most important restrictions:

■ There is no validation that the rows in the external partition satisfy the definition of the VALUES clause for that partition.

■ You cannot perform MODIFY PARTITION, EXCHANGE PARTITION, MERGE PARTITIONS, SPLIT PARTITION, COALESCE PARTITION, or TRUNCATE PARTITION operations on a partitioned external table.

■ Reference, automatic list, and interval partitioning are not supported.

■ Incremental statistics are not collected for partitions of a partitioned external table.

The first restriction is the one you need to carefully consider when evaluating partitioned external tables: your partition for CA could have non-CA rows in it and the query processing would not validate the partitioning key because it only accesses the corresponding external CSV file when the partition key in the WHERE clause matches the value in the VALUES clause. Adding a line in **cust_ca.csv** that has a state code of IL produces unexpected results:

```
select * from customers_ext where cust_st_cd = 'CA';

CUSTOMER_ID CU C
----------- -- -
        110 CA C
        120 CA B
        201 IL B
```

Therefore, when using partitioned external tables, you'll have to perform additional validations to ensure that the partitioning key column matches the value of the partition key as defined in the corresponding VALUES clause.

# Materialized View Performance Improvements

Materialized views, available since Oracle Database 10g, provide huge scalability benefits in terms of reduced execution time at the expense of additional disk space. For example, if you have users in several departments who will aggregate employee or sales data several times a day, you can use materialized views to pre-aggregate the results of a query that has a GROUP BY clause. Even if a typical query only accesses a subset of departments or customer orders, the materialized view rewrite feature, enabled with the ENABLE QUERY REWRITE clause, will still use the aggregated query results in the materialized view and only return the rows relevant to the subset of departments.

The problem you often run into with materialized views is unexpected degradation in elapsed time when a materialized view becomes stale. For example, let's say that after the nightly ETL you build an aggregated materialized view that sums daily order total by customer. It takes about 15 minutes to build the materialized view and each department's query during the day only takes a few seconds to run since the order totals have already been computed for yesterday's sales.

However, let's say there was a duplicate item on one customer order and the duplicate item was deleted from the ORDER_ITEMS table—the materialized view you create every morning has now become stale and won't be used for query rewrite for the rest of the day. You could potentially refresh the materialized view every time a change is made during the day to the ORDERS and ORDER_ITEMS table, but that takes 15 minutes and the impact on overall system performance will be high.

To address this problem (and prevent users from calling you when their reports suddenly take too long to run), Oracle Database 12c Release 2 now supports *real-time materialized views*. A real-time materialized view will still use a stale materialized view to support a query against the base tables and temporarily apply any changes to the base tables *on the fly*. To use this feature, you add the ENABLE ON QUERY COMPUTATION clause to your CREATE MATERIALIZED VIEW command, as in this example:

```
create materialized view log
    on orders
    with rowed
    (order_id,customer_id,order_dt,order_total)
    including new values;

create materialized view order_totals_mv
    refresh fast on demand
    enable query rewrite
    enable on query computation
as
    select customer_id, trunc(order_dt) order_dt, sum(order_total)
cust_orders_total
    from orders
    group by customer_id, trunc(order_dt);
```

There are two new clauses you need to specify if you want to use real-time materialized views:

- **INCLUDING NEW VALUES**   When you create the materialized view logs to support the refresh of your materialized view, you need to specify the INCLUDING NEW VALUES clause so that any new rows in the base tables are marked to make it more efficient for the real-time materialized view refresh to occur.

- **ENABLE ON QUERY COMPUTATION**   In the CREATE MATERIALIZED VIEW command itself, you add the clause ENABLE ON QUERY COMPUTATION so that a stale materialized view will not prevent a user query from leveraging the materialized view if only a few rows in the base table have been updated, inserted, or deleted.

Whether or not you use real-time materialized views depends on the size of the materialized view and the typical number of changes made to the base tables during the day but before the next full refresh. If the materialized view is millions of rows and only one or two rows in the ORDERS table have changed, the slight additional work needed to merge the contents of the existing materialized view with the latest changes is minor compared to using the base tables instead of the materialized view to satisfy the query.

# Summary

The enhancements to partitioning in Oracle Database 12c Release 2 revolve around additional list partitioning features. The new automatic list partitioning feature saves you time when a new partition is created for a partition key value that you didn't expect—meaning that the new key value will have its own partition instead of ending up in a default partition. The multicolumn list partitions feature means you'll have even more granular control over which rows end up in which partition based on more than just one column. External tables have also been enhanced to allow for list partitioning, meaning that you can save disk space by leaving more types of data outside of your database (Hadoop and Apache Hive data, for example) as well as save I/O by leveraging partition pruning.

Materialized views have also been fine-tuned to be more granular—it's no longer "all or nothing" when attempting to leverage query rewrite against a materialized view when it becomes stale due to DML on the base tables. Real-time materialized views will take a stale materialized view and apply recent base table changes on the fly for the duration of a query. This will reduce the need for more frequent materialized view refreshes as well as keep user queries from experiencing wide variations in run times due to stale materialized views.

In the next chapter, I'm going to switch gears a bit from big data and analytics features to the Oracle security and utility realm by introducing an enhanced security analysis tool along with significant improvements to Oracle Data Pump.

# CHAPTER
## 10

# Utilities and Scheduler
# New Features

I n Oracle Database 12*c* Release 2, the utilities and built-in stored procedures that you probably use every day have been enhanced not only to integrate and support database new features but also to expand the scalability and ease of use of the utilities themselves. In this chapter I'll cover three of the most significant enhancements to those utilities: parallel-enabled Data Pump metadata management, external table access driver types, and enabling scheduler jobs to be even more lightweight than in Oracle Database 12*c* Release 1!

# Oracle Data Pump Parallel Metadata Management

Oracle Data Pump has evolved over the last several releases of Oracle Database into the most robust and powerful logical data backup and recovery tool. You can export and import database objects at the table, schema, tablespace, and (of course) database level. There was still one significant bottleneck in Data Pump performance that is now addressed in Oracle Database 12*c* Release 2: parallel import/export of Data Pump metadata.

To ensure that your Data Pump operations are scalable, you want to leverage multiple CPUs and I/O channels if those resources aren't being fully utilized by other user jobs. In Oracle Database 12*c* Release 1 and previous releases, you can run both the Data Pump import (**impdp**) and export (**expdp**) commands with the PARALLEL parameter, as in this example:

```
[oracle@db122dev /u01/app/oracle/dp]$ expdp c##rjb/c##rjb@db122dev/dev02a
    directory=dpdir dumpfile=dev02a%U.dmp logfile=dev02a.log parallel=4 full=y
Export: Release 12.2.0.1.0 - Production on Thu Apr 20 16:28:04 2017
Copyright (c) 1982, 2017, Oracle and/or its affiliates.  All rights reserved.
Connected to: Oracle Database 12c Enterprise Edition Release 12.2.0.1.0 -
    64bit Production
Starting "C##RJB"."SYS_EXPORT_FULL_01":  c##rjb/********@db122dev/dev02a
directory=dpdir dumpfile=dev02a%U.dmp logfile=dev02a.log parallel=4 full=y
Processing object type DATABASE_EXPORT/PRE_SYSTEM_IMPCALLOUT/MARKER
Processing object type DATABASE_EXPORT/PRE_INSTANCE_IMPCALLOUT/MARKER
Processing object type DATABASE_EXPORT/EARLY_OPTIONS/VIEWS_AS_TABLES/TABLE_DATA
. . .
Master table "C##RJB"."SYS_EXPORT_FULL_01" successfully loaded/unloaded
******************************************************************************
Dump file set for C##RJB.SYS_EXPORT_FULL_01 is:
  /u01/app/oracle/dp/dev02a01.dmp
  /u01/app/oracle/dp/dev02a02.dmp
  /u01/app/oracle/dp/dev02a03.dmp
  /u01/app/oracle/dp/dev02a04.dmp
Job "C##RJB"."SYS_EXPORT_FULL_01" completed with 3 error(s)
    at Thu Apr 20 16:30:45 2017 elapsed 0 00:02:37
[oracle@db122dev /u01/app/oracle/dp]$ ls -l
total 29968
```

```
-rw-r-----. 1 oracle dba 10133504 Apr 20 16:30 dev02a01.dmp
-rw-r-----. 1 oracle dba 19976192 Apr 20 16:30 dev02a02.dmp
-rw-r-----. 1 oracle dba   167936 Apr 20 16:30 dev02a03.dmp
-rw-r-----. 1 oracle dba   393216 Apr 20 16:30 dev02a04.dmp
-rw-r--r--. 1 oracle dba    12836 Apr 20 16:30 dev02a.log
[oracle@db122dev /u01/app/oracle/dp]$
```

This example uses four parallel servers by specifying PARALLEL=4 along with the %U wildcard in the dump file specification to more quickly create the four Data Pump export dump files. However, there is a potential bottleneck even when you want to leverage parallelism in Data Pump operations. Mixed in with those four dump files is the *database metadata*. If you wanted to extract just the metadata from those dump files in releases previous to Oracle Database 12c Release 2, you would run something like this:

```
[oracle@db122dev /u01/app/oracle/dp]$
impdp c##rjb/c##rjb@db122dev/dev02a directory=dpdir dumpfile=dev02a%U.dmp
   logfile=dev02a_meta_in.log content=metadata_only sqlfile=dev02a_meta.sql
[oracle@db122dev /u01/app/oracle/dp]$ ls -l
total 33032
-rw-r-----. 1 oracle dba 10133504 Apr 20 16:30 dev02a01.dmp
-rw-r-----. 1 oracle dba 19976192 Apr 20 16:30 dev02a02.dmp
-rw-r-----. 1 oracle dba   167936 Apr 20 16:30 dev02a03.dmp
-rw-r-----. 1 oracle dba   393216 Apr 20 16:30 dev02a04.dmp
-rw-r--r--. 1 oracle dba    12836 Apr 20 16:30 dev02a.log
-rw-r--r--. 1 oracle dba     3650 Apr 20 21:07 dev02a_meta_in.log
-rw-r--r--. 1 oracle dba  3132090 Apr 20 21:07 dev02a_meta.sql
```

In a database with thousands of database objects and users, the metadata export file can be quite large—potentially larger than the export of the database itself! Therefore, having an option to use multiple CPUs and I/O channels to extract metadata from a dump file is very appealing. The PARALLEL parameter for both Data Pump import and export now applies to the metadata as well.

To give you even more control over the degree of parallelism that you will use for metadata export, you can add the MAX_METADATA_PARALLEL parameter to your Data Pump jobs.

**NOTE**
*You can only use the MAX_METADATA_PARALLEL parameter for the **expdp** command to set the maximum degree of parallelism for export of metadata to a Data Pump dump file.*

The previous **expdp** example would look like this with the MAX_METADATA_PARALLEL parameter added:

```
expdp c##rjb/c##rjb@db122dev/dev02a directory=dpdir dumpfile=dev02b%U.dmp
   logfile=dev02b.log parallel=4 full=y max_metadata_parallel=2
```

**NOTE**
*In a RAC environment, set PARALLEL=1 or MAX_METADATA_PARALLEL=1 to keep all Data Pump processes on a single node in the cluster.*

Notice that I specified a different number of parallel server processes for the metadata part of the export so as not to take too many resources away from the rest of the export process; conversely, I can set MAX_METADATA_PARALLEL to a value *larger* than PARALLEL if I want to prioritize creating the metadata in the Data Pump file.

# External Table Access Driver Improvements

When you create external tables in the database, one of the key parameters in the definition of the external table is the ORGANIZATION EXTERNAL clause. That clause identifies the type of external table, where it's located, and how to process it. Here's the CUSTOMERS_EXT table definition from Chapter 9, to which I'll make changes to demonstrate the enhancements for Hadoop and the ORACLE_DATAPUMP driver:

```
create table customers_ext
(
 customer_id     number,
 cust_st_cd      varchar2(2),
 cust_typ_cd     varchar2(1)
)
organization external
(
 type oracle_loader
 default directory cust_ext
 access parameters
 (
  records delimited by newline
  badfile 'bad_cust%a_%p.bad'
  logfile 'log_cust%a_%p.log'
  fields terminated by ","  optionally enclosed by "'"
 )
);
```

When using Oracle Loader for Hadoop (OLH), you use files that are exported and imported by the ORACLE_DATAPUMP access driver. The problem with OLH and ORACLE_DATAPUMP is that the files written by the ORACLE_DATAPUMP driver have a header block that has to be updated when the export is done, but since HDFS is a *write-once* file system, that header block cannot be updated. To solve this issue and avoid multiple passes over the same data, you still use the ORACLE_DATAPUMP access driver but add the HADOOP_TRAILERS parameter to the ACCESS PARAMETERS clause, as in the following example. Here is the external table created with the ORACLE_DATAPUMP driver, based on the existing CUSTOMERS_EXT table:

```
create table customers_ext_pump
    organization external
    (
      type oracle_datapump
      default directory dpdir
      access parameters (hadoop_trailers enabled)
      location('cust_ext_dp.dmp')
    )
as
    select customer_id,cust_st_cd,cust_typ_cd
    from customers_ext
;
```

Syntactically, you won't have to change your CREATE TABLE statement other than the addition of the new access parameter, but under the covers, the amount of I/O that needs to be done in a Hadoop environment when accessing an HDFS file system is dramatically reduced. The Hadoop-friendly external table shows up in the file system much like any other external table:

```
[oracle@db122dev /u01/app/oracle/dp]$ ls -l cust*
-rw-r--r--. 1 oracle dba      20480 Apr 21 07:37 cust_ext_dp.dmp
-rw-r--r--. 1 oracle oinstall   192 Apr 21 07:44 customers_ext_pump_9295.log
[oracle@db122dev /u01/app/oracle/dp]$
```

# In-Memory Scheduler Jobs

As early as Oracle Database 11g Release 2, there were several enhancements to the Oracle job scheduler to make it more scalable and reduce its footprint. One of these enhancements was to offer lightweight jobs, which had several advantages such as reduced create and drop times, smaller disk footprints, and RAC load balancing. Lightweight scheduler jobs made it much easier to set up a new scheduler job and run it much more frequently than a traditional scheduler job due to database overhead, especially in terms of job startup and shutdown resources. However, you still had to store the jobs in the data dictionary along with the accompanying I/O requirements.

In Oracle Database 12c Release 2, these limitations are addressed by memory-resident scheduler jobs. You can use in-memory jobs to enhance performance even beyond the performance gains from using lightweight jobs. In-memory jobs occupy a bit more memory but can almost eliminate I/O when jobs start and stop, which translates into significantly reduced elapsed time during the job startup and shutdown phases. There are two types of in-memory jobs: *in-memory runtime* and *in-memory full*.

## In-Memory Runtime Jobs

In-memory runtime jobs are based on lightweight jobs, so they are persistent; you can run them multiple times on a schedule with a repeat interval. In releases previous to Oracle Database 12c Release 2, you would create a job template and submit a lightweight job like this:

```
-- table holding the status of the DUAL table
create table check_dual_status
(
  status_timestamp     timestamp,
  status_code          number(2)
);

-- create the scheduler object, don't run it yet but enable it
begin
   dbms_scheduler.create_program(
      program_name => 'rjb.dual_check',
      program_action =>
         'begin
              insert into rjb.check_dual_status
              values (systimestamp,
                      decode((select count(*) from dual),1,1,2));
          end;',
      program_type => 'PLSQL_BLOCK',
      enabled => true);
end;
/


-- submit the program as a lightweight job
begin
   dbms_scheduler.create_job (
      job_name => 'lightweight_job_1',
      program_name => 'rjb.dual_check',
      job_style => 'LIGHTWEIGHT',
      comments => 'Check if DUAL has extra rows'
   );
end;
/
```

The job type for in-memory runtime jobs is IN_MEMORY_RUNTIME and in the job class DEFAULT_IN_MEMORY_JOB_CLASS, which does no job logging—therefore, you won't see job completion or status information in views like DBA_SCHEDULER_JOB_RUN_DETAILS. To instead submit the DUAL_CHECK program as an in-memory runtime job that starts now and runs every 15 seconds, you'd create the job like this:

```
-- submit the program as an in-memory runtime job, every 15 seconds
begin
    dbms_scheduler.create_job (
        job_name => 'lightweight_job_2',
        program_name => 'rjb.dual_check',
        start_date => systimestamp,
        repeat_interval => 'freq=secondly;interval=15',
        job_style => 'IN_MEMORY_RUNTIME',
        comments => 'Check if DUAL has extra rows'
    );
end;
/
```

## In-Memory Full Jobs

In-memory full jobs are even more lightweight since they only exist in memory, unlike in-memory runtime jobs, which are based on lightweight jobs. The primary use case for in-memory full jobs is to run them once and exit. The job type for in-memory full jobs is IN_MEMORY_FULL. Because in-memory full jobs only exist in memory, they must have a program associated with them, can't have a repeat interval, and aren't saved on disk. Using my DUAL_CHECK example again, here is how to create that job:

```
-- submit the program as an in-memory full job, only once!
begin
    dbms_scheduler.create_job (
        job_name => 'super_lightweight_job',
        program_name => 'rjb.dual_check',
        job_style => 'IN_MEMORY_FULL',
        comments => 'Check if DUAL has extra rows only once'
    );
end;
/
```

Since you can't specify either START_DATE or REPEAT_INTERVAL, the job is going to run right now and only once.

# Summary

There is definitely a theme apparent when looking at most of the changes in Oracle Database 12c Release 2. Although there are many new features, the vast majority of the changes are enhancements to existing features to make the database more scalable, more interoperable, and less resource-intensive.

For the Oracle Data Pump utility, you can get your database metadata into and out of the dump file in parallel, which is especially useful if the database metadata is all you need. External tables can now interoperate more easily with Hadoop data stores and reduce I/O requirements significantly. Finally, even Oracle scheduler jobs are leveraging in-memory technologies with two new types of scheduler jobs that reduce your disk, I/O, and CPU overhead and make it even easier than before to create either one-time jobs or scheduled lightweight jobs.

In the next chapter, I'll talk about several new features that can make life easier for developers, DBAs, and report writers alike, such as the new built-in database functions.

# CHAPTER
## 11

# New Features for Developers, Report Writers, and Power Users

I f you're an Oracle developer, report writer, DBA, or call yourself a power user, Oracle Database 12c Release 2 has some new features for you. For developers in particular, many of these new features will make your job easier. First, I'll show how most of the existing conversion functions (and a couple of new ones) give you the opportunity to recover from conversion issues more gracefully. As a report writer, you'll be able to return results more quickly by using the existing approximation functions more automatically. As a DBA, you'll be able to help report writers by changing just one or two initialization parameters, and you'll also be able to document database objects more thoroughly by leveraging the new limits for identifier lengths.

## New and Enhanced Functions

Oracle's function library is the backbone of report queries, ETL processes, and PL/SQL code. This includes both single-row and multi-row functions ranging from simple transformations to complex analytical functions. Every release of Oracle Database contains new and enhanced functions so that you don't have to write them.

The following sections review many of these new and revised functions, such as CAST, VALIDATE_CONVERSION, and LISTAGG. The main focus of these functions is enhanced error checking and recovery: in many cases, you can move your error handling out of the client and into the database—avoiding extra PL/SQL code as well!

## CAST

The CAST function is an ANSI-standard SQL method to convert a built-in data type to another. It's very powerful in two ways. First, you can specify any constant, column, or expression as the argument and convert it to almost any Oracle data type. Second, the argument can be a collection type; in other words, it can be the result of a query, which can then return that result set as a new collection whose elements are of a different data type. For example, you may want to convert string expressions to numeric, or vice versa. Other functions such as TO_CHAR and TO_NUMBER are shorthand versions of the CAST function.

The downside of using CAST, however, has always been that bad data ends up in the argument to the CAST function, such as non-numeric characters in a string expression that you want to convert to a number. Sometimes, you have to deal with raw data that the front-end application could not or cannot clean up, such as the following output, as you've no doubt seen hundreds of times:

```
[oracle@db122dev /home/oracle]$ sqlplus c##rjb/c##rjb@db122dev/dev01
SQL*Plus: Release 12.2.0.1.0 Production on Mon Mar 27 20:26:32 2017
Connected to:
Oracle Database 12c Enterprise Edition Release 12.2.0.1.0 - 64bit Production
```

```
SQL> select cast('105.4.1' as number(8,2)) conv_val from dual;
select cast('105.4.1' as number(8,2)) from dual
              *
ERROR at line 1:
ORA-01722: invalid number
SQL> select cast('2018/02/30' as date) conv_date from dual;
select cast('2018/02/30' as date) conv_date from dual
              *
ERROR at line 1:
ORA-01840: input value not long enough for date format
```

To deal with these scenarios prior to Oracle Database 12c Release 2, you had a couple of options. You could make sure that the data entry system would validate the numeric and date fields before sending the contents of the web form to the database. That's still a good idea, but you might not catch all possible conversion scenarios. You could also use a PL/SQL processing step that would catch errors like these with an EXCEPTION WHEN OTHERS block. But that logic can be complex and requires PL/SQL programming knowledge, and gets even more complicated when you have to deal with hundreds of data elements.

In Oracle Database 12c Release 2, you have another option to deal with bad data you encounter when converting the field in a SELECT statement. Figure 11-1 shows the expanded syntax of the CAST function.

The addition to the syntax for the CAST function is the DEFAULT clause. In the DEFAULT clause, you specify a valid value for the function's result if the conversion fails. Using this feature, the CAST function will never generate an error, although you may still want to do some post-processing on return values that had to be mapped to the default. Here is what the previous examples look like when we add the DEFAULT clause:

```
SQL> select cast('105.4.1' as number(8,2)
  2                  default 0.0 on conversion error) conv_val
  3   from dual;
```

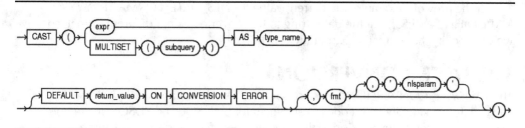

**FIGURE 11-1.** *Enhanced CAST function syntax*

```
CONV_VAL
----------
         0

SQL> select cast('2018/02/30' as date
  2                  default '2000/01/01' on conversion error) conv_date
  3  from dual;

CONV_DATE
-------------------
2000/01/01 00:00:00
SQL>
```

The element *return_value* in the DEFAULT clause must be a constant or bind variable, unfortunately; maybe in Oracle Database 12*c* Release 3 it will be an expression:

```
SQL> select cast('2018/02/30' as date
  2                  default trunc(sysdate) on conversion error) conv_date
  3  from dual;
             default trunc(sysdate) on conversion error) conv_date
                  *
ERROR at line 2:
ORA-43907: This argument must be a literal or bind variable.
SQL>
```

But wait, there's more! Notice in Figure 11-1 that you can also use a format mask for the converted value regardless of whether a conversion error was triggered. In this example, I'm converting a string to a DATE data type:

```
SQL> select cast('28-feb-2018' as date,'DD-MON-YYYY') conv_date from dual;

CONV_DATE
-------------------
2018/02/28 00:00:00
SQL>
```

Per the previous example, the current value for NLS_DATE_FORMAT is 'YYYY/ MM/DD HH24:MI:SS', but the date string to be converted is in a different format, so we can specify that format as part of the function call.

## VALIDATE_CONVERSION

The VALIDATE_CONVERSION function is new to Oracle Database 12*c* Release 2 and can further simplify your code development for both SQL and PL/SQL. It attempts to convert a specified expression to the specified data type and returns 1 if the conversion will be successful and 0 otherwise. Figure 11-2 shows the syntax for VALIDATE_CONVERSION.

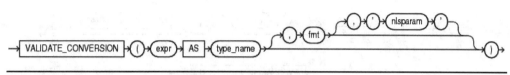

**FIGURE 11-2.** *Syntax diagram for VALIDATE_CONVERSION*

This function would be useful not only in a SQL SELECT statement, but also in a PL/SQL procedure where you don't necessarily want to rely on an EXCEPTION block to handle conversion errors (save the EXCEPTION code for truly serious errors!). Here is how you might use VALIDATE_CONVERSION in a PL/SQL procedure:

```
declare
    bad_or_good_num         varchar2(100);
begin

    bad_or_good_num := '117.4E10';
    case validate_conversion(bad_or_good_num as number)
        when 1 then
            dbms_output.put_line(bad_or_good_num || ' will convert successfully.');
        else
            dbms_output.put_line(bad_or_good_num || ' won''t convert.');
    end case;

    bad_or_good_num := '117.4E';
    case validate_conversion(bad_or_good_num as number)
        when 1 then
            dbms_output.put_line(bad_or_good_num || ' will convert successfully.');
        else
            dbms_output.put_line(bad_or_good_num || ' won''t convert.');
    end case;
end;
/

117.4E10 will convert successfully.
117.4E won't convert.
PL/SQL procedure successfully completed.
```

You can use the *fmt* parameter with string expressions that you want to convert to DATE values, as in this example:

```
SQL> select validate_conversion('2018/02/28' as date,'DD-MON-YYYY') from dual;

VALIDATE_CONVERSION('2018/02/28'ASDATE,'DD-MON-YYYY')
-----------------------------------------------------
                                                    0

SQL>
```

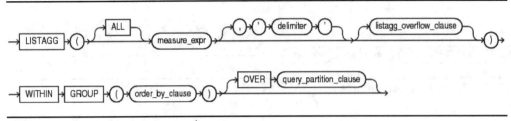

**FIGURE 11-3.** *LISTAGG syntax diagram*

The string '2018/02/28' is a valid date string, but only if the NLS_DATE_FORMAT is 'YYYY/MM/DD'. Attempting to convert it using a date mask of 'DD-MON-YYYY' will fail.

# LISTAGG

The LISTAGG function has been available for several Oracle Database releases and is very useful to group rows based on the ORDER BY clause, then take a specified column or expression and concatenate that column's values into a single string. If you use the LISTAGG function in a SELECT statement with GROUP BY, you get one aggregate per grouping, and the items within the group are ordered.

Until Oracle Database 12c Release 2, there was a major complication with using LISTAGG—the rolled-up string value returned might exceed the maximum length of a VARCHAR2 data type. The problem is that you don't know ahead of time that you'll have some really long string values, a fact that you discover after you run the SELECT statement, at which point the SELECT statement fails with an ORA-01489 and you get no results. Thus, prior to Oracle Database 12c Release 2, using LISTAGG was an "all or nothing" proposition, whereas most of the time you might be happy with *almost* all of the results you're looking for instead of no results. Figures 11-3 and 11-4 present the syntax diagrams for the revised LISTAGG function.

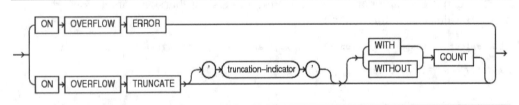

**FIGURE 11-4.** *LISTAGG overflow clause*

**NOTE**
*The maximum length of a VARCHAR2 column is 4000 if MAX_STRING_SIZE=STANDARD and is 32767 if MAX_STRING_SIZE=EXTENDED. The default is STANDARD.*

Figure 11-4 shows two options: ON OVERFLOW ERROR or ON OVERFLOW TRUNCATE. Using ON OVERFLOW ERROR means that you want to use the previous behavior: the SELECT statement fails with an ORA-01489 if *any* of the aggregated strings exceeds the maximum length for a VARCHAR2. For the ON OVERFLOW TRUNCATE clause, the string is truncated at the nearest complete measure, and you specify these options when the aggregated string is too long:

- *Truncation-indicator* is the string to append to the truncated results and defaults to "..."

- WITH COUNT (the default) appends the number of truncated measures to the end of the string.

- WITHOUT COUNT does not append the count of truncated measures after the *truncation-indicator*.

A practical example will show you how LISTAGG works when string truncation occurs (without generating an ORA-01489 error!). Suppose I want a report for the DBA that shows the largest database segments by type and ordered by size within each type. I could easily use a standard SELECT statement with GROUP BY and ordering by segment type within all segment type groups, but I want a much more compact report that the DBA can review every week. The following version of the query I wrote in Oracle Database 12*c* Release 1 was not very useful because it failed most of the time:

```
select segment_type,
    listagg(owner || '.' || segment_name || ' [' || blocks || ']',';' ')
        within group (order by bytes desc) biggest_files
from dba_segments
group by segment_type
having segment_type like 'TABLE%'
order by segment_type;

Error report -
ORA-01489: result of string concatenation is too long
```

Now that I have the ON OVERFLOW TRUNCATE option available, I'll use that:

```
select segment_type,
    listagg(owner || '.' || segment_name || ' [' || blocks || ']',';'
                on overflow truncate 'more...' with count)
        within group (order by bytes desc) biggest_files
from dba_segments
group by segment_type
having segment_type like 'TABLE%'
order by segment_type;

SEGMENT_TYPE         BIGGEST_FILES
-----------------    ---------------------------------------------------------
TABLE                SYS.IDL_UB2$ [1792]; C##RJB.MY_OBJECTS_NO_CI [1536
                     ]; C##RJB.MY_OBJECTS_WITH_CI [1536]; C##RJB.MY_OBJ
                     ECTS_WITH_RCA1_LOW [1536]; C##RJB.MY_OBJECTS_WITH_

. . .
                     _SNAPSHOT [8]; MDSYS.SDO_FEATURE_USAGE [8]; MDSYS.
                     SDO_GEOR_XMLSCHEMA_TABLE [8]; MDSYS.SDO_PREFERRED_
                     OPS_SYSTEM [8]; MDSYS.SDO_PRIME_MERIDIANS [8]; MDS
                     YS.SDO_PROJECTIONS_OLD_SNAPSHOT [8]; MDSYS.SDO_STY
                     LES_TABLE [8]; MDSYS.SDO_UNITS_OF_MEASURE [8]; mor
                     e...(475)

TABLE PARTITION      SYS.WRI$_OPTSTAT_HISTGRM_HISTORY [640]; SYS.WRI$_O
                     PTSTAT_HISTGRM_HISTORY [640]; SYS.WRI$_OPTSTAT_HIS
                     TGRM_HISTORY [256]; SYS.WRI$_OPTSTAT_HISTHEAD_HIST
                     ORY [256]; SYS.WRI$_OPTSTAT_HISTHEAD_HISTORY [256]
                     ; SYS.WRI$_OPTSTAT_HISTHEAD_HISTORY [256]; SYS.WRI
                     $_OPTSTAT_HISTGRM_HISTORY [128]; SYS.WRI$_OPTSTAT_
                     HISTGRM_HISTORY [96]; SYS.WRI$_OPTSTAT_HISTHEAD_HI
                     STORY [48]; SYS.WRI$_OPTSTAT_HISTHEAD_HISTORY [48]
                     ; AUDSYS.AUD$UNIFIED [8]; SYS.WRI$_OPTSTAT_HISTGRM
                     _HISTORY [8]; SYS.WRI$_OPTSTAT_HISTHEAD_HISTORY [8
                     ]
```

Here are a few things to point out in the preceding example:

- As part of the output, I'm including the number of blocks for each table in the list, but sorting by the number of bytes—as long as I have only one block size in my database, the lists will sort the same either way.

- I'm using the HAVING clause to limit my results to just tables, so only tables and table partitions appear in the output.

- Because there are too many tables to fit into a VARCHAR2, the list is truncated at the last complete table, indicated by the "more . . ." label. After the label, I show the number of tables left off the list, and in this case there were 475 tables that didn't make the list.

■   There are not very many table partitions in this database, so they all fit
    within the limits for a VARCHAR2 and there is no need for a "more . . ."
    label or the count.

# Approximate Query Processing

Databases and computer technology in general are all about automation, precision,
and accuracy. When we want to know how many orders went out yesterday, we
typically want the exact number—and the accountants want to know for those
orders exactly how many payments were made, what types of payments were made,
and the total amount of money that was paid for goods and services. However, we
when we are looking at trends over the last few months or even the last few weeks,
accuracy to the closest thousand orders and sales to the nearest thousand dollars
may be good enough.

Calculating statistics on every table every day may not be necessary for overall
database performance and will require lots of CPU and I/O resources that may not
always be available. In addition, an analyst may run many "what if" queries across
decades of historical tables every day but only needs approximate answers,
especially in the early stages of analysis. The *approximate query processing* feature
can cut down processing time by orders of magnitude for typical "big data"
analytics while providing results that are approximate but close enough for their
intended purpose.

You may already be using the approximation-based function APPROX_COUNT_
DISTINCT introduced in Oracle Database 12*c* Release 1, but what if you have
thousands of PL/SQL applications that already have COUNT(DISTINCT . . .) in the
SELECT statements and you'd like to use approximation on the fly? To address this
scenario, Oracle Database 12*c* Release 2 adds features to approximate query
processing to avoid code changes when you might need results more quickly.

The new built-in functions related to approximation include the following:

■   APPROX_COUNT_DISTINCT_DETAIL

■   APPROX_COUNT_DISTINCT_AGG

■   TO_APPROX_COUNT_DISTINCT

■   APPROX_MEDIAN

■   APPROX_PERCENTILE

■   APPROX_PERCENTILE_DETAIL

■   APPROX_PERCENTILE_AGG

■   TO_APPROX_PERCENTILE

The algorithms, according to Oracle, will provide a 99 percent accurate result. They were introduced in Oracle Database 12*c* Release 1, but they have been enhanced in Oracle Database 12*c* Release 2 by adding a few new initialization parameters.

## Configuring Approximate Query Processing

It's great to have the APPROX_* functions available, but what if you won't be able to change all of your code right away, or better yet, what if you want to automatically use the approximation functions on demand with no code changes? Three new parameters help you control this behavior:

- APPROX_FOR_COUNT_DISTINCT
- APPROX_FOR_AGGREGATION
- APPROX_FOR_PERCENTILE

All three of those parameters can be set either at the system level or at the session level. However, you should avoid setting these at the system level so that queries with existing COUNT(DISTINCT . . .) clauses won't suddenly return imprecise results when the report writer expected exact results!

Both APPROX_FOR_COUNT_DISTINCT and APPROX_FOR_AGGREGATION default to FALSE, and APPROX_FOR_PERCENTILE is not set. Setting any of these parameters is as easy as any ALTER SESSION command:

```
alter session set approx_for_count_distinct=true;
```

These can also be set with the OPT_PARAM query hint if including an ALTER SESSION command in your code is not feasible.

## Using Approximate Query Processing

The value of approximate query processing is in the accuracy of the results and how fast you get the results back. How do you know if the approximation is kicking in? First, you'll get the results back a lot faster. But to make absolutely sure that the approximation is happening, you can look at the execution plan. For example, when I run this SELECT statement after setting APPROX_FOR_COUNT_DISTINCT to FALSE:

```
alter session set approx_for_count_distinct=false;
select count(distinct object_name) from my_objects_arch;

COUNT(DISTINCTOBJECT_NAME)
--------------------------
                     60336
```

the execution plan appears as shown in Figure 11-5, as expected.

| OPERATION | OBJECT_NAME | OPTIONS | CAR |
|---|---|---|---|
| ⊟ ● SELECT STATEMENT | | | |
| ⊟ ⬦ SORT | | AGGREGATE | |
| ⊟ ⊞ VIEW | SYS.VW_DAG_0 | | |
| ⊟ ● HASH | | GROUP BY | |
| ⌞ ⊞ TABLE ACCESS | MY_OBJECTS_ARCH | FULL | |

**FIGURE 11-5.** *Execution plan for non-approximate COUNT(DISTINCT)*

**NOTE**
*The default value for APPROX_FOR_COUNT_
DISTINCT is FALSE, but when you're not sure if the
target database will have it set to either TRUE or
FALSE, programming best practices dictate that you
set it explicitly in your code.*

Next, I change the APPROX_FOR_COUNT_DISTINCT parameter at the session
level to TRUE and run the query again:

```
alter session set approx_for_count_distinct=true;
select count(distinct object_name) from my_objects_arch;
```

```
COUNT(DISTINCTOBJECT_NAME)
--------------------------
                     61007
```

Figure 11-6 shows the new execution plan. Notice the different execution plan
option AGGREGATE APPROX.

In this case, the execution time is considerably less and gives me a result that is
within 1.1 percent of the actual count. That's close enough for my CFO to figure out
if our last quarter was profitable or not and whether a bonus is possible at the end of
the year!

| OPERATION | OBJECT_NAME | OPTIONS | CARD |
|---|---|---|---|
| ⊟ ● SELECT STATEMENT | | | |
| ⊟ ⬦ SORT | | AGGREGATE APPROX | |
| ⌞ ⊞ TABLE ACCESS | MY_OBJECTS_ARCH | FULL | |

**FIGURE 11-6.** *Execution plan for approximate COUNT(DISTINCT)*

# Data Dictionary and Data Type Enhancements

A few new data dictionary views in Oracle Database 12c Release 2 help both DBAs and developers alike. DBA_INDEX_USAGE gives the DBA a more fine-grained approach to index monitoring, and DBA_STATEMENTS helps PL/SQL developers cross reference SQL statements in their code.

For everyone who uses Oracle Database, the expansion of identifier lengths to 128 bytes is a welcome change! I'll demonstrate this new feature in detail.

## Identifier Length Changes

From a developer's perspective, the 30-byte identifier length limitation has been an impediment to database documentation. The more you have to abbreviate each table name, column name, constraint, and so forth, the less readable your code will be and the more likely it is that errors will occur when automated code-generation tools push identifier lengths over the 30-byte limit: for example, materialized view logs prepend MLOG$_ to the name, which further restricts what you can name your table if it ever becomes the master table for a materialized view.

To address all of these concerns, most Oracle objects now can have a name with up to 128 bytes. There are still a few identifiers that have lower limits:

- Database names are limited to 8 bytes.

- These database objects have a limit of 30 bytes:

    - ASM disk groups

    - Pluggable databases (PDBs)

    - Rollback segments

    - Tablespaces

    - Tablespace sets

To leverage the longer identifier length, the COMPATIBLE parameter must be set to 12.2 or higher.

**NOTE**
*The identifier length limit is 128 bytes. Therefore, depending on the national character set for your database, the number of characters for an identifier may be less than 128.*

These identifiers with lower length limits will likely not have an impact on your development, even if you have 4000 PDBs in your CDB! Think of the possibilities. Your schema names, table names, and column names can each be 128 bytes. So this works:

```
grant create session, create table to   VeryLongSchemaNameXXXXXXXXXXXXXXXXXXXXXX-
XXXXXXXXXXXXXXXXXXXXXXXXXXXXXXXXXXXXXXXXXXXXXXXXXXXXXXXXXXXXXXXXXXXXXXXXXXXXXXXXXX-
XXXXXXXXXXX
identified by X;
Grant succeeded.

create table   VeryLongSchemaNameXXXXXXXXXXXXXXXXXXXXXXXXXXXXXXXXXXXXXXXXXXXXXXXXX-
XXXXXXXXXXXXXXXXXXXXXXXXXXXXXXXXXXXXXXXXXXXXXXXXXXXXXXXXXX.VeryLongTableN-
ameXXXXXXXXXXXXXXXXXXXXXXXXXXXXXXXXXXXXXXXXXXXXXXXXXXXXXXXXXXXXXXXXXXXXXXXXXXXXXXX-
XXXXXXXXXXXXXXXXXXXXXXXXXXXXXXXXXXXXX
    (VeryLongColNameXXXXXXXXXXXXXXXXXXXXXXXXXXXXXXXXXXXXXXXXXXXXXXXXXXXXXXXXXXXXXXX-
XXXXXXXXXXXXXXXXXXXXXXXXXXXXXXXXXXXXXXXXXXXXXXXXXXXXX number);
Table VERYLONGSCHEMANAMEXXXXXXXXXXXXXXXXXXXXXXXXXXXXXXXXXXXXXXXXXXXXXXXXXXXXXXXXX-
XXXXXXXXXXXXXXXXXXXXXXXXXXXXXXXXXXXXXXXXXXXXXXXXXXXXX.VERYLONGTABLENAMEXXXXXX-
XXXXXXXXXXXXXXXXXXXXXXXXXXXXXXXXXXXXXXXXXXXXXXXXXXXXXXXXXXXXXXXXXXXXXXXXXXXXXXXXXX-
XXXXXXXXXXXXXXXXXXXXXXXXXXXX created.

describe VERYLONGSCHEMANAMEXXXXXXXXXXXXXXXXXXXXXXXXXXXXXXXXXXXXXXXXXXXXXXXXXXXXXXX-
XXXXXXXXXXXXXXXXXXXXXXXXXXXXXXXXXXXXXXXXXXXXXXXXXXXXX.VERYLONGTABLENAMEXXX-
XXXXXXXXXXXXXXXXXXXXXXXXXXXXXXXXXXXXXXXXXXXXXXXXXXXXXXXXXXXXXXXXXXXXXXXXXXXXXXXXXX-
XXXXXXXXXXXXXXXXXXXXXXXXXXXXX
Table VERYLONGSCHEMANAMEXXXXXXXXXXXXXXXXXXXXXXXXXXXXXXXXXXXXXXXXXXXXXXXXXXXXXXXXX-
XXXXXXXXXXXXXXXXXXXXXXXXXXXXXXXXXXXXXXXXXXXXXXXXXXXXX.VERYLONGTABLENAMEXXXXXX-
XXXXXXXXXXXXXXXXXXXXXXXXXXXXXXXXXXXXXXXXXXXXXXXXXXXXXXXXXXXXXXXXXXXXXXXXXXXXXXXXXX-
XXXXXXXXXXXXXXXXXXXXXXXXXXXX created.

Name
Null? Type
--------------------------------------------------------------------------------
--------------------------------------------------- ----- ------
VERYLONGCOLNAMEXXXXXXXXXXXXXXXXXXXXXXXXXXXXXXXXXXXXXXXXXXXXXXXXXXXXXXXXXXXXXXXXXXX-
XXXXXXXXXXXXXXXXXXXXXXXXXXXXXXXXXXXXXXXXXXXXXXXXXXXXXX           NUMBER
```

If you decide to use *quoted* identifiers (that is, use lowercase characters in your identifier names), you have to count the double quote character " in the length of the identifier. Using lowercase in a column name is generally not recommended from a development perspective, so stick with uppercase Oracle object names.

# New Data Dictionary Views

For almost every new or enhanced feature in Oracle Database 12c Release 2, there is some kind of a change to an existing data dictionary view, and many of the new features are supported by a new data dictionary view. We'll cover three of the most consequential new data dictionary views in this section: DBA_INDEX_USAGE, DBA_STATEMENTS, and DBA_IDENTIFIERS.

## DBA_INDEX_USAGE

From Oracle Database 11g through Oracle Database 12c Release 1, you can mark an existing index with the MONITORING USAGE clause to see if that index is referenced in a SELECT statement over some arbitrary period of time. If the index doesn't get used during that time, the dynamic performance view V$OBJECT_USAGE indicates this, thereby identifying that index as one you could potentially drop to save space and index maintenance time during ETL.

There are several deficiencies with that strategy. First, even if the index is flagged as having been referenced, you don't know how many times it was referenced or how many blocks were retrieved from the index. In addition, the index might have been flagged as used when operations other than SELECT statements accessed the index; for example, an EXPLAIN PLAN run on the query may have indicated that the index was *probably* going to be used when the query is run, but the index may not have *actually* been used at run time.

To address these deficiencies, in Oracle Database 12c Release 2, the data dictionary view DBA_INDEX_USAGE has been added to provide a much more granular level of detail for *all* indexes—they don't have to be marked to be monitored. Here is what the view looks like:

```
describe dba_index_usage
```

```
Name                               Null?       Type
---------------------------------- --------    -------------
OBJECT_ID                          NOT NULL    NUMBER
NAME                               NOT NULL    VARCHAR2(128)
OWNER                              NOT NULL    VARCHAR2(128)
TOTAL_ACCESS_COUNT                             NUMBER
TOTAL_EXEC_COUNT                               NUMBER
TOTAL_ROWS_RETURNED                            NUMBER
BUCKET_0_ACCESS_COUNT                          NUMBER
BUCKET_1_ACCESS_COUNT                          NUMBER
BUCKET_2_10_ACCESS_COUNT                       NUMBER
BUCKET_2_10_ROWS_RETURNED                      NUMBER
BUCKET_11_100_ACCESS_COUNT                     NUMBER
BUCKET_11_100_ROWS_RETURNED                    NUMBER
BUCKET_101_1000_ACCESS_COUNT                   NUMBER
BUCKET_101_1000_ROWS_RETURNED                  NUMBER
BUCKET_1000_PLUS_ACCESS_COUNT                  NUMBER
BUCKET_1000_PLUS_ROWS_RETURNED                 NUMBER
LAST_USED                                      DATE
```

The data dictionary view DBA_INDEX_USAGE is covered in more detail in Chapter 7.

## DBA_STATEMENTS and DBA_IDENTIFIERS

If you are a developer and you use PL/Scope in your PL/SQL development, the two new views DBA_STATEMENTS and DBA_IDENTIFIERS will help you automatically identify occurrences of static and native dynamic SQL statements in each PL/SQL unit. You might not need these views if your PL/SQL application is only a couple hundred lines, but if you have hundreds of procedures and thousands of lines, you want to know how often and where a particular SQL statement is referenced. Here is what DBA_STATEMENTS looks like:

```
Name                                              Null?     Type
-------------------------------------------- --------  ----------------------
OWNER                                                   NOT NULL VARCHAR2(128)
SIGNATURE                                               VARCHAR2(32)
TYPE                                                    VARCHAR2(17)
OBJECT_NAME                                             NOT NULL VARCHAR2(128)
OBJECT_TYPE                                             VARCHAR2(12)
USAGE_ID                                                NUMBER
LINE                                                    NUMBER
COL                                                     NUMBER
USAGE_CONTEXT_ID                                        NUMBER
SQL_ID                                                  VARCHAR2(13)
HAS_HINT                                                VARCHAR2(3)
HAS_INTO_BULK                                           VARCHAR2(3)
HAS_INTO_RETURNING                                      VARCHAR2(3)
HAS_INTO_RECORD                                         VARCHAR2(3)
HAS_CURRENT_OF                                          VARCHAR2(3)
HAS_FOR_UPDATE                                          VARCHAR2(3)
HAS_IN_BINDS                                            VARCHAR2(3)
TEXT                                                    VARCHAR2(4000)
FULL_TEXT                                               CLOB
ORIGIN_CON_ID                                           NUMBER
```

When using PL/Scope, all the metadata from functions and procedures is stored in DBA_STATEMENTS. The column TYPE shows what kind of statement was referenced, such as a SELECT, DELETE, FETCH, or even EXECUTE IMMEDIATE. This view is a big time-saver when your development manager wants to know how many times you reference the ORDER_ENTRY table or open a cursor in your e-commerce application, for example.

# Summary

Oracle Database 12c Release 2 brings many developer-related enhancements to the table (no pun intended). One of the biggest changes is the addition of more error checking to conversion-specific functions such as CAST, VALIDATE_CONVERSION, and LISTAGG. These new and enhanced functions enable you to move some of your validation logic to the database layer, where it makes sense and avoids many error conditions that would otherwise cause delays in report processing due to bad data making it through to the data warehouse tables.

For agility and improved response time of ad hoc analytic queries, you can more easily leverage the approximate query functions even when you're not directly referencing functions such as APPROX_COUNT_DISTINCT. At the session level, you can change an initialization parameter to transparently substitute one of the APPROX_ functions for a query with a traditional SELECT DISTINCT clause.

Developers benefit as well: new data dictionary views such as DBA_STATEMENTS help a PL/SQL developer keep track of statement and column references in their PL/SQL applications.

The next and final chapter takes a look at Oracle Enterprise Manager Cloud Control 13c Release 2 and its new features related to the new features of Oracle Database 12c Release 2.

# CHAPTER
## 12

# Integrating with Oracle Enterprise Manager Cloud Control 13c Release 2

E ven though this book is about the new features of Oracle Database 12c Release 2, it's important to cover some of the new features of Oracle Enterprise Manager Cloud Control 13c Release 2 (Cloud Control) because this latest version of Cloud Control fully supports all of the new features of Oracle Database 12c Release 2 and, of course, makes those features available in a very convenient GUI.

In this chapter, I first cover some of the prerequisites for installing Cloud Control, including the setup of the database needed to hold the metadata for Cloud Control. Then, for readers who haven't installed Cloud Control recently, I provide a brief overview of how to install Cloud Control and configure agent software on all of your target servers and databases.

Once you have completed the setup of the Cloud Control repository database and Cloud Control itself, I'll introduce you to the most important new features in Cloud Control that support Oracle Database 12c Release 2.

# Configuring a Cloud Control Repository

Every Cloud Control deployment requires an Oracle database in which to keep the target metadata and other statistics and configuration information. The configuration and size of your database depends on the number of targets you intend to monitor. To help you configure your Cloud Control database repository correctly, Oracle provides three Database Configuration Assistant (DBCA) templates that you can use to easily create a Cloud Control repository:

- Small_deployment.dbc

- Medium_deployment.dbc

- Large_deployment.dbc

**NOTE**
*See Figures 2-12 and 2-13 in Chapter 2 for the first two steps when creating a database with DBCA.*

You'll have to select "Advanced Configuration" on the "Select Database Creation Mode" window to be able to select one of these templates. These templates are available in the same location where you download the Cloud Control software itself, as shown in Figure 12-1, where I have launched the DBCA and specified the small deployment template to create my repository.

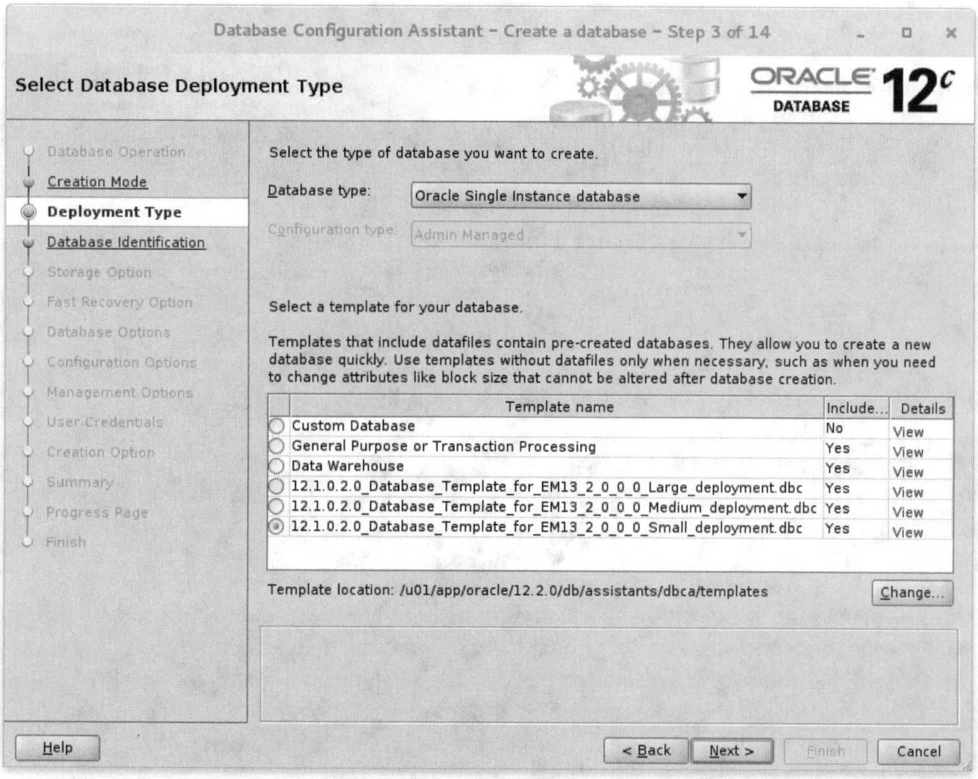

**FIGURE 12-1.**   *Selecting a Cloud Control repository template*

In the next step of the DBCA, Specify Database Identification Details, shown in Figure 12-2, name your database (as you would for any new database creation). Note that for Cloud Control 13c Release 2, the repository must *not* be a multitenant database, which is why the Create as Container Database check box is not available. Click Next.

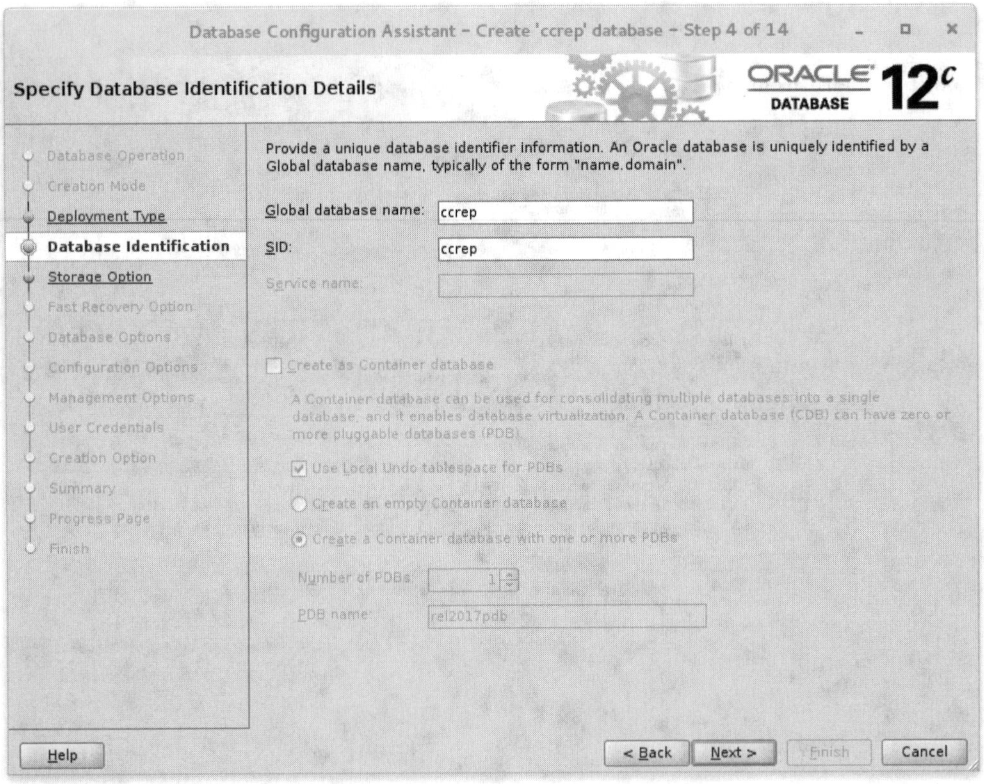

**FIGURE 12-2.** *Specifying the repository name and database type*

The storage specification for the Cloud Control repository database is also much like any other database creation: use ASM storage along with Oracle-Managed Files (OMF), as configured in Figure 12-3. Click Next.

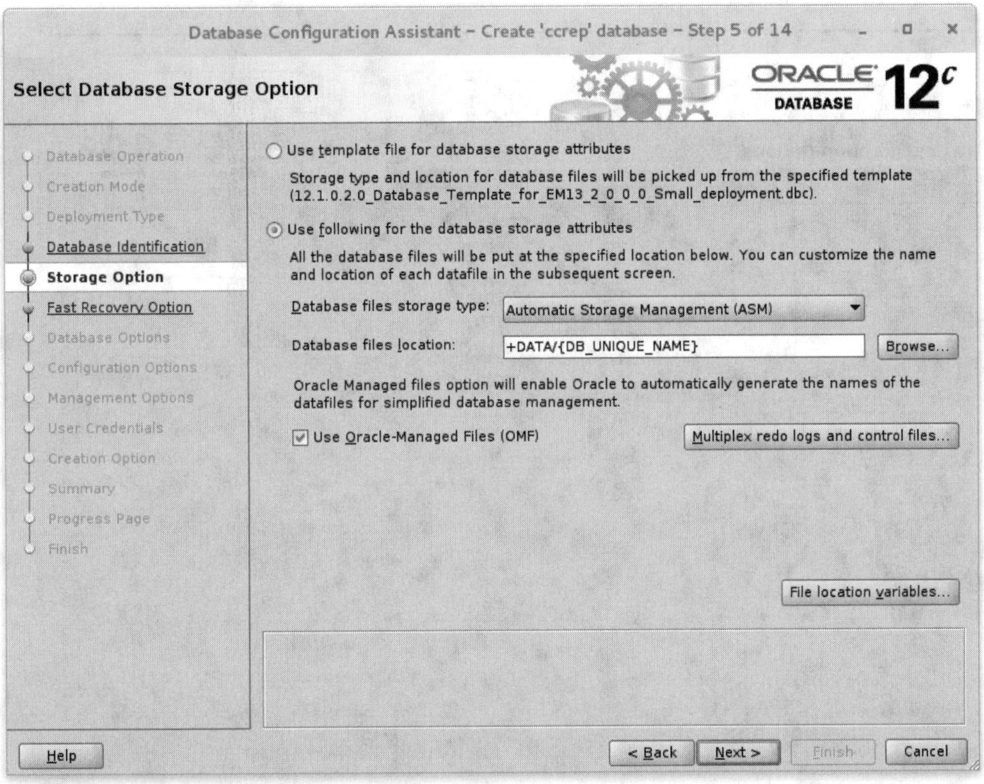

**FIGURE 12-3.**   *Repository database storage options*

Figure 12-4 shows you one of the benefits of using the Oracle-provided DBCA template: many settings such as SGA and PGA size are filled in for you. Assuming you have selected the small deployment template, your SGA does not need to be larger than 3 GB and your PGA is only 1 GB. In addition, the Database options window is not needed since those options are specified in the template.

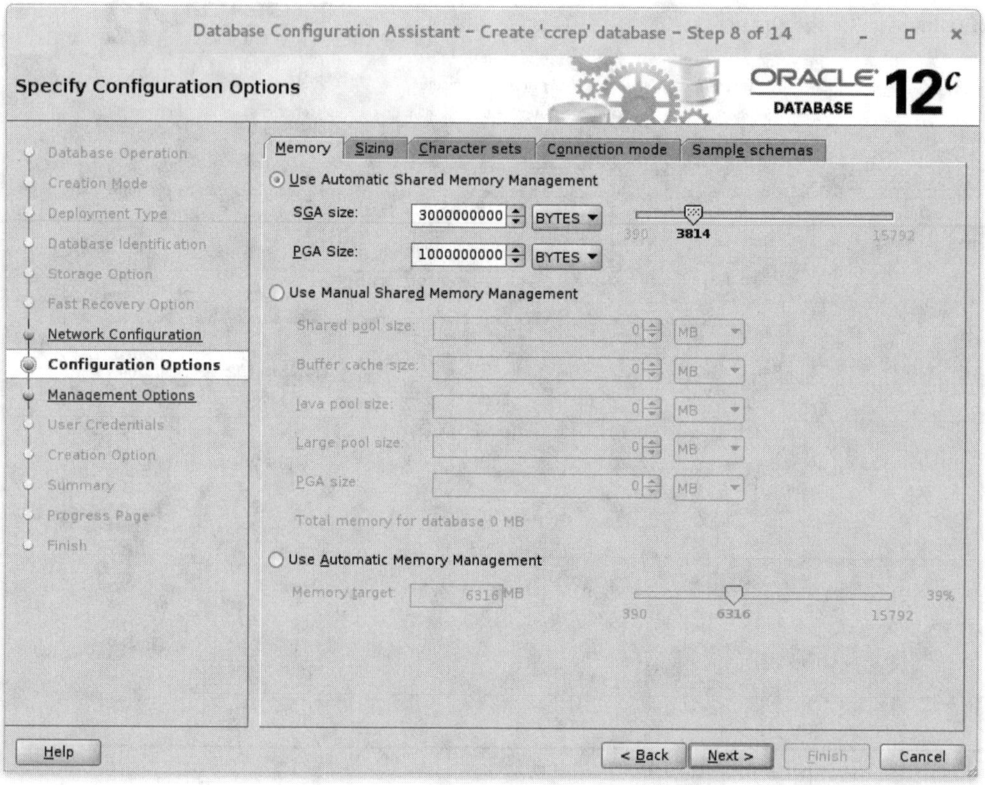

**FIGURE 12-4.** *Memory settings provided in the DBCA template*

Specify a fast recovery area if needed, and you'll supply SYS and SYSTEM passwords on the user credentials window as you would for any database installation. Figure 12-5 shows the Summary page before creating the database. Once you click Finish and the database is created, you can proceed with installing Cloud Control 13*c*!

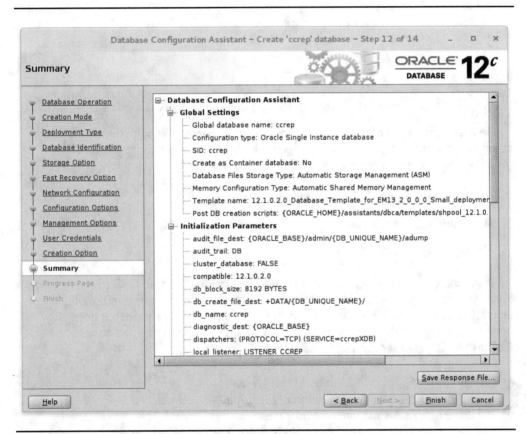

**FIGURE 12-5.**   *Repository database creation summary*

# Installing Cloud Control 13*c*

The Cloud Control installer consists of seven files, one ZIP file, and a binary installer. Here are the filenames for version 13.2:

```
[oracle@db122dev /install/cloud]$ ls
12.1.0.2.0_Database_Template_for_EM13_2_0_0_0_Linux_x64.zip
em13200p1_linux64-2.zip
em13200p1_linux64-3.zip
em13200p1_linux64-4.zip
em13200p1_linux64-5.zip
em13200p1_linux64-6.zip
em13200p1_linux64-7.zip
em13200p1_linux64.bin
EMBSC.pdf
[oracle@db122dev /install/cloud]$ ./em13200p1_linux64.bin
```

To begin the installation, change the **.bin** file to be executable with the **chmod +x** command and run it as in the previous example. In the example that follows, I'll be installing the following components in these locations:

- Middleware repository: **mw_home**

- Software library: **swlib**

- Agent base: **agent_base**

Installing Cloud Control is similar to installing Oracle Database or Grid Infrastructure, so many of these steps will look very familiar. Keep in mind, though, that this is a different type of Oracle software—it's middleware, although it does need an existing database for its metadata, so we'll use the database we created earlier in the chapter for this purpose.

**NOTE**
*Even though I used the latest version of the "small" database template, I still had to adjust these parameters during the Cloud Control install:*

```
alter system set "_allow_insert_with_update_check"=true scope=spfile;
alter system set shared_pool_size=800m scope=spfile;
alter system set session_cached_cursors=350 scope=spfile;
```

When you reach the Software Updates step of the installation, shown in Figure 12-6, you are prompted by default to search online for updates using your My Oracle Support account. This makes it much easier to deploy patches across all monitored targets. In this case, however, I skip the update check since I know I have the latest version and patches.

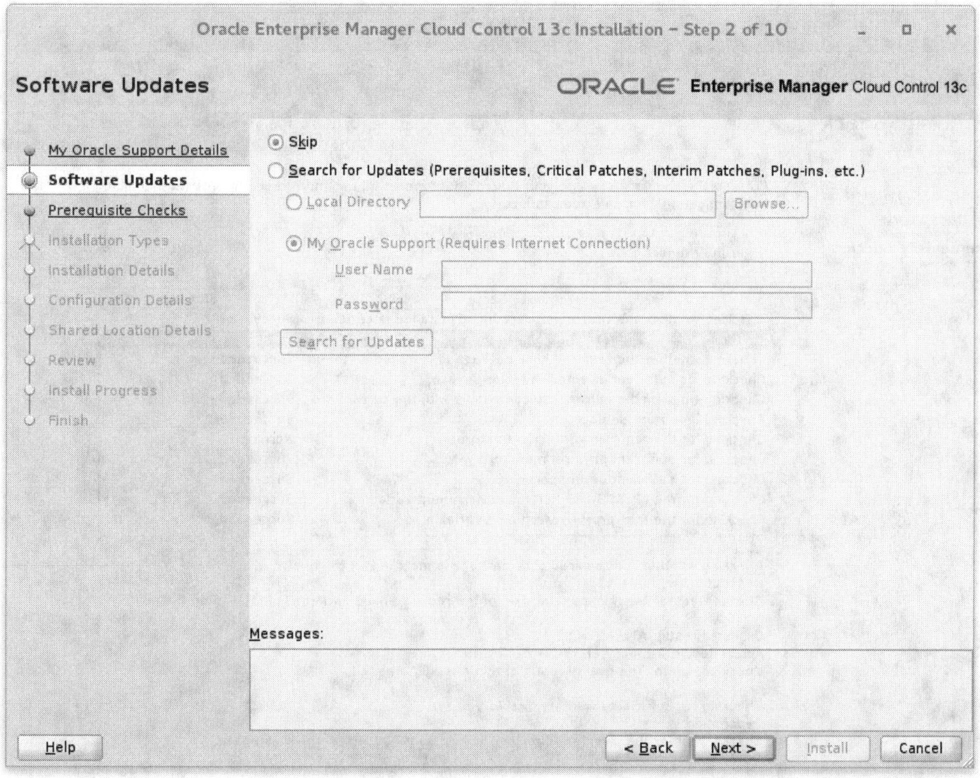

**FIGURE 12-6.** *Enterprise Manager searching for software updates*

In the next step, Prerequisite Checks, shown in Figure 12-7, the installer checks to ensure that your OS parameters are set correctly and that you have the minimum set of packages at the right version to support Cloud Control. Depending on what the installer finds, you can make corrections at the OS level and retry the prerequisite checks; a more serious configuration issue may require you to cancel the installation, fix the issue, and restart the installation later.

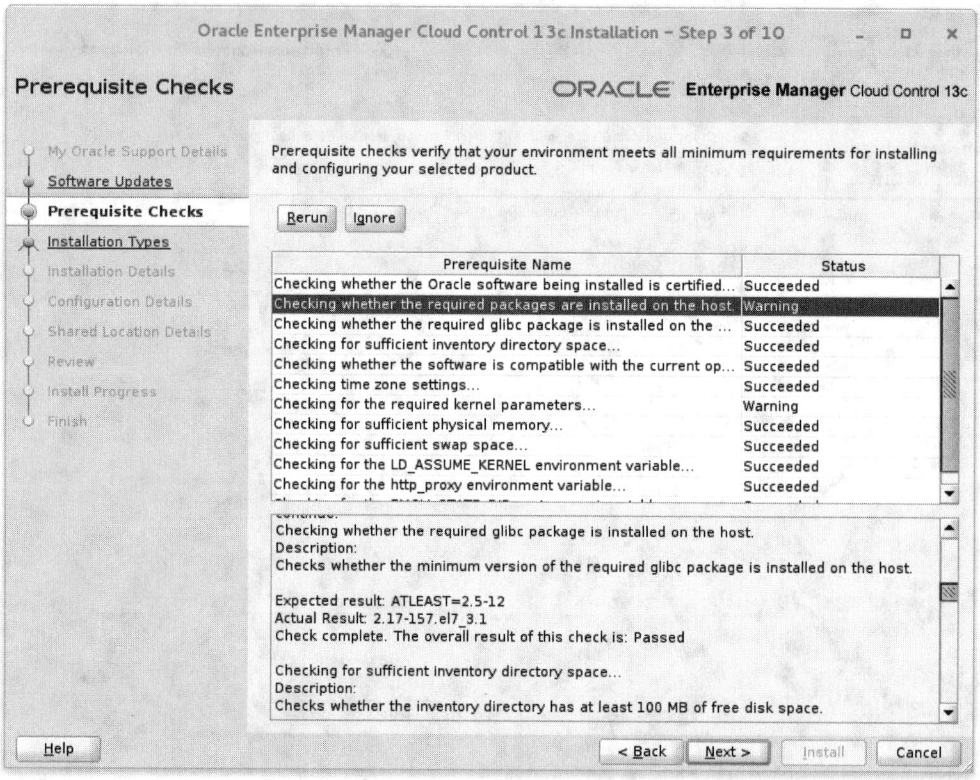

**FIGURE 12-7.** *Cloud Control prerequisite checks*

The Installation Types step, shown in Figure 12-8, gives you the option to choose a more advanced installation as well as the option to install just the software and postpone the configuration until later. Figure 12-9 shows the Installation Details step, where you specify the locations for each part of the software, such as the primary middleware binaries, as well as the location for all of the agent software you will deploy on your targets.

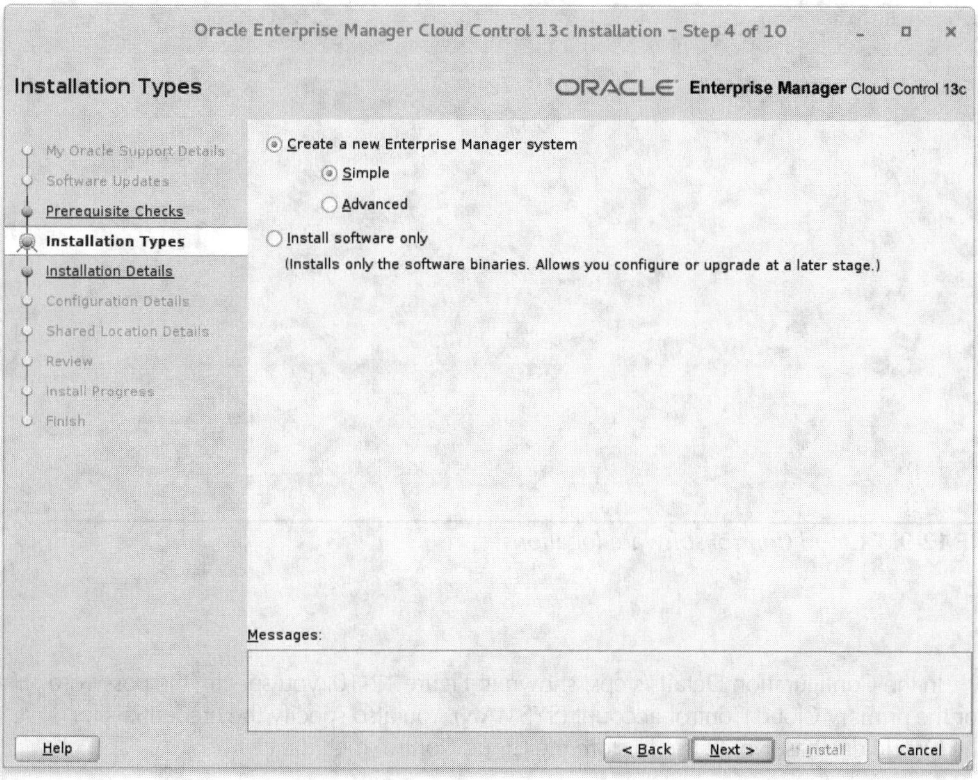

**FIGURE 12-8.**    *Cloud Control installation types*

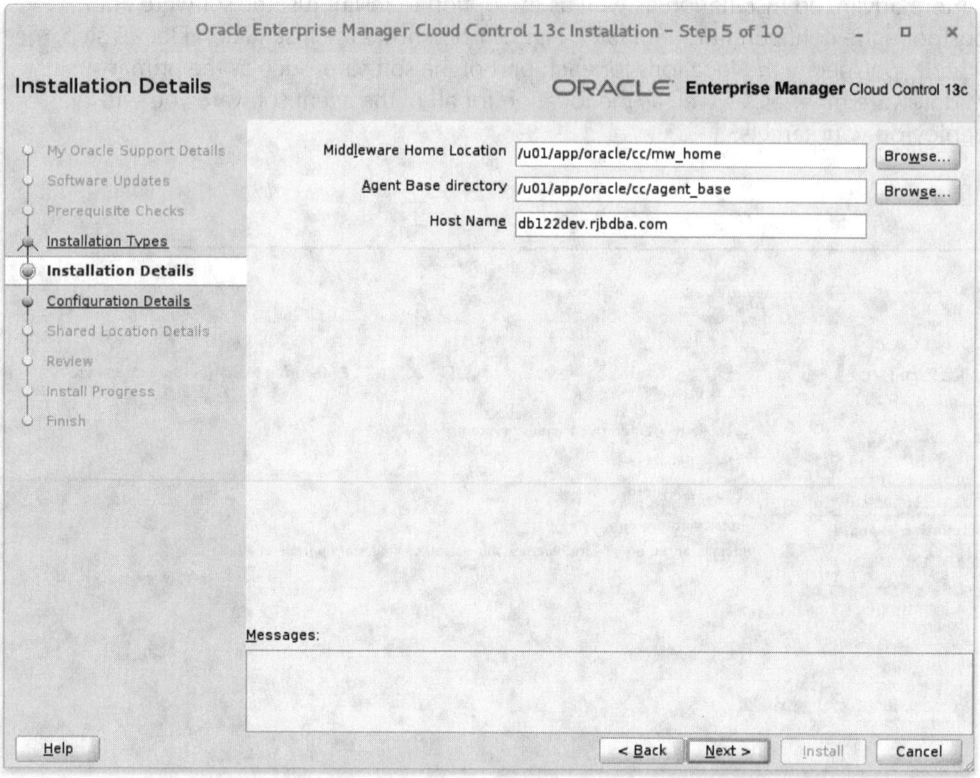

**FIGURE 12-9.** *Cloud Control software locations*

In the Configuration Details steps, shown in Figure 12-10, you specify the password for the primary Cloud Control account (SYSMAN). You also specify the credentials for the Oracle database you'll use to store the Cloud Control metadata.

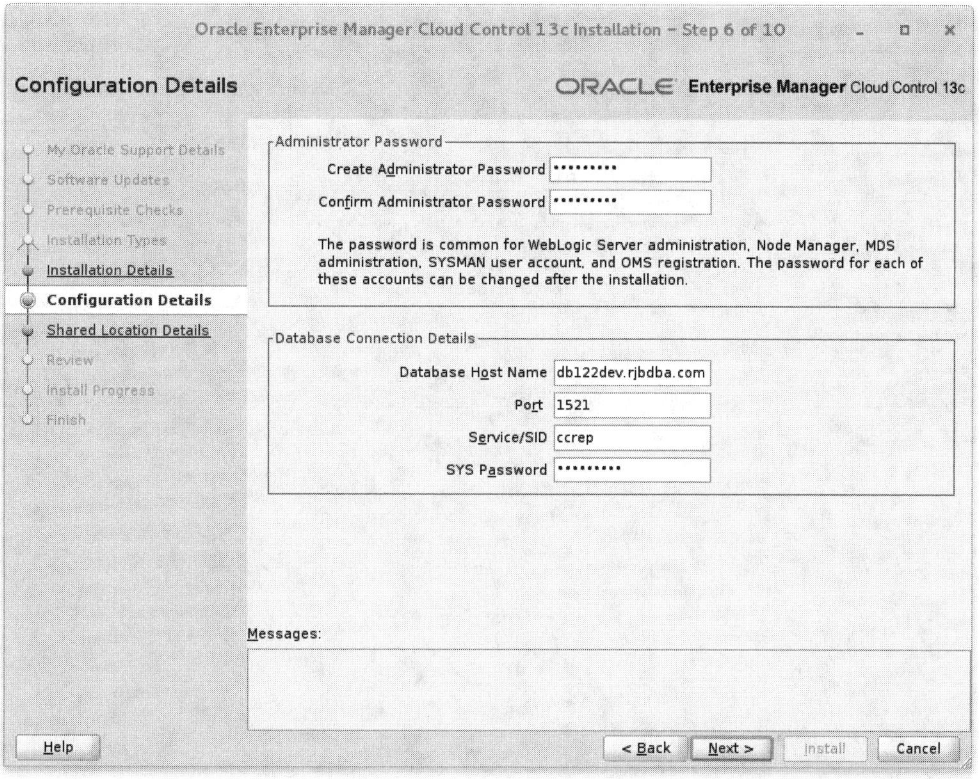

**FIGURE 12-10.** *Cloud Control administrator password and database credentials*

If you're going to have a multi-server Cloud Control environment, you specify the directory for the shared software library in the Shared Location Details step, shown in Figure 12-11. The location specified, **/u01/app/oracle/cc/swlib** in the example, must be accessible from all nodes in the multi-server environment.

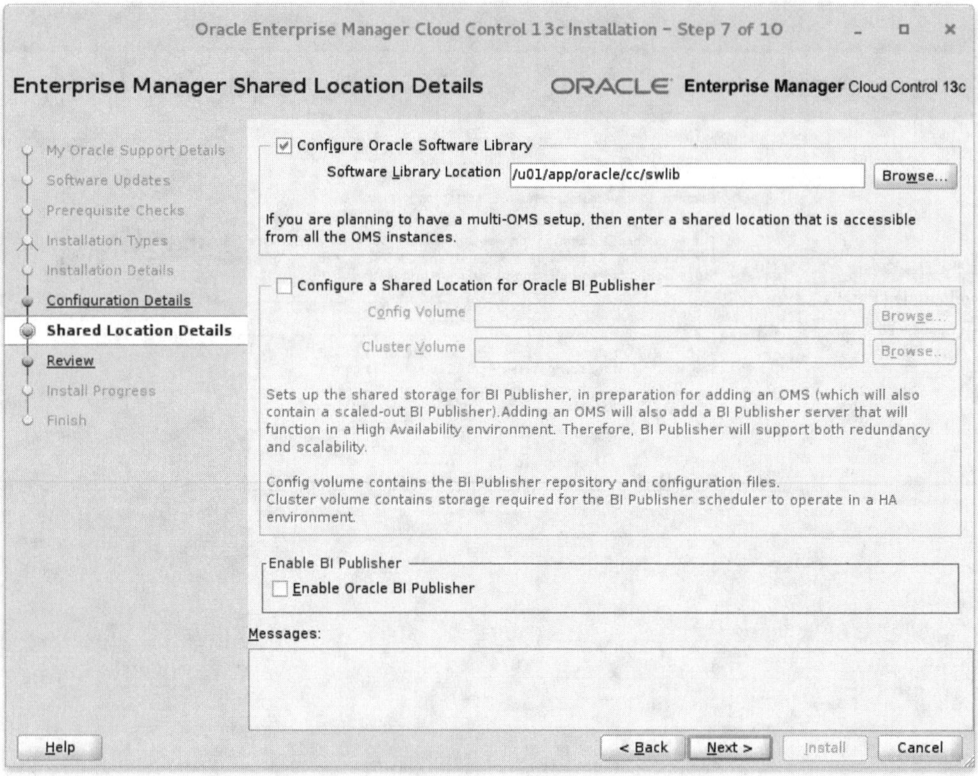

**FIGURE 12-11.** *Cloud Control shared software library location*

Before the installation starts, you can review a summary of the installation parameters, as shown in Figure 12-12.

Each step in the Cloud Control installation process is shown in the Installation Progress Details screen, shown in Figure 12-13. While each step is running, you can view the log by clicking the hyperlink provided in the Log Details column. This link is especially useful if that step fails! In most cases, you can fix the issue and retry the step with the Retry button.

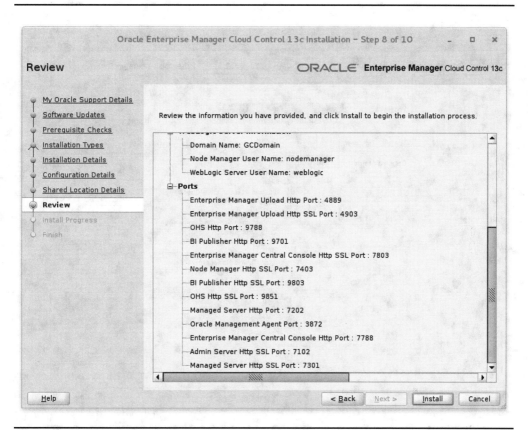

**FIGURE 12-12.** *Cloud Control preinstallation summary*

Most Oracle software installs contain at least one step requiring **root** access, and the Cloud Control installation is no exception! Figure 12-14 identifies the script that has to run as **root** to finish the installation.

After a successful installation of Cloud Control, you'll see the window shown in Figure 12-15.

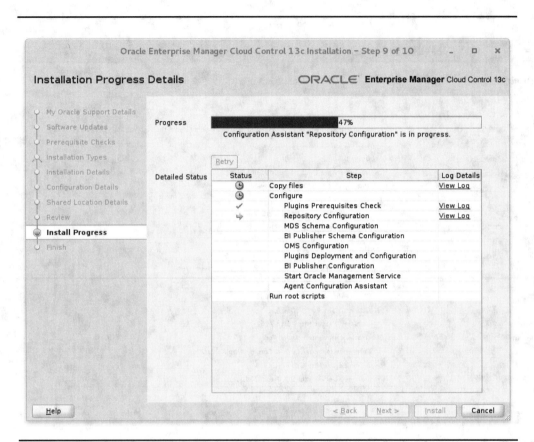

**FIGURE 12-13.** *Cloud Control installation progress window*

Here are the key portions of the file referenced in Figure 12-15:

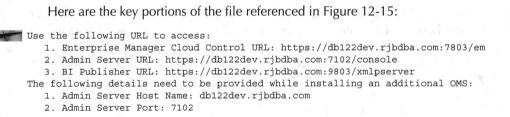

```
Use the following URL to access:
    1. Enterprise Manager Cloud Control URL: https://db122dev.rjbdba.com:7803/em
    2. Admin Server URL: https://db122dev.rjbdba.com:7102/console
    3. BI Publisher URL: https://db122dev.rjbdba.com:9803/xmlpserver
The following details need to be provided while installing an additional OMS:
    1. Admin Server Host Name: db122dev.rjbdba.com
    2. Admin Server Port: 7102
```

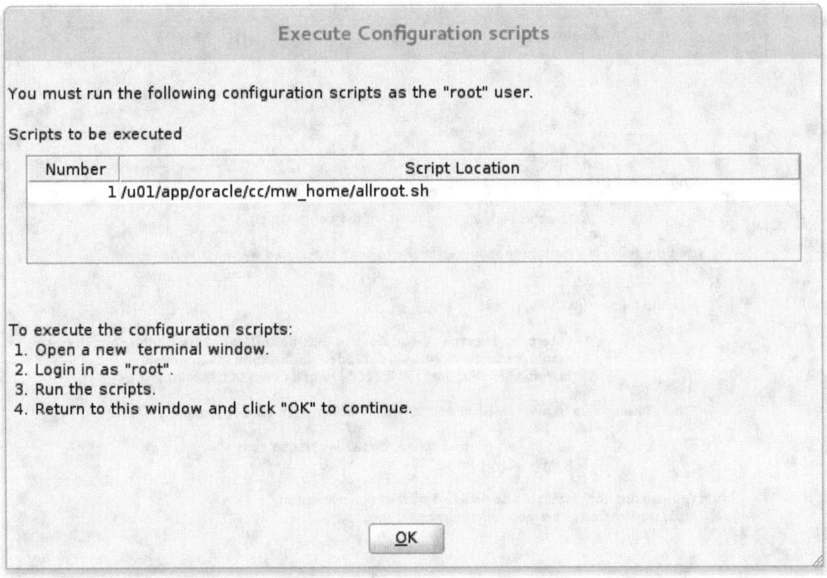

**FIGURE 12-14.**  *Cloud Control installation root script*

Create bookmarks for those URLs! Adding targets is even more straightforward and automated than it was in Enterprise Manager 12*c* Release 5, primarily due to UI improvements. Figure 12-16 shows the automated discovery process for the other databases I've created for demonstrating the new features of Oracle Database 12*c* Release 2 throughout this book.

Starting with Enterprise Manager Cloud Control 12*c* Release 5, multitenant databases are fully supported. Enterprise Manager Cloud Control 13*c* Release 2 fully supports the new features of Oracle Database 12*c* Release 2, such as switching a PDB to use local undo mode and managing application containers.

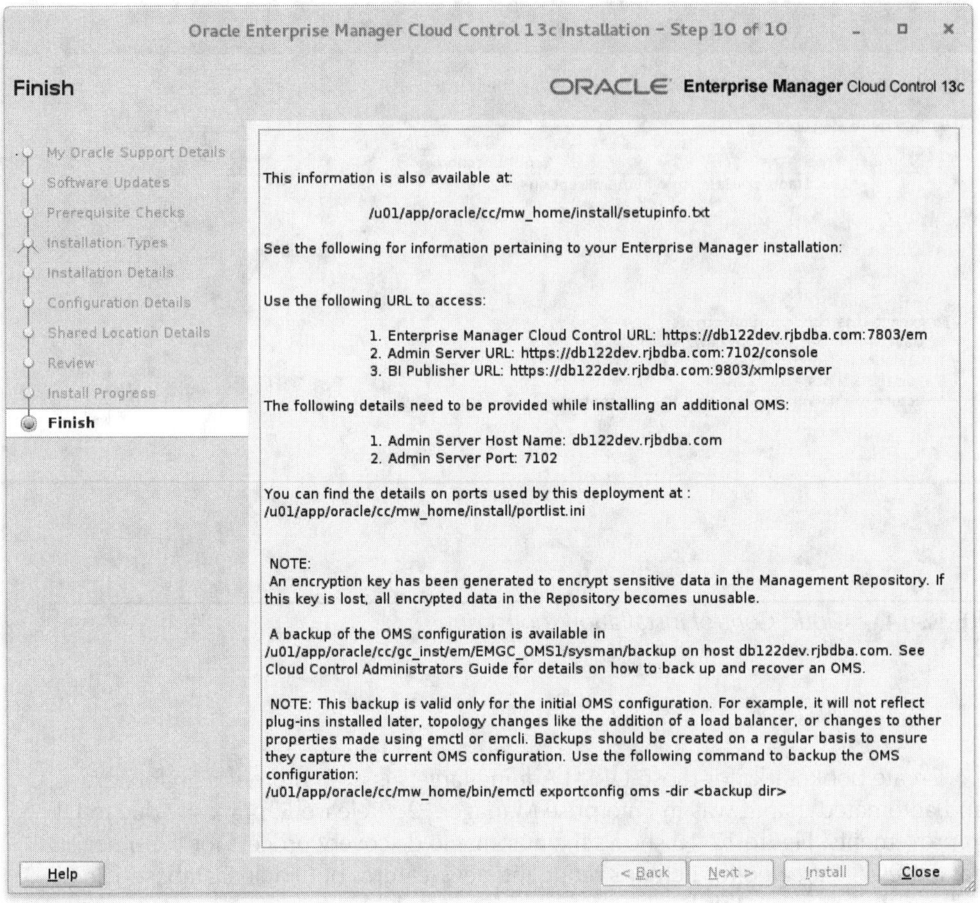

FIGURE 12-15. *Cloud Control installation summary*

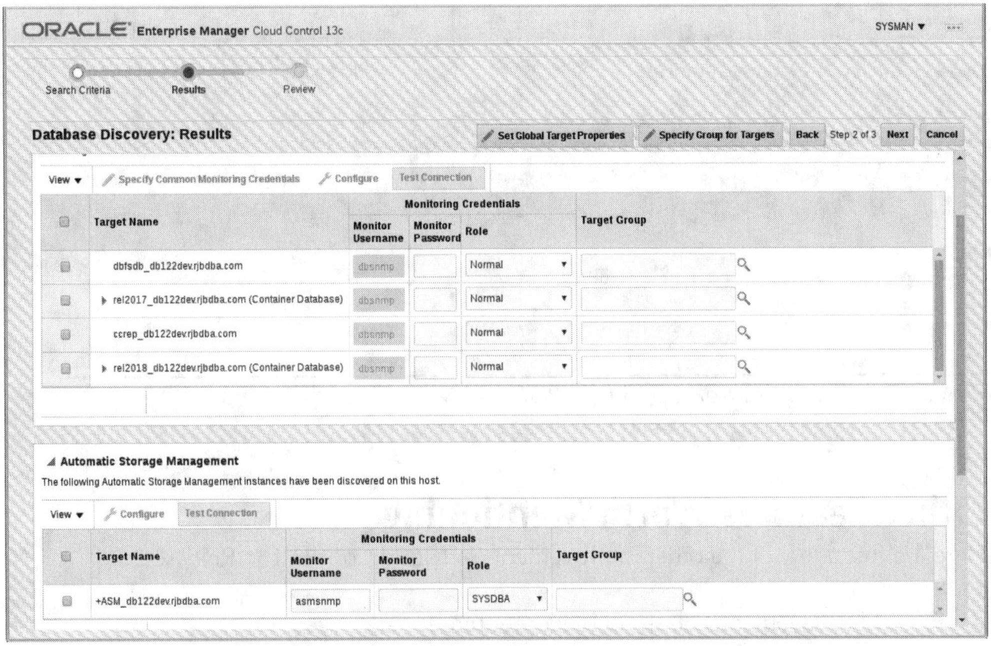

**FIGURE 12-16.**  *Target discovery process for databases and storage*

# Leveraging New Cloud Control 13c Features

The SYSMAN account is the default account for managing assets (servers, databases, listeners, and so forth). In the example that follows I use the SYSMAN account in the CCREP database. In a larger deployment, you will likely have several users or administrators, each with different levels of security and access to different resources.

## Support for Oracle Database 12c Release 2

Cloud Control stays ahead of each Oracle Database release in this respect: any new features in a given database release are fully supported in Cloud Control. For example, Oracle Database 12c Release 2 can create PDB archives (see Chapter 3) and, as you can see in Figure 12-17, Cloud Control supports several different methods for unplugging a PDB, including two ways to create a PDB archive.

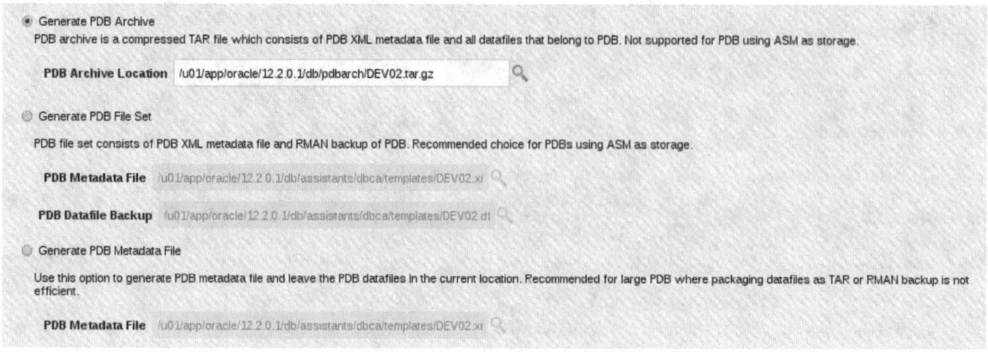

**FIGURE 12-17.** *Cloud Control support for PDB archives*

## Other Features Worth Mentioning

Here are just a few of the other improvements in Cloud Control 13c Release 2:

- UI improvements: Flash no longer required!

- Intelligent incident compression: compress multiple events into a single incident

- New job type for cookbooks and recipes

- Installation and migration improvements

- Gold image lifecycle management

- Database consolidation workbench

- Snap clone enhancements

- Exadata virtual machine provisioning

# Summary

Both Oracle Database and Oracle Enterprise Manager Cloud Control move ahead in tandem and are designed to work together. This chapter showed you how easy it is to implement Cloud Control along with the database used to hold the metadata for hundreds if not thousands of managed targets, whether they be servers, databases, storage arrays, listeners, or even engineered systems such as Exadata. This chapter concludes this book. Given all of the new features of both Oracle Database and Cloud Control, there is no reason not to upgrade both in your environment right now!

# Index

# O

# Join the Largest Tech Community in the World

 Download the latest software, tools, and developer templates

 Get exclusive access to hands-on trainings and workshops

Grow your professional network through the Oracle ACE Program

 Publish your technical articles – and get paid to share your expertise

**Join the Oracle Technology Network**
**Membership is free. Visit community.oracle.com**

🐦 @OracleOTN   f facebook.com/OracleTechnologyNetwork

# Push a Button
## Move Your Java Apps to the Oracle Cloud

<u>Same</u> Java Runtime
<u>Same</u> Dev Tools
<u>Same</u> Standards
<u>Same</u> Architecture

# ... or Back to Your Data Center

**cloud.oracle.com/java**

Reach More than 640,000 Oracle Customers
with Oracle Publishing Group

Connect with the Audience that Matters Most to Your Business

**Oracle Magazine**
The Largest IT Publication in the World
Circulation: 325,000
Audience: IT Managers, DBAs, Programmers, and Developers

**Profit**
Business Insight for Enterprise-Class Business Leaders to Help Them Build
a Better Business Using Oracle Technology
Circulation: 90,000
Audience: Top Executives and Line of Business Managers

**Java Magazine**
The Essential Source on Java Technology, the Java Programming Language,
and Java-Based Applications
Circulation: 225,00 and Growing Steady
Audience: Corporate and Independent Java Developers, Programmers,
and Architects

For more information
or to sign up for a FREE
subscription: Scan the
QR code to visit Oracle
Publishing online.

# Beta Test Oracle Software

Get a first look at our newest products—and help perfect them. You must meet the following criteria:

✔ **Licensed Oracle customer or Oracle PartnerNetwork member**

✔ **Oracle software expert**

✔ **Early adopter of Oracle products**

## Please apply at: pdpm.oracle.com/BPO/userprofile